A Muslim Woman IN TITO'S YUGOSLAVIA

NUMBER TWENTY-FOUR:
Eastern European Studies

A Muslim Woman

IN TITO'S YUGOSLAVIA

Munevera Hadžišehović

Translated by THOMAS J. BUTLER *and* SABA RISALUDDIN
Foreword by SABRINA P. RAMET

Texas A&M University Press
College Station

First edition

The paper used in this book
meets the minimum requirements
of the American National Standard
for Permanence
of Paper for Printed Library Materials,
Z39.48-1984.
Binding materials
have been chosen for durability.

∞

Library of Congress Cataloging-in-Publication Data
Hadžišehović, Munevera.
[Muslimanka. English]
A Muslim woman in Tito's Yugoslavia / Munevera Hadžišehović ; translated by Thomas J. Butler
and Saba Risaluddin; foreword by Sabrina P. Ramet.— 1st ed.
p. cm. — (Eastern European studies ; no. 24)
Includes index.
ISBN 1-58544-269-0 (cloth : alk. paper) - ISBN 1-58544-304-2 (pbk. : alk. paper)
1. Hadžišehović, Munevera. 2. Muslims—Yugoslavia—Sandžak (Serbia and Montenegro)—
Biography. 3. Sandžak (Serbia and Montenegro)—Biography. I. Butler, Thomas J., 1922-
II. Title. III. Eastern European studies (College Station, Tex.) ; no. 24.
DR1350.S25 H3313 1997
305.48'69710497'0904—dc21
2003003575

To Kenan and Amir

Contents

Illustrations

Series Editor's Foreword

Munevera Hadžišehović has written a partly autobiographical and partly sociological book on the experiences of being a Muslim woman in the former Yugoslavia. Her book stands alongside yet in sharp contrast to Tone Bringa's *Being Muslim the Bosnian Way.* Bringa offers important insights, but they can never be more than the insights of an outsider, a Norwegian anthropologist who tries to empathize yet cannot penetrate to the genuine inner emotions of the people she studied. This is a chronic limitation in field studies: no matter how well trained, the participant-observer can never really participate in the "actor's point of view." Bringa starts on the outside—describing the sorry state of Muslim, Croat, and Serbian ethnic relations in Bosnia-Herzegovina—and attempts to move inside, showing how Bosnian Muslims in general and Bosnian Muslim women in particular felt and adjusted to this state of affairs. Bringa is more an observer than a participant. Hadžišehović, on the other hand, writes from the inside out, starting with her emotions and experiences, then moving outward to the "objective" facts that concern scholars in diverse fields, such as the role of the Ustaše, Chetniks, and Germans in World War II; the attitude of Serb-dominated Yugoslavia toward Muslims; and the same tragic state of ethnic relations that led to war again in the 1990s. She is more a participant than an observer.

Thus, Hadžišehović gives the reader a loving yet accurate portrait of Bosnian Muslim customs pertaining to the household, gardens, meals, dating—in short, everyday life. It is a portrait of what David Riesman has called tradition-directed society, one whose function was to integrate society at the cost of repressing women's aspirations for schooling and success. It is only by the standards of other types of societies, such as the inner-directed type, that such traditions can be perceived as damaging in certain regards. Nevertheless, Hadžišehović managed to cherish the traditions yet find sufficient inner-directed drive and ambition to break out of the traditional woman's role and find success in academia, the Communist Party, and Belgrade, the seat of anti-Muslim prejudice. Serb-dominated Yugoslavia was perennially anti-Muslim—scores of historical texts document that fact. Hadžišehović describes how this oppressive attitude was experienced emotionally by Bosnian Muslims in general, and Bosnian Muslim women in particular. The

Bosnian Muslims were caught in a no-man's-land of cultural identity: not sufficiently Muslim by Turkish Ottoman standards, yet clinging to some traditions by Yugoslav standards. The constant charge leveled at Bosnian Muslims by other ethnic groups in Yugoslavia is that the Muslims tried to avoid taking sides. On one hand, this so-called ambivalence seemed to be the only way to preserve their cultural identity in an atmosphere that tried to eradicate it. On the other, this attitude betrays a tradition-directed innocence analogous to the sheep's ignorance of the wolf's intentions.

Hadžišehović writes with childlike innocence when describing these hostile cultural forces. This can be explained easily with regard to her childhood memories, because she is recounting how a child perceived aggression. Yet, there is more to it than that. She writes that no one in her town knew enough to be frightened when the Germans bombed and occupied it. She describes the Italian occupiers as being kind of nice because they handed out candy and chocolates, and notes that some Muslim-Italian marriages worked out. She does not delve into the reasons why the Chetniks were bent upon exterminating the Muslims, and, like other victims, seems bewildered by such evil intentions. Following World War II, Tito gave the Bosnian Muslims a sense of limited cultural autonomy and opportunity, but not as much as the Christian Serbs and Croats. Was Tito being cynical? Like some other Bosnian Muslims, Hadžišehović took the opportunity to advance herself when the window was opened partway, but she documents her experience of constantly feeling discriminated against and being caught in political crosswinds, even though she tried to find the best intentions in these realities. She also recounts the story of her intimate life and eventual success in a paternity suit that she initiated in order to give her son a sense of social status in relation to both the traditional culture that raised her and the modernist communist system in which she lived. Her son officially had a father. Yet even in this regard, as an adult she betrays certain traditional values, such as not wishing to undermine the authority of her son's father. Some readers will probably be amazed at her lack of anger at the man who evaded his responsibilities as a father and provider. A sociologist would probably note that tradition-directed society did not prepare her for such callousness in men whose behavior is not bounded by traditions.

There is an innocence to traditional societies that is both refreshing and astounding, yet ultimately self-destructive. Hadžišehović displays some of this tradition-directed naiveté and bewilderment in the last chapter of her book at the fact that the horrors of World War II were being revisited on Yugoslavia in the 1990s. Despite her sophistication as a natural scientist, she writes about her surprise at the expression of hatred against Croats and Muslims in Belgrade preceding the eruption of war. She seems to interpret the advice of her Serb neighbors to move out of her apartment as perhaps well intentioned, whereas a more cynical reader might conclude that the neighbors did not want to deal with the trouble and danger to themselves of having a Muslim neighbor. Perhaps Hadžišehović captures the genuine bewilderment of many Bosnian Muslims at becoming the objects of hatred in Yugoslavia again, despite wanting to believe in the ideal of brotherhood and unity left by Tito. I believe this is the real value of Hadžišehović's book. Bringa and other anthropologists and academics who have studied Yugoslavia's ethnic relations are—because of their training and expertise in ethnic tension—too sophisticated and cynical to comprehend why the Bosnian Muslims seemed not to think that the violence inflicted on the Slovenes and Croats could happen to them. Innocence is dangerous and cynicism is corrosive. Hadžišehović's book is an important contribution toward understanding the inside story of tradition-directed women in war-torn Bosnia-Herzegovina.

—Stjepan G. Meštrović

Foreword

This is a book about injustice, the injustice of Serbs toward Muslims, and the injustice of the Communist Party toward honest people, rewarding informers regardless of competence and punishing integrity. At a more personal level, it is about the injustice perpetrated by Derviš, the man the author thought she might marry, toward the woman to whom he once promised marriage. It is also a record of how one woman coped with injustice and survived—without seeking revenge and without allowing herself to be crushed by bitterness. What apparently kept her going was her refusal to be crushed, her spirit of defiance. That spirit was just as evident in her dealings with Derviš as it was in her refusal to work as an informer for the Communist Party. Through her eyes, we relive the history of Yugoslavia from the interwar kingdom to the breakup of socialist Yugoslavia. In the kingdom, she recalls, Muslims of the Sandžak and of Bosnia-Herzegovina had the paradoxical experience simultaneously "of belonging and alienation."[1] It was their country insofar as they made their life there; but they were alienated insofar as the Serbian establishment claimed Muslim songs and other cultural artifacts as their own while excluding the history of Islamic culture in Yugoslavia from the school curriculum. But that was officialdom. At the local level, in her native town of Prijepolje, Serbs and Muslims, though living in separate neighborhoods, interacted in a normal way. The Serbs of Prijepolje even showed their respect for Muslim traditions by refraining from eating in public during Ramadan and by not selling pork at the shops.

In fact, in the author's account, her early years in Prijepolje emerge as the most "normal" time in her life, and, for that matter, for the Muslims of the Sandžak, at least during the past eighty years. The traditional setting of town life was governed by clear rules of behavior in which even the details of courtship were tightly prescribed. One knew at all stages of life how to behave—what constituted proper behavior and what was improper. Propriety, in turn, assured a certain amount of predictability or security in life. The outbreak of World War II began the process of shattering that ostensibly secure world. The author remembers Chetnik depredations against Muslims—depredations that destroyed some towns altogether, moved populations around, and left survivors to deal with the legacy of the annihilation of the traditional setting in which the traditional codes of behavior had been sustained. What World War II did not destroy, the communists often attacked, as in their 1950 campaign against female veiling. There were other pressures, too, in communist times, including of a political nature. Some Yugoslav Muslims, including members of the author's family, responded by declaring themselves Turks in order to gain refuge in Turkey. The old traditions were forgotten after a generation in Turkey, and members of the second generation came to regard Turkey "as their only homeland."

Although Hadžišehović is not concerned with analyzing the reasons for the breakup of socialist Yugoslavia, her story throws some light on this issue. Readers will look in vain for any evidence here that the breakup resulted either from "ancient hatreds" or from constitutional "blueprints" drawn up in Slovenia and Croatia. Nor does she present the breakup in 1991 (or rather, 1987–2002) as the final stage of World War II, or even of a rekindling of its embers. The collapse of socialist Yugoslavia was instead a failure of the socialist system itself, in which, among other things, disaffected professionals "without prospects or social status" were mobilized by nationalist rhetoric that tapped into their discontent, directing it toward members of other ethnic groups. In the mid-twentieth century, Jean-Paul Sartre and Martin Heidegger challenged people to live "authentically." That "authenticity" embraced integrity, an acceptance of the responsibility entailed in one's own freedom, however limited one's choices may sometimes be, and the courage to do what one thinks is right. If that concept of authenticity may be considered as definitional of *existentialism,* then one may characterize Hadžišehović's book not only as a series of reflections about forms of injustice, but also as an existential personal history.

Hadžišehović's account unfolds against the background of huge political upheavals in the land of the South Slavs. The country was born under dubious circumstances. In 1918, as the Austro-Hungarian Empire was falling apart, Yugoslav politicians declared the creation of a state consisting of Slovenes, Croats, and Serbs under the authority of a national council. This council, operating as a provisional government for Slovenia, Croatia, and Bosnia-Herzegovina, sent a delegation to Belgrade to negotiate terms of unification with the kingdom of Serbia. Instead of negotiating, however, the delegation—worried about the threat of an Italian military incursion into Slovenia and Croatia—asked the Serbian regent to proclaim unification without any conditions. Although the delegation had exceeded its mandate, there was no turning back. Even the warnings of Stjepan Radić, leader of the Croatian Peasant Party, that the union would not be stable until it reached a consensus on the internal organization of the state, were ignored. In fact, no such consensus was reached. The leading Serbian parties—the Radical Party and the Democratic Party—were bent on taking the centralized form of government used in Serbia as the model for the new Kingdom of Serbs, Croats, and Slovenes, as the new state was called. They therefore were opposed to either federalism or any form of autonomy. Nonetheless, the Croatian Peasant Party, Croatia's largest party, favored a federal or even confederal arrangement for the state. The Yugoslav Muslim Organization, the leading political party in Bosnia-Herzegovina, wanted autonomy for Bosnia-Herzegovina and special autonomy for Muslim religious institutions. The Slovenes preferred a federal arrangement ideally, but were prepared to reach a deal with the Serbs. Other national groups, specifically the Macedonians and the Montenegrins, were not recognized as nationally distinct, which meant that Macedonian children—whose parents spoke a form of Bulgarian—were taught to speak Serbian rather than their own language in the schools. Kosovar Albanians were treated the worst of all: they were discouraged from attending school at all. Moreover, the Belgrade government seized more than 150,000 acres of Albanian land, turning much of it over to Serb "colonists," and negotiated with Turkey for the emigration of up to forty thousand Albanian families.[2]

The "Vidovdan" constitution of June 28, 1921, was not the product of consensus, and it was never accepted as legitimate by Croats, let alone Macedonians or Kosovar Albanians.[3] In 1928, Radić was shot by a Serb deputy while attending a session of the National Assembly; Radić himself thought that Prime Minister Vukićević had known in advance of the plot to shoot him and had given his approval. Radić's death a little over a month later had an enormous impact on Croats. It also made clear just how dysfunctional the Vidovdan system was.

Rather than addressing the sources of the system's dysfunctionality, King Aleksandar Karađorđević decided to abolish the constitution and the parties and take all power into his own hands. Thus, on January 6, 1929, he declared a royal dictatorship. He had some of the leading political figures in the country, including Radić's successor as Croatian Peasant Party leader, Vlatko Maček, arrested and incarcerated, and imposed strict censorship on the press. By 1931, the king had concluded that he could not maintain his authoritarian system without creating a formal party structure. As a result, he issued a constitution and the Yugoslav Radical Peasant Democracy—a party whose name was designed to appeal to all major interests—was subsequently created. In the meantime, however, the radical fringe of the Croatian political spectrum had gone into exile in Italy, Hungary, and Belgium, creating the Ustaše movement. Headed by Ante Pavelić, the erstwhile head of the Croatian Party of the Right, the Ustaše organization made several attempts on the king's life before finally killing him on October 9, 1934, while he was visiting Marseilles. The new king, Petar II, was under age (eleven in 1934); so the deceased king's cousin, Prince Pavle, became regent. Within two months, the regent had removed the ruling clique from power and had put his own man, Bogoljub Jevtić, in the prime minister's office. But Jevtić lasted barely six months, and in June, 1935, Milan Stojadinović, who had worked efficiently as minister of finance, became the new prime minister. Stojadinović remained in office for almost four years—by far the longest continuous term served by any prime minister in interwar Yugoslavia. He is best remembered today for having adopted some of the external trappings of fascism (among other things, having crowds of uniformed followers chant "Leader! Leader!" in the Italian style), and for having failed, in spite of his best efforts, to obtain passage of the concordat the Roman Catholic Church had been seeking. Meanwhile, the Croatian Peasant Party was organizing a paramilitary force known as the Croatian Peasant Defense, obtaining weaponry from revisionist states in the region. By 1939, the regent felt that the unitary (centralized) system of government had become a complete absurdity and looked for a prime minister who would prioritize the solution of what was coming to be called "the Croatian question," because the Croats were the most vocal in demanding changes. In February, 1939, Dragiša Cvetković (a moderate member of the Radical Party) became prime minister and, after several months of negotiations, reached an agreement with Vlatko Maček, leader of the Croatian Peasant Party (in August, 1939), creating a large *banovina* (governate) of Croatia, which was granted extensive autonomy. Portions of what had historically been Bosnia-Herzegovina (including Brčko, Derventa, and Travnik) were assigned to the *banovina* of Croatia, provoking angry protests throughout Bosnia. The Bosniaks, in particular, demanded the creation of a comparable *banovina* of Bosnia-Herzegovina, to which the alienated lands would be restored.[4] In fact, the creation of the Croatian *banovina* fell so far short of what might have satisfied most citizens (namely federalism) that it could scarcely be said to have solved the problem.

This was the Yugoslavia in which Hadžišehović grew up. It was an overwhelmingly peasant society, with up to 85 percent of the population working in agriculture. Illiteracy was also high in most parts of the country. In Bosnia-Herzegovina, illiteracy stood at 80.5 percent in 1921. Only Macedonia had a higher rate of illiteracy in the Yugoslav kingdom.[5]

If interethnic and interconfessional resentments had been growing in the years after 1918 (or, in the case of Bosnia-Herzegovina, after 1878), the experiences of World War II deepened them profoundly, sowing deep hatred among its peoples.[6] The country was broken up into several parts, with Germany, Italy, Hungary, Bulgaria, and Italian-occupied Albania taking over portions of the country outright. The Axis also created two quisling states: Croatia and Serbia. Ante Pavelić headed the Independent State of Croatia (NDH)—which is somewhat a misnomer as it was not independent at all—and Gen. Milan Nedić, who had previously served as the Yugoslav kingdom's minister of war, led the Nazi satellite of Serbia. Both quisling regimes collaborated with the Nazis by liquidating Jews, rounding up and killing communists, and attacking other perceived enemies. The Pavelić regime, which also targeted Serbs for annihilation or expulsion, is generally considered to have been the more brutal of the two "Yugoslav" quisling regimes.

The Yugoslav Communist Party organized the "Partisan" resistance to the occupation, under communist leader Josip Broz Tito. A Serbian colonel, Draža Mihailović, organized a rival force called the Chetniks, who pledged their loyalty to the Yugoslav government-in-exile in London and hoped to restore the kingdom on the basis of unambiguous Serb hegemony. The Chetniks also hoped to make the restored kingdom as homogeneously Serb as possible.[7] Although the Chetniks advertised themselves as an anti-Axis resistance force, they decided after the first few months that this posture was counterproductive, that the Serbs' real enemy was the increasingly multiethnic Partisans. The Chetniks therefore began collaborating with the Italians, receiving weapons and supplies both from them and from Milan Nedić's quisling government. Despite the slaughter of Serb civilians by the Ustaše, and the slaughter of Muslim (Bosniak) and Croat civilians by the Chetniks, the Croatian Ustaše and the Serbian Chetniks had a common enemy: the Partisans.[8] By June, 1942, NDH authorities had established collaborative relations with several local Chetnik leaders, including Momčilo "Duke" Djujić.[9]

Altogether, some 1,027,000 Yugoslavs died in the course of the war—most of them as a result of slaughters or combat, although a typhus epidemic in Chetnik ranks in January, 1945, contributed to the number of Serbian dead. In absolute numbers, the groups with the largest wartime losses were the Serbs (530,000 dead), the Croats (192,000 dead), and the Bosniaks (103,000 dead). In proportional terms, the groups with the largest wartime losses were the Jews (80 percent of all Jews killed), the Bosniaks (8.1 percent), the Serbs (7.3 percent), and the Croats (5 percent).[10]

After the war, Tito's communists were by far in the strongest position, and quickly snuffed out rival parties that tried to reestablish themselves. The communists, taking the measure of the kingdom's failure, established a federal system made up of six republics, with borders largely reflecting historic frontiers. An exception was made in the case of Croatia, which was compelled to give up most of eastern Srijem to Vojvodina because the majority of the local population was by then Serbian. The borders of Bosnia-Herzegovina corresponded closely to the borders fixed by the Congress of Berlin in 1878. The communists now recognized five "nations" in Yugoslavia—the Serbs, Croats, Slovenes, Macedonians, and Montenegrins—with other groups being called "nationalities" (a term that gave them lesser status). The Bosniaks were not recognized as a nation for more than two decades, and on census forms could choose among three possibilities: "Serbs of Muslim faith," "Croats of Muslim faith," and "nationally undecided." Under the circumstances, many Bosniaks declared that they were "undecided." In February, 1968, however, the eighteenth session of the League of Communists of Bosnia-Herzegovina declared that Bosnia-Herzegovina's Muslims constituted a sixth nation in the Yugoslav community of nations.[11] This declaration was subsequently endorsed at the federal level, and in the 1971 census Bosniaks were given the option of declaring themselves "Muslims in an ethnic sense."[12]

To a foreign audience, Tito seemed awe-inspiring. He had defied the Soviets in 1948, cofounded the nonaligned movement, and set up a system of workers' councils that he called self-management and which attracted considerable interest and attention around the globe. There were problems at home, however, and, as in the case of the interwar kingdom, some of them had to do with the perspectives shared by the members of certain national groups. In Croatia, for example, there was widespread discontent—expressed openly in the Croatian countryside—after Tito removed the liberal leadership of Mika Tripalo and Savka Dabčević-Kučar in December, 1971. Serbs were upset about the 1974 constitution for a number of reasons, but above all because it declared Kosovo and Vojvodina to be "federal units" and enhanced their status and autonomy. They remained provinces of Serbia, but in Kosovo, Albanians, who by 1971 constituted 73.3 percent of the province's population, comprised 61.7 percent of the membership of the Central Committee of the Kosovar Party organization in 1973, and 62.5 percent by 1974.[13] Although the Albanians were proportionally underrepresented in the organs of power, local Serbs resented their gains and wanted to reverse them. Albanians, for their part, felt that they remained the victims of discrimination and rioted in 1968 and again in 1981.

As for the Bosniaks, there were currents of opposition that came to the surface in August, 1983, when the communists put eleven prominent Bosniaks on trial on charges of having plotted to eliminate the Serb and Croat populations in Bosnia-Herzegovina and to establish an Islamic state there. Among the accused was Alija Izetbegović, the future president of Bosnia-Herzegovina. The eleven were, in the course of things, found guilty and sentenced to prison terms averaging eight years in length. A key document for the prosecution was an "Islamic declaration" written by Izetbegović a number of years earlier, which, according to the prosecution, outlined the program for a militant Islamic state. Izetbegović, for his part, disputed this interpretation both at the time and later. In the meantime, Tito had died (in May, 1980), and within a few years the combination of economic deterioration (which began in the late 1970s), crumbling faith in self-management and other institutions of state, and rising currents of nationalism, especially among the Serbs, brought Yugoslavia to the edge of collapse.[14] However, it was the rise to power of Slobodan Milošević in Serbia that pushed the country over the edge. Milošević and his collaborators violated the constitution and laws of the land on repeated occasions;[15] organized mass rallies to destabilize and overthrow the governments of Vojvodina, Kosovo, and Montenegro; made plans for a war against Croatia and Bosnia-Herzegovina through which they hoped to create a "Greater Serbia"; and sat down with Croatian president Franjo Tuđman in March, 1991, to decide on the partition of Bosnia. More than twenty thousand persons were killed in the course of the war in Croatia, whereas about 215,000 persons lost their lives in the Bosnian war of 1992–95.[16] Quite apart from the loss of lives, the legacy of the war included revived hatred and intolerance; the displacement of 2.7 million persons, only a minority of whom have been able to return to their prewar homes; the destruction of much of Bosnia-Herzegovina's economic infrastructure; and the eradication of many historically and culturally important places of worship and other cultural landmarks.[17]

As I have already noted, Hadžišehović's book takes up the twin themes of justice and injustice. Injustice takes various forms. There is the injustice of personal betrayal (exemplified in this book by the character of Derviš); the injustice of misrepresentation with malice; the injustice of discrimination and prejudice; the injustice entailed in hypocrisy, when affirmations of noble intent and of principle are betrayed in the event; and there is the kind of injustice that colors an entire system, subverting it, one might say, from its soul outward. This was the kind of injustice with which Plato was concerned when he praised justice as a form of social proportion (in *The Republic*) and demanded that the laws of a state be in accord with the (higher) Natural Law (in *The Laws*). It is also the kind of injustice that plagued Yugoslavia in all three incarnations—the interwar kingdom (1918–41), the communist system (1945–91), and the nationalist rump state dominated from its inception until October, 2000, by Slobodan Milošević (1992–2002). To cure a state of this kind of "injustice of the soul" would seem to require a thoroughgoing political "exorcism." But what form would such a "political exorcism" take? Rewriting the constitution? Staging elections? Replacing the incumbents? Ultimately, the foregoing "solutions"—which to many minds may seem like the obvious remedies—are usually not adequate to the task unless they are accompanied by that most-essential nostrum of all: a comprehensive reorientation of the educational system to move the next generation away from the value system that underpinned an unjust system (whether a Serb-hegemonic system or a collectivist system disrespectful of individual rights or a nationalist regime committed to a program of "ethnic cleansing"). Such a reform of textbooks and educational curricula has been under way recently in most of the postcommunist states of Central and Eastern Europe, including Serbia and Bosnia-Herzegovina.[18] Among the Balkan states (including Greece), a preliminary review undertaken by experts found, evidently without exception, tendencies toward national self-glorification, and toward de-emphasizing the sufferings and perspectives of other nations while stressing the sufferings and perspectives of one's own nation.[19] In other words, the textbooks were found to be suitable for preparing the younger generation for future wars against neighbors, and had the side effect of stimulating intolerance toward local members of ethnic minorities. Churches have also had ideas for educational reform, centering on getting denominational religious instruction in the state schools as a regular (that is, not after-hours) subject. Given that some of the religious associations in the area have been active in promoting sexual, religious, and ethnic intolerance, the establishment of a religious presence in the state school curriculum is not necessarily a boon. On the contrary, it may actually render the process of building a stable and legitimate system far more complicated. Justice, then, has something to do with some rather definite values—chief among them being tolerance of all that does no harm, and a respect for fundamental human equality.

Americans have three typical illusions about justice: (1) that there are no higher standards of justice at all, that everything is relative, so that one ultimately does not even have a basis for condemning, let us say, the mass murder of Bosniaks at Srebrenica by Bosnian Serb forces in the summer of 1995; (2) that justice does not matter because it is no more than "good wishes" (a perverse point of view that opens the door to a far-ranging cynicism in which neither truth nor life is respected); and (3) that ordinary citizens cannot make a difference and that they therefore have no responsibility, not even the responsibility to speak out. These illusions were specifically championed by some Western apologists for Karadžić and Milošević (who, in defending the Serbs' demons, imagined that they were somehow on the side of "the Serbs") during the Serbian Insurrectionary War of 1991–95. Politicians rarely appeal to mere convenience or even to mere security requirements in justifying wars and conquests, however. On the contrary, there is often some "principle" cited—such as the doing of God's work (for the Spanish conquistadors in the sixteenth century and for other European colonizers later), or the notion of intrinsic national superiority (as in the case of the Nazi doctrine of "*Deutschland über Alles*"), or the Serb nationalist conceit that all Serbs should live within a single state (a "right" that was not extended to other peoples but which became the unofficial motto of the Milošević regime). The Yugoslav case illustrates the principle that the farther a state deviates from universal values of tolerance, equality, rule of law, and respect for human rights, the more vulnerable it becomes to decay and collapse.[20] Values matter not only in themselves, but also for rather practical reasons as well.

—Sabrina P. Ramet

Notes

1. The most useful English-language books dealing with the history of Bosnia-Herzegovina are: Robert J. Donia and John V. A. Fine Jr., *Bosnia and Hercegovina: A Tradition Betrayed* (New York: Columbia University Press, 1994); and Noel Malcolm, *Bosnia: A Short History* (Washington Square: New York University Press, 1994). Among the many fine works written in Bosnian, Mustafa Imamovic's *Historija Bošnjaka,* 2d ed. (Sarajevo: Bošnjačka zajednica kulture, 1998), is especially useful.
2. Ivo Banac, *The National Question in Yugoslavia: Origins, History, Politics* (Ithaca, N.Y.: Cornell University Press, 1984), 299–300; and Noel Malcolm, *Kosovo: A Short History* (London: Macmillan, 1998), 285–86.
3. The most useful English-language books dealing with the interwar kingdom are: Banac, *National Question;* Mark Biondich, *Stjepan Radić, the Croatian Peasant Party, and the Politics of Mass Mobilization, 1904–1928* (Toronto: University of Toronto Press, 2000); J. B. Hoptner, *Yugoslavia in Crisis, 1934–1941* (New York: Columbia University Press, 1962); Frank C. Littlefield, *Germany and Yugoslavia, 1933–1941: The German Conquest of Yugoslavia* (Boulder, Colo.: East European Monographs, 1988); and James J. Sadkovich, *Italian Support for Croatian Separatism, 1927–1937* (New York: Garland, 1987). For a concise and clear-headed summary of interwar Yugoslav politics, see Joseph Rothschild, *East Central Europe between the Two World Wars* (Seattle: University of Washington Press, 1974), chap. 5, "Yugoslavia."
4. Šaćir Filandra, *Bošnjačka politika u XX. stoljeću* (Sarajevo: Sejtarija, 1998), 107, 111, 113–26.
5. Dušan Bilandžić, *Hrvatska moderna povijest* (Zagreb: Golden Marketing, 1999), 105.
6. The most useful English-language books dealing with Yugoslavia's experiences in World War II are: Philip J. Cohen, *Serbia's Secret War: Propaganda and the Deceit of History* (College Station: Texas A&M University Press, 1996); Milovan Djilas, *Wartime,* trans. from Serbo-Croatian by Michael B. Petrovich (New York: Harcourt Brace Jovanovich, 1977); Walter R. Roberts, *Tito, Mihailović and the Allies, 1941–1945* (New Brunswick, N.J.: Rutgers University Press, 1974); Jozo Tomashevich, *War and Revolution in Yugoslavia, 1941–1945: The Chetniks* (Stanford, Calif.: Stanford University Press, 1975); and idem., *War and Revolution in Yugoslavia, 1941–1945: Occupation and Collaboration* (Stanford, Calif.: Stanford University Press, 2001).
7. Cohen, *Serbia's Secret War,* 44.
8. Fikreta Jelić-Butić, *Četnici u Hrvatskoj, 1941–1945* (Zagreb: Globus, 1986), 149–150.
9. Ibid., 110.

10. Vladimir Žerjavic, *Gubici stanovništva Jugoslavije u drugom svjetskom ratu* (Zagreb: Jugoslavensko Viktimološko Društvo, 1989), 61–66; and Ivo Goldstein, *Croatia: A History,* trans. from Croatian by Nikolina Jovanović (Toronto: McGill-Queens University Press, 1999), 158.
11. Hamdija Pozderac, *Nacionalni odnosi i socijalisticko zajedništvo* (Sarajevo: Svjetlost, 1978), 44.
12. The most useful English-language books dealing with communist-era Yugoslavia are: Ivo Banac, *With Stalin Against Tito: Cominformist Splits in Yugoslav Communism* (Ithaca, N.Y.: Cornell University Press, 1988); Duško Doder, *The Yugoslavs* (New York: Random House, 1978); Vojislav Koštunica and Kosta Čavoški, *Party Pluralism or Monism: Social Movements and the Political System in Yugoslavia, 1944–1949* (Boulder, Colo.: East European Monographs, 1985); Sabrina P. Ramet, *Nationalism and Federalism in Yugoslavia, 1962–1991,* 2d ed. (Bloomington: Indiana University Press, 1992); and Dennison I. Rusinow, *The Yugoslav Experiment, 1948–1974* (Berkeley and Los Angeles: University of California Press, 1977).
13. Sednica predsedništva CK SK Srbije (May 17, 1976), in *Zadaci SK Srbije u razvoju medjunacionalnih odnosa i borbi protiv nacionalizma* (Belgrade: Komunist, 1978), 165; and Ivan Stojanović, "Problemi zapošljavanja i medjunacionalni odnosi," in *Gledišta* 15, no. 7–8 (July-August 1974): 747.
14. See discussion in Tim Judah, *The Serbs: History, Myth, and the Destruction of Yugoslavia* (New Haven, Conn.: Yale University Press, 1997).
15. See the partial list of violations in Sabrina P. Ramet, *Balkan Babel: The Disintegration of Yugoslavia from the Death of Tito to the Fall of Milošević,* 4th ed. (Boulder, Colo.: Westview Press, 2002), 71–72.
16. Official Croatian government statistics for the period through August, 1993, showed 6,651 dead and 12,706 persons missing and presumed dead. See *Slobodna Dalmacija* (September 1, 1993), as cited in Reneo Lukić and Allen Lynch, *Europe from the Balkans to the Urals: The Disintegration of Yugoslavia and the Soviet Union* (Oxford: Oxford University Press, 1996), 193. The casualties for Bosnia are the estimates of Vladimir Žerjavic, the distinguished Croatian demographer, as reported in *Globus* (Zagreb), January 9, 1998, 24.
17. Quite a number of variously misleading, ill informed, or maliciously mendacious books have been written about the war. The *most useful* English-language books about the Yugoslav collapse and the Serbian Insurrectionary War of 1991–95 are: Norman Cigar, *Genocide in Bosnia: The Policy of "Ethnic Cleansing"* (College Station: Texas A&M University Press, 1995); Lukić and Lynch, *Europe from the Balkans to the Urals;* Viktor Meier, *Yugoslavia: A History of Its Demise,* trans. from German by Sabrina Ramet (London: Routledge, 1999); Ramet, *Balkan Babel;* Laura Silber and Allan Little, *The Death of Yugoslavia* (London: Penguin Books and BBC Books, 1995); and Mark Thompson, *Forging War: The Media in Serbia, Croatia, Bosnia and Herzegovina,* completely revised and enlarged ed. (Luton: University of Luton Press, 1999).
18. See Dubravka Stojanović, "The Balkans, Wars and Textbooks: The Case of Serbia," *Association for Social History* (2001), available at www.udi.org.yu/Founders/Stojanović/textbooks.htm, 10; and Robert J. Donia, "The Quest for Tolerance in Sarajevo's Textbooks," *Human Rights Review* 1, no. 2 (January-March, 2000).
19. Christina Koulouri, ed., *Teaching the History of Southeastern Europe* (Thessaloniki: Center for Democracy and Reconciliation in Southeast Europe, 2001).
20. Regarding universal values, see Oto Luthar, Keith A. McLeod, and Mitja Žagar, eds., *Liberal Democracy, Citizenship, and Education* (Niagara Falls, N.Y.: Mosaic Press, 2001).

Acknowledgments

I wrote the book *A Muslim Woman in Tito's Yugoslavia* in the Bosnian language on my own. But in preparation for the English version of this book, Prof. Thomas J. Butler of the Department of Slavic Languages and Literatures at Harvard University provided especially important help with the supplemented and revised manuscript. As translator, he translated the most difficult parts of the manuscript, which was rich in Bosnian ethnographic and local expressions. Professor Butler's professional experience allowed him to complete this painstaking job successfully and his advice in helping me choose a publisher for the English translation was of enormous importance to me. I also want to thank Saba Risaluddin from Sarajevo, who translated several parts of the manuscript very quickly and with accuracy, greatly saving me time and reducing my expenses.

I am grateful to Texas A&M University Press's two anonymous readers who recommended the manuscript for publication. They gave the comments and suggestions necessary to complete the text and gave it its finishing touches. I am grateful to Texas A&M University Press's editors for their cooperation and patience. Ayman Hanash from Paterson, New Jersey, was helpful in scanning the photographs for the illustrations.

It was a great responsibility of mine to find the exact definitions and translations of Bosnian and oriental words used by local Muslim people for this book. To do this in the best way, I asked for, and received, very useful information from many professionals in that field. I am indebted to Mustafa Tanović and Ezol Avdović from New York, who were kind enough to read the manuscript in Bosnian as well as the glossary of Bosnian terms and make comments on both of them. Mohammad Qatanani, the imam at the Islamic Center of Passaic County, New Jersey, edited the English translations of the Qur'anic verses used in this book. By courtesy of Mustafa Jahić, the director, I was able to use the Gazi Husrev Beg Library's archives of photos and data in Sarajevo. Lamija Hadžiosmanović of the Sarajevo Faculty of Arts and Literatures reviewed the manuscript, emphasizing that "in addition to its other qualities, is a valuable historical document of a turbulent period for the Bosniak people. Hadžišehović addresses them with full intellectual and human respect." Lamija and Aleksandra Vagner from New York expressed my feelings in these words: "As both participant in and witness of events that fundamentally altered her life, and—which is more important—the life of the people, the nation to which she belongs, Munevera Hadžišehović is more astonished than embittered, more confused than aggrieved." Thanks, Lamija and Aleksandra, for this beautiful passage about my book.

I wrote this book day by day after finishing my work in the lab, often times being very tired. I want to thank my lawyer, Michael R. Steinberg from New York, and my friends for their encouragement and their firm belief in my project. I also want to thank my colleagues Fahra Bašić, Nezahat Ruždić, and Zlatan Šehović in Sarajevo, Mehmed Hadžišehović in Prijepolje, and in Belgrade, Đorđe Bek-Uzarov, Nada Miljević, Sakib Šehović, and especially Vera Marković. They were always prompt in providing me with data and photos for the book, and they welcomed my efforts to write this English version. By using the information they provided, and through exchanging e-mails and letters with them, I sensed the old times and the atmosphere from my Belgrade and Sarajevo days. Many thanks to them for all they have done from so far away.

I do not want to forget both my son, Kenan, and my friend Victor Ismail Sedlar from the United States for supporting the book, for helping me with my English writing, and for checking and verifying the correctness of historical events cited or described in the book.

I am indebted to those who made contributions to this book project. They are the people, mainly workers, of the different religions and nations from the area of the former Yugoslavia, who found the United States as their other country for life: Hedija and Hamdija Tahiri, Azrudin Karalić, Šaćir Šabani, Dana Kesler, Hasan Kolenović, Kadrija and Mehmed Ramičević, Kemal Bekteši, Eko Sadiković, and Ilija Jurić. I must mention the contributions and the kindness of Rahman Perwaiz of Gainesville, Texas, Nagia and Abdel Latif Moharram, Muhamad Aslam, and Hussain Zavi's family of Dallas, Texas, in whose home I started writing the book in Bosnian in 1994. My gratitude certainly goes to my employers, Susan and Omar Baturay, who were supportive and understanding when an aged refugee sought to exist in an alien country.

To those who offered me their hospitality, help, meals, time, and, most importantly, their love, I owe a debt of gratitude—the numbers are too great to be acknowledged. Nevertheless, I would like to mention these people from New Jersey: Nezrina-Nena Berberištanin, the Čajević family, Jasmina and Sead Bakić, Dino Bakić, Mirsada and Burhaneddin Bilali, Azra and Ljupčo Kojčevski, Ramiza Krlić, Mubera and Esad Malagić, Šefketa and Ruždija Đerlek, Mujesira and Muzafer Melajac, Fatima-Maca Čarovac,

Mersa Kapidžić, Ana and Slavko Pejić, Hanifa and Osman Kevac, and Ivo Čutura.

I loved writing this book. In the deepest sense, this book is my gift to those people who believe in the common life and in our diversity. *Kalu inna lillahi ve inna ilejhi radžiun*—"To God we belong, and to Him is our return" (Qur'an, chapter Baqara, verse 156).

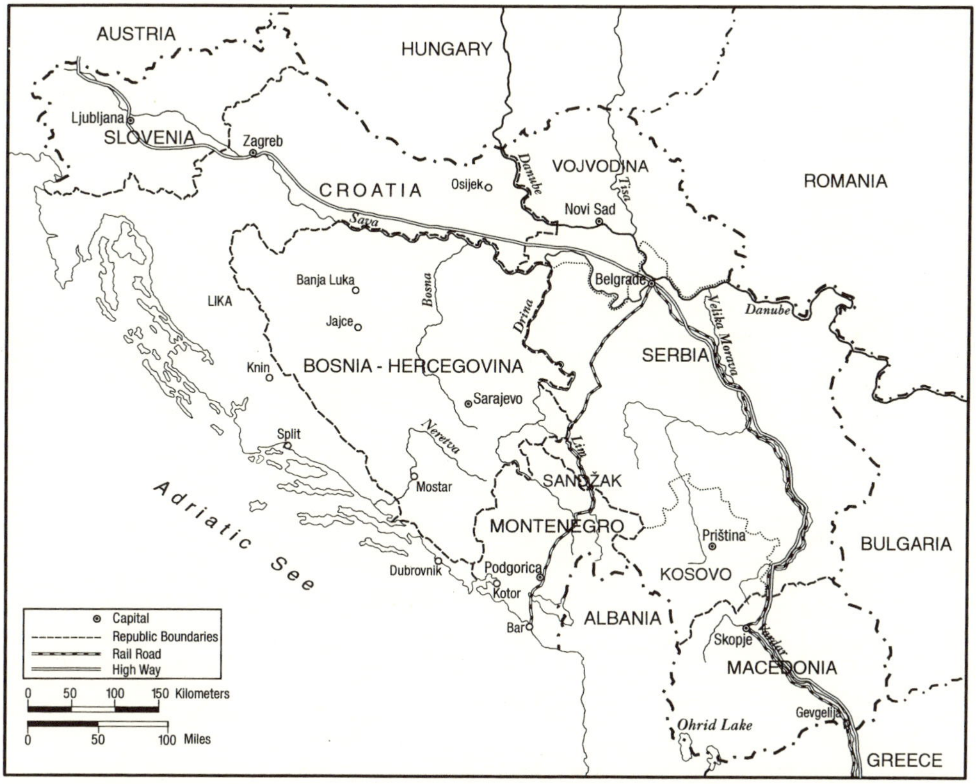

Map 1. The republics and autonomous provinces of the former Yugoslavia (1945–92). Republics: Bosnia and Herzegovina, Croatia, Macedonia, Montenegro, Serbia, and Slovenia. The autonomous provinces are Kosovo and Vojvodina, which belong to Serbia.

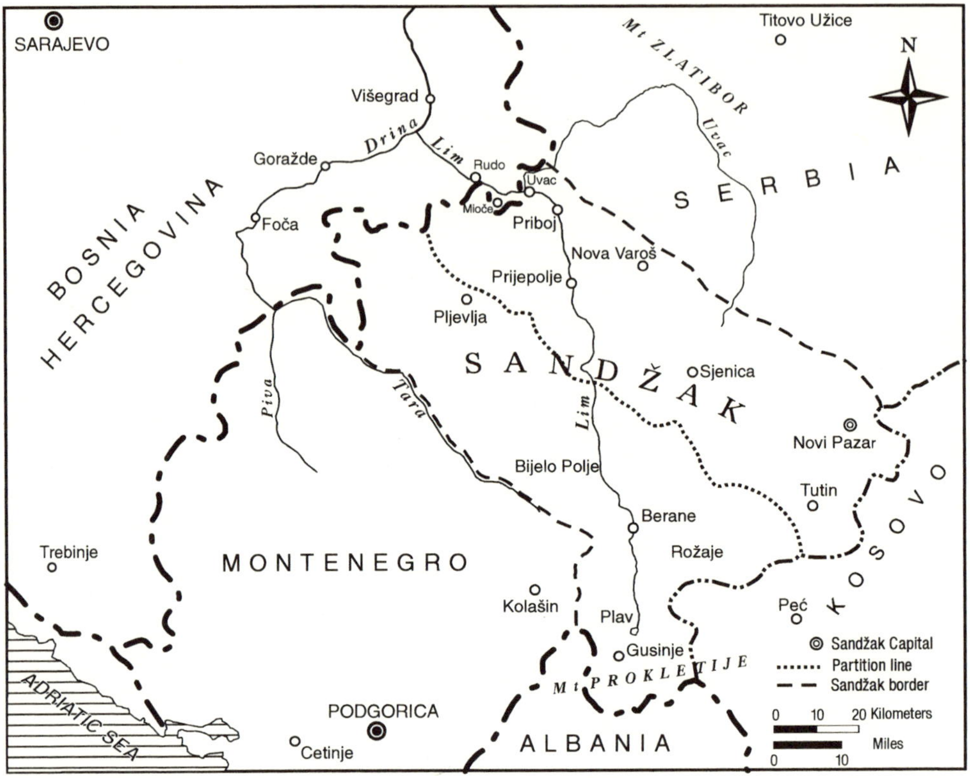

Map 2. The location of the Sandžak in relation to Bosnia, Montenegro, and Serbia. In 1946, Sandžak was partitioned between Montenegro and Serbia.

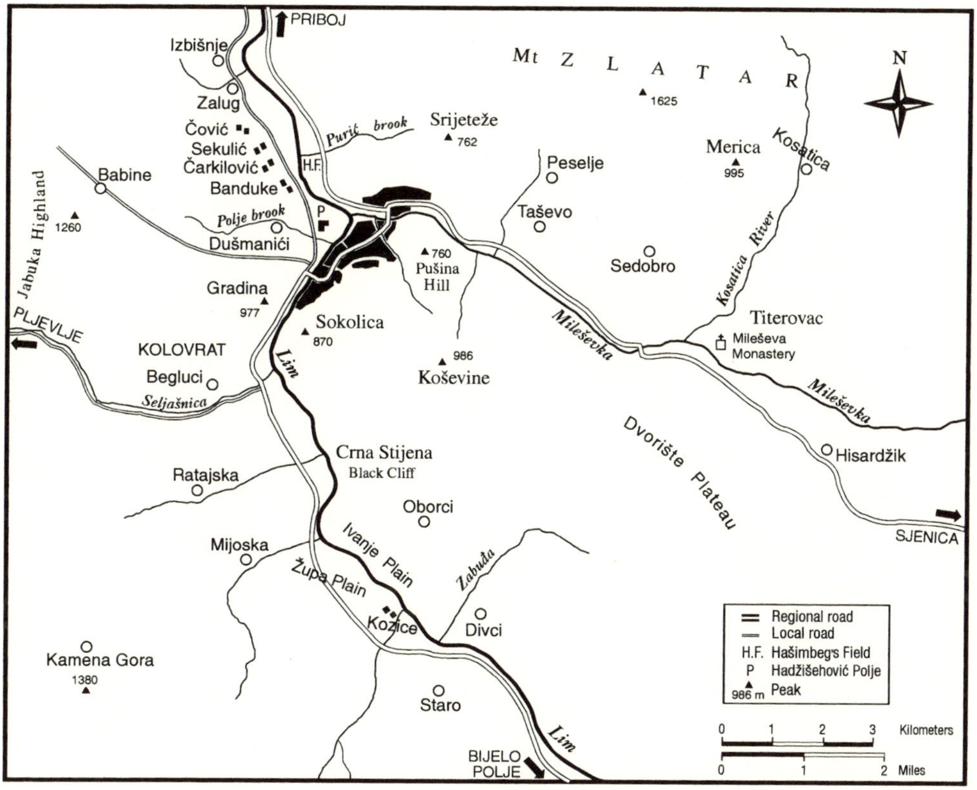

Map 3. Prijepolje and surrounding villages with the regional roads linking Serbia, Bosnia, Montenegro, and the Adriatic Sea.

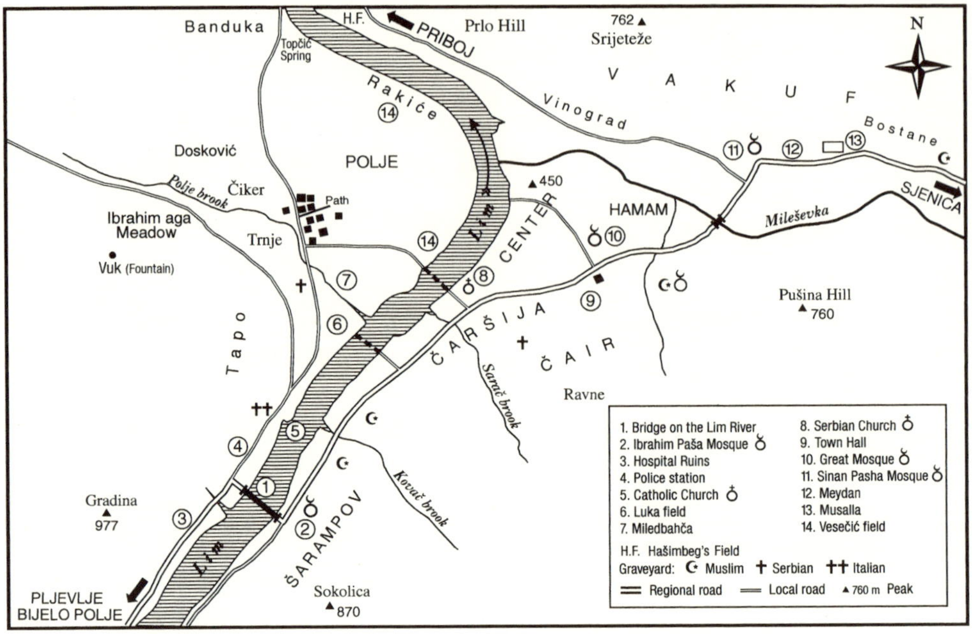

Map 4. The town of Prijepolje and its urban districts (in detail).

Part I: My Sandžak

Prijepolje and Hadžišehović Polje 1

Prijepolje is located in the Sandžak, at the juncture of three borders: Serbia, Montenegro, and Bosnia. During my childhood, before World War II, it was a kasaba, a small town of about a few thousand inhabitants. The River Lim approaches it from the south in a gentle curve, then splits Prijepolje into two parts: the town itself, and Polje (field), on the left bank, which our family settled ages ago.

Muslims and Serbs lived in Prijepolje, with Muslims being in the majority. There were a few Catholics and Jews, as well as others. A settlement of Muslim Gypsies was situated in Bostane (Melon Patch). At the other end of town, in Šarampov (Military Trench), the Gypsies had workshops called "Gypsy Foundries," from which the pounding of hammers on glowing iron could be heard all day long. They forged all kinds of tools and implements for the home and for work in the fields, and they shoed horses—which the children did not like to watch, thinking that it hurt the animals.

Muslims and Serbs lived in separate neighborhoods. Among the Muslim families, Vinograd, a hilly ancient vineyard, was the home of the Hašimbegović, or Hašimbeg's family; Vakuf was home to the Bakićs, the Salihbegovićs, and the Pašanovićs; the neighborhood of Hamam (Public Bath) contained the Čuturić and Kurtović families; Čair (Hilly Meadow) held the Jusufagićs; and the Veljovićs lived in Šarampov. The Serbs lived near their church in the center of town, as well as in a suburb in the direction of the Mileševa monastery and Kolovrat. The Muslim and Serbian peasants likewise lived apart. The Serbian villages were mainly in the foothills of Mount Zlatar (Golden Mountain) in the direction of Nova Varoš, and in the western hinterlands of Jabuka (Apple), toward Pljevlje, whereas the Muslim villages were to the southeast, toward Sjenica and Bijelo Polje. Prijepolje also had a small Roman Catholic church atop the cliff above the Lim. It was built in 1878, when the region belonged to the Austro-Hungarian Empire, but was later abandoned.

Like the whole of the Sandžak, Prijepolje had no industry. The town's population engaged in commerce and the trades, while those living in the countryside raised livestock, farmed, or cut and exported lumber down the Lim. The small coal-powered electrical plant operated only a few hours a day, providing electricity for the dim street lights, the Polimlje (Lim Valley) Hotel, the hospital and police station, and maybe a few homes. There was no light in Polje. Electricity was not introduced there until after World War II. Before that time we used lamps that we cleaned each evening, filled with kerosene, and hung from a peg in the room where we planned to spend the night.

The Serbs were already involved in the professions: they were doctors, lawyers, mechanics, clerks, and elementary and secondary schoolteachers. They occupied positions in the administration and in the police force. There were also a number of Russian doctors and teachers in the lower grades of the gymnasium. They had settled in town after the October Revolution in Russia in 1917. In many cases, Serbian peasants occupied the former estates of Muslim landlords, whose land had been confiscated after the Agrarian Reform of 1918 when the Kingdom of Serbs, Croates and Slovens—officially known as Yugoslavia after 1929—came into being with Aleksandar, Serbia's former regent, as king.

Most Muslims were small-scale tradesmen and merchants, although some in town continued to live off the income generated by what was left of their estates. There were very few Muslims in the town administration. Those who managed to obtain an education in places like Sarajevo, Istanbul, and Cairo rarely came back to Prijepolje.

Both the old Serbian and Muslim families lived in their own houses, which usually had two stories. The Muslims' houses had courtyards and gardens enclosed by walls or fences, whereas Serbian homes were more often built with workshops, either in the homes themselves or nearby. Serbian and Muslim children played together, and the young lads and girls went around together. On special occasions—such as Bairam, Christian holidays, or when there was a funeral or a wedding—Muslim and Christian neighbors visited one another. Yet even on these occasions, the men only rarely visited one another's houses, preferring to meet in the *čaršija* or market district. Serbs in town did not keep pigs, nor was there pork in the butcher shops. During Ramadan, Serbs in the *čaršija* did not eat in public out of respect for Muslims fasting during this period.

Intermarriage was almost nonexistent. A Muslim woman from Šarampov, who was married to a policeman of Hungarian origin, lived for a short time in our cousin, Salihaga's, former house. The woman came from a poor family and none of the people from the neighborhood visited her. She loved children, however, so she would invite us in for cakes and candies. Her kitchen, with its cupboard, white enameled stove, table, and small rug—which one could enter with one's shoes on—was in stark contrast to our rug-covered rooms, which had none of these innovations that seemed so strange to us children. We were told not to take anything from her because she might use fat when cooking, so we avoided her apartment. Sometimes, though, we took her candies and small shreds of cloth to make puppets.

Market day was very important for every Sandžak town. Saturday was market day in Prijepolje. In the early dawn, summer and winter, the peasants came to town on foot, some from distant places that were hours away, bringing whatever small things they had to sell. Each region was famous for something or other: Sjenica for its cheese and smoked meat; Babine for its *kajmak,* a thick cream; and Hisardžik for its chesnuts and pears, called *budale* (crazy). From Kosatica came meat, mountain-grown fruits, bilberries, and wool. From Mount Zlatar they brought wooden tubs, milking stools, kindling for lighting a fire, and various kinds of medicinal tars. The lowlanders brought wheat, and mountain villagers came with cattle and wool. The houses were supplied with these products even though we had our own but in smaller quantities. For the sake of variety and because of their exceptional taste, we bought dark-red cherries, fragrant and sweet apples, barley pears, and wild strawberries in buckets made from bark. In the fall, there were the tart but sweet and juicy *jerbasma* pears; the sweet, large *buzdohanka* pears; and the milky *budale* pears—picked as soon as they were ripe, sweetened with sugar, and served with soft chestnuts and walnuts.

All of the shops in the *čaršija* were open on market day, making it difficult to make your way through the market district because of the throngs of people. Tradesmen and merchants sent supplies home via their apprentices. Muslim women did not go to the market until after World War II, and even then shopping was largely a man's job. Women usually sent word to their men, instructing them what to buy from the apprentices and the children who trotted from house to men's shops.

If Saturday fell on major Serbian holy days or on household saints' days, the peasants would congregate early in the morning at the fair in the area around the church and below the River Lim. Brass orchestras came from Serbia and played all day. Such fairs were frequent in the wintertime, when, at summer's end, the saints' days began—for example, Our Lady's great and small feast days, Saint Demetrius's Day, and Saint Nicholas's Day. Our Lady's small feast day (September 19) was also the patron saint's day of the monastery at Mileševa. Fairs were held right at the monastery doors, and large gifts of cattle, grain, and milk products were given to the monastery. For the feast of the Epiphany (January 19), the holy liturgy was celebrated all night in the church. Before dawn, a cross was thrown into the frozen Lim and water was taken from the river. The water was preserved for a long time in copper vessels or glass bottles in which a copper coin would be inserted.

Serbs blessed the bodies of the dead with this water or gave it to sick people hoping that they would get well. The Muslims had a similar custom, but the water they brought came from a well in Mecca called "Zemzem."

Rakija (brandy) was downed at the fairs, and girls of marriageable age appeared, decorated with necklaces made of coins and wearing embroidered white-linen blouses and dark pleated skirts reaching to just below their knees. The skirts were woven from fine linen with barely visible lines. They wore woven woolen stockings embroidered with red and blue yarn and Serbian *opanci*—leather shoes with long "noses." Many were won right there at the fair. Sometimes young lads who had not already made up their minds about whom they were going to marry fought over girls.

The crowd became quiet with the first hint of twilight, and the musicians went away. Those who were too drunk to walk left on horseback; others walked beside horses carrying bags full of market goods: kerosene for lamps, tobacco, sugar, matches, and dye for yarn. Girls and young married women changed into their workday clothes in our courtyards and then set off for their villages, many of them embracing each other, singing peasant songs in a drawn out, throaty wail. Their voices filled the twilight and were evocative of some far-off call of the wild. They were accompanied by young lads, husbands, and relatives who also sang and hugged each other while walking and passing around a flask of *rakija* from hand to hand.

Polje was called "Hadžišehovićs's Field" after our family. Its main branch lived in the Hamam area, whereas the family's estates extended throughout Polje, Mijoska, Zalug, and farther on through the villages in the Lim Valley. Ahmo Šehović, my father's first cousin, kept track of the family tree. According to his data, Mustafa Čuturić was born in our family around 1800. He took on the title of *hadži* after going on a *hadž:* the pilgrimage to Mecca prescribed as a religious duty for Muslims. His son Ibrahim—they called him Šeho—also went to the Kaaba, so he got the nickname of Hadži Šeho, and his descendants became the Hadžišehović. My *amidža,* Osman, who lives in Turkey, adds that the Čuturić family came from the Bakarević of Pljevlje, who in turn originated from the Bakaroĝlu family of Konya in Turkey. Bakarević and Bakaroĝlu (the Turkish form) are the same name, indicating their descent from a coppersmith.

Besides our family, Polje had two other old families—the Musabegović and Selmanović—as well as some smaller families that settled there later. In the First Yugoslavia, Serbs also moved in, including Jovan Koković, who kept a small barroom on the road to Zalug, and a policeman named Grdanić. The latter joined the Chetniks during World War II, and his family moved away. All trace of them was lost after the war, and their house was taken over by refugees. Farther on, in the foothills toward Zalug, the family of Vojin Dosković lived on a rather large estate bought from Salihaga when he emigrated to Turkey in 1921. The estate consisted of meadows with sweet-smelling and medicinal herbs like savory, thyme, peppermint, wormwood, and burdock, as well as some cleared farmland bordered by woods right up to Čiker, a small hill above Polje. It had a stream with potable cold water and a barley pear tree whose tiny yellow fruit came at the beginning of July, when the barley was being harvested. A great mulberry tree located just behind the house filled with reddish-black mulberries at the beginning of each summer. Duša, Vojin's younger daughter, and I would climb the tree and sit on its branches, eating mulberries until her mother, Tijana, would call us in her drawn-out voice: "Oh . . . oh . . . children, come here, I have something for you to do." Tijana wore a peasant's long black skirt, a white linen blouse with long sleeves, and covered her head with a gray kerchief. Her call meant that it was time to go on one of the errands that children used to go on in those days. In the summertime we shucked the wheat, carried in the grass to be boiled with flour for cattle feed, and drove the cows to pasture early in the morning before sunrise and again in the afternoon when the unbearable heat had begun to die down.

The branch of the great Selmanović family that lived in several Sandžak towns, mainly Pljevlje, had inhabited Polje for centuries. The family was extinguished when its last two members, Zijah-Zika, who was deaf and dumb, and his sister Nedžiba, who was mentally impaired, died in 1943.

They lived in the largest and oldest house, built of stone and thick beams, which had been cut from the beech forests that once encircled Polje. Part of the house, along with its nearby meadows, was called "Banka" or "Bankino" in my time because it had been taken from the family for its debts. In the *avlija* (courtyard), which was enclosed by a wall made of unbaked bricks, stood the gaping ruins of the Konak, the separate house in which guests and chance visitors had at one time stayed for free. The house had an interior kitchen in which food was prepared over the great hearth, where oak and beech logs burned almost day and night. Grandmother Nina, the matron of the Beganović house in Zalug, where I spent my school vacations, had learned to cook as a young girl in that house. Her meatless peas in milk were acclaimed far and wide, as was her sweetened, thickly layered cornbread, baked under an iron lid covered with red-hot wood ashes.

The children did not dare to enter the courtyard because of Zika, but we were tempted by his vegetable garden below the house. We would peer through holes in the fence, waiting for him to go out into the neighborhood, so that we could enter and gather sweet, sticky, reddish-yellow peaches. That did not happen very often, though. We had to make our move when

Nedžiba was sleeping, so that she would not see us and scream for Zika to come home. Sometimes, Nanna, as I called my mother, would send me over with fresh milk for them. Zika would open the door for me and I would fearfully enter the *hajat* (anteroom). I would look around at the large, semi-darkened room, its *kilim*-covered floor, the cushioned wall seats and built-in, carved wooden shelves, and its deep windows. Silently, I would look for Nedžiba. She usually was playing with the nearly life-size dolls that Zika made for her. She gave them the names of my uncles, aunts, and other neighbors, who were her age and with whom—as a young girl—she used to play when her mother would take her out into the neighborhood. Entranced, I would make an effort to take everything in because Zika did not like us to linger. However, I would sometimes see her take a rolling pin and shoot at the dolls, mumbling: "Haso, Hanefija, Hanko bu . . . u . . . u. . . ."

The smell of stale air filled the room, and chickens cackled in the anteroom and along the spacious wooden stairway above. For some reason I still do not understand, Zika kept the chickens on the upper floor. Sometimes I would follow him upstairs when he was spreading wheat and corn for them to eat. They ran through the *kamrija,* the interior hallway on the upper floor, and the rooms with their still-preserved wooden floors and ceilings, which were like new. There was no one anywhere—everything was empty, except that chickens had laid eggs in the corner. Probably someone had picked up the furnishings from Zika, or they simply gave them away—I doubt that the neighbors would have taken them.

The house was wide and covered with an old tile roof that had survived the wartime bombing. At one time it was divided into four parts, with separate entrances, yards, and gardens. Besides Zika's and the empty "Banka" sections, Jakupaga Hodžić lived in a third part—where we sometimes took shelter during the war. The town war council put refugees in the remaining quarter. The garden below the house was separated from the fields by a partly destroyed stone wall beside which we passed on the way to our house. In the evenings, we were careful not to pass too close to the walnut tree beside the ruins of the even older Konak on the corner, where one sometimes saw "ghosts." Zika used to come into the neighborhood to sit and carve wood. People gave him cooked food, which he did not really need—he had everything, including wheat—but it was customary that part of our meals be set aside for him and Nedžiba. When they got seriously ill, it was Nedžiba who died first and Zika died not long afterward, probably from grief. After the war, instead of preserving what was almost certainly the oldest house in Prijepolje and maintaining it as a monument of fine architecture and the lifestyle of great families, it was destroyed.

The Musabegović family—which included in a cluster of houses Smailbeg and his relative Mehmedbeg, was at that time still well off. The fields below their houses stretched toward the Lim and they also owned estates in the neighboring villages of Dušmanići and Begluci. They lived in large two-story houses, with auxiliary buildings—barns, kitchens, racks for drying corn and plums, and stalls—in the lower courtyards. The houses had storerooms on the ground floor where flour, cheese, foods rich in fat, jam, and pickled foods were kept. Picked winter apples, pears, and dried fruit were kept in the attic or in rooms that were not in use during the winter. One small room alone would be almost full of nuts.

The Musabegović's spent almost the entire summer on the estate where the winter food was being prepared. In late fall—after the wheat had been harvested, the corn and fruit plucked, and the vegetables picked from the garden—they would return to Polje.

Smailbeg's son Nedžibeg was the only one from Polje who worked for the state at that time. He had a job as a clerk in the post office. He was married to Azizehanma (Lady Aziza), who had had two daughters from her first marriage to Osmanagić of Višegrad: Hamida and my best friend, Vasvija. She had three sons with Nedžibeg, whom the boys called *adžo* (uncle), so they would not hurt their half-sisters. It was a long time before I learned that "Adžo" was not Vasvija's father. Azizehanma's wealth was considerable. When she was quite young, her Aunt Sejdehanma, who was married to Mahmutaga Veljović of Šarampov, brought her to Prijepolje from the Pljevlje. Since her aunt and Mahmutaga did not have any children, Azizehanma inherited the Veljović family's wealth through her aunt: several houses in Šarampov, an estate and mill in Seljašnica and, from the property of Osmanagić, a field along the Lim known as Luka, the "Public Garden"—called Miledbahča—with the buildings of the old and new hospitals in it, and the house in which they lived, together with the land below, extending all the way to the River Lim.

I remember Sejdehanma leaning back against the chair in their house's "small room" on the upper floor, as she took in what was happening around our fountain on the road. She wore a flower on a twig behind her ear, a silk *mintan,* blouse with a silver and gold embroidered collar, and *dimije,* baggy pants made of fine wool tucked in at the waist. In the cabinets of her room, which one seldom entered, there were vases, small bowls, decorated glass cups, and little plates made of expensive colored glass and stone, edged in silver—all brought from Arabia, Damascus and Aleppo, when the Veljović *agas* used to trade in those days. We were all sad when "Teza," as we called her, passed away in 1943.

2 Families, Households, Food, and Animals

During my childhood, what was left of the Hadžišehović family after the emigration to Turkey numbered five households with about thirty-five members.

My grandfather, Avdaga, who was the seventh child, had six brothers and four sisters. Except for Nazifa, they all had large families. Nazifa, whom they affectionately called Aunt "Pila" ("Chick") because of her frail figure, did not marry. She lived with her youngest brother, Arifaga, a merchant.

There remains in my memory a picture of her walking up the finely paved courtyard with Lato's tied-up dog, Džono, behind her, pulling on his chain. Džono, whom we children feared, had the habit of running into the outdoor kitchen and stealing meat. My mother used to tell me that when it was her turn to cook, the hardest for her were Džono and Uncle Osman—at that time a young lad—who both wanted to be served out of turn so they could get the best. Lato, Arifaga's oldest son, and Osman left for Turkey in 1933. The greater part of the family emigrated to Turkey between 1923 and 1933. The First Yugoslavia's Agrarian Reform program was carried out during that period, which deprived them of their best lands. Families became impoverished and were scattered. That was one of the reasons for the emigration. The other, more important, reason was fear of the new Serbian government. Those who remained engaged in commerce and the trades. One part of the family was well off. Mujaga and Arifaga had businesses, houses, and rather large estates in Polje, Zalug, and Mijoska. My father, Ćamil, and his brother Abid, were *abadžije,* tailors who sewed and embroidered traditional clothes. Ahmo, their youngest cousin, was a barber. The remaining fields they owned in the villages of Izbišnje, Mijoska, and Zalug were sold off gradually for various reasons: the departure of family members to Turkey or to school, or because the people in the house could not adjust to the new way of life. They were accustomed to living in the old style, with plenty of guests, gifts, and expenditures. There still remained in my family the smaller lands around the houses in Polje and Zalug.

Muslims call their fathers "babba" or "babo." We used to call my father Babba. Old Serbian families, especially those living in the countryside, also used to call their fathers "babo." Babba had three brothers and two sisters. My grandfather and grandmother had lost three sons before my father was born, so they brought Ahmo Hasanagić, my grandmother Džemila's nephew, from Priboj to raise him together with Babba. People believed this was a cure when children were not surviving. It was said that Ahmo was a strong and mischievous child.

In his youth, Ahmo got married in an original manner: He abducted a girl from the Hadžimurtović's—the family of his mother, Fatima—because her father would not let her marry him. My Babba had to ride on horseback to Priboj that night in order to ask for the girl's hand from her father, so that neither the girl nor her family would lose face because she had fled with the young man on her own. While growing up with Ahmo, Babba spent part of his childhood in Priboj, thus becoming friends with Ahmo's younger brother, Tahir. Tahir was to marry a girl from the Hašimbegović family of Prijepolje. It was customary at that time for boys and girls to marry someone from their own *vilajet* (province). This meant that their prospective mate would come from one of the old Sandžak families. It also was customary to arrange marriages between people of the same social class. This social aspect was scrutinized very closely.

I remember as through a mist Tahir's visits to Polje. He would drive up in his own car, which was a real rarity in those days. Nanna and my aunts took advantage of the situation by getting him to drive them to our fields in Mijoska, where they would have a cup of coffee with our relatives living in the countryside. That was probably the first time I sat in an automobile. I remember being squeezed between grownups in the backseat. Not long afterward, in 1939, Tahir drove Nanna and me to visit my sister Šehza in Sjenica when she had her first child. They had sewn for me a beautiful, multicolored little coat for the occasion. We spent the night in Prijepolje at a friend's house, which was at the head of the *čaršija.* This made it easier for Tahir to pick us up before dawn, when he would be driving with some mail from Priboj to Sjenica. I know that I was very excited and barely slept, waiting anxiously for Tahir's arrival. I could hear the night watchmen calling to one another in the distance, and the shrill sound of their whistles down below in the *čaršija.* In Turkish times, guards would make their presence known by beating on a drum. They used to guard houses and shops from break-ins, especially in the *čaršija.*

The *fijaker,* as we used to call a car, finally arrived. Nanna and I got into it in front of the coffee shop that served as a waiting room and headed off toward the monastery of Mileševa and Hisardžik on the road to Sjenica. The *čaršija* remained in darkness behind us, except for the flickering light of the oil lamp in the coffee shop. It was the route taken for centuries by merchants as well as emigrants from Sarajevo and the Sandžak traveling to Salonika, Dubrovnik, and Istanbul. The only difference was that they were on horseback.

As the oldest child, Babba had been the head of our household for forty years. That meant that he did not belong to my sisters and me any more than he did to the rest of the family, nor was any distinction made between us children. We were all equal, no matter what house we lived in. In my day, Babba lived with his younger brother Abid, while others in the family were scattering throughout the world. Uncle Ibrahim, a *šerijat* (Muslim canon law) judge, went off to work in Macedonia. Uncle Osman emigrated to Turkey, and his sisters Zina and Hanka got married. His mother Džemila, whom we all called "Mother," came from the Hadžimurtović family of Priboj. We often had houseguests from Priboj, including Aunt Zina, who was married to Fehimbeg Hasanagić. She brought with her Juso, her first son and the oldest male child in the extended family. My sister Šehza was much older, but she was not a male. Later, Uncle Abid had a son named Muhamed who took primacy over the rest of us children.

We liked it when there were guests, because the lower house would fill with people. The rooms were all lighted up and people would sit around until late in the evening, telling stories about olden times, or about relatives in Turkey, and about fields and villages where they had once held estates. For example, the field in the village of Izbišnje, a little farther down the Lim Valley, was famous for a snake that used to come to its stream, and "for that reason they sold it." Another piece of land, this one with fruit trees along the road, became dangerous because Serbs would go there to provoke trouble. It eventually had to be let go because the neighbors wanted it that way.

Rice and *burek,* a kind of meat pastry made from wild game that our guests brought as a gift, were served at such parties. My relatives would retell stories about skating in winter after dinner. It was at one of those events that our relative Zuhdija, who had just been in Ankara, descended like an arrow down our path because Hanka ("No, it was Hata," someone interjected), had poured water on our path in order to freeze it. She thus paid him back in kind for having wrapped himself all in white in order to spook her when he emerged one evening from behind the summer kitchen at the lower house.

I learned more about my grandmother Džemila from these stories: she used to go on her bay horse around her father's estate to help him because he did not have a male child. She was rather tall and had a dark complexion. Babba, Uncle Ibrahim's daughter Šadija, and I took after her the most, both in stature and appearance. They used to say that I was similar to her in nature: "like a male."

Babba was an *abadžija,* a profession that was in decline. Together with his brother Abid, he used to sew peasant clothes on a sewing machine, whereas the baggy pants and vests he would embroider by hand, using various silk braids and trimmings. We lived in two houses: the upper house at the top of Polje and the lower house at the bottom of the path, closest to the Lim. The upper, smaller house, in which my parents lived, was situated below a small hill, Trnje, which was traversed by a road in the direction of Dušmanići. It was separated from the other houses in Polje by a brook that emerged from its crevice between Trnje and another small hill, Čiker, next to our house. The lower house, which we called "Mother's," was the last in a string of Hadžišehović and Musabegović houses.

My mother was Babba's second wife. His first wife, who died young, left behind my half-sisters Šehza and Ferida. Before getting married, Nanna was a teacher and later a teacher of religion. During Turkish times, my parents finished both the *iptidaija* and *ruždija,* that is, the primary and secondary/junior schools, as they were called in those days. They learned to write Turkish in Arabic letters because the schools for Muslim and non-Muslim children were separate before 1912. After the Turks pulled out of the Sandžak in 1912, there was a shortage of teachers and so, while still a *ruždija* student, Nanna replaced the Turkish teachers, who often were the wives of officers who had resettled in Turkey. She used to receive her pay in Turkish and English gold liras, some of which we have kept as souvenirs to this day.

Nanna continued to receive her pay during World War I, when school was not open and Prijepolje was already in Serbian hands. Her father would take her to the courthouse—just as in Turkish times—to collect her pay. She already wore the veil, and she used to tell me that Petar I Karađorđević paid her from exile, sending her money from London.

Nanna kept her work booklet in a box. It had a cloth binding and fine paper with printed Cyrillic titles for each column. The school official, Gojko Zejaković, who filled the same position after 1945, used to certify each column in black ink and signed each page. He wrote in the fine hand that was taught in school in those days. The booklet clearly shows that in 1929 Nanna received twenty-nine Yugoslav dinars a month. A year earlier she had bought—for eight thousand dinars, through the teacher's cooperative—a Singer sewing machine of the latest design with its own case. The black metal trestle had the trademark "SINGER" embossed on its footing and there was also a box with a special adapter for embroidery. That was a great novelty, because until that time, women had done all embroidery by hand. Nanna cleaned the machine regularly, teaching me to do the same. Nanna's Singer was always in working condition, except for minor repairs, and remains in our family to this day.

Nanna and Babba often spoke Turkish at home, corresponding with friends and Uncle Ibrahim in Turkish written with Arabic letters. It seems to me that besides Nanna there were no other older Muslim women who were educated. There were few young people who could even read and write decently. As far as the older generation was concerned, the situation was basically the same with the Serbian women. However, at least some of them finished pedagogical school outside Prijepolje.

During the short period of Austro-Hungarian rule, the government organized courses and special sessions in which Muslim teachers were taught to write in Latin and even in Cyrillic. About seventy teachers and important Muslim figures from the Sandžak attended the training course in Prijepolje. Among them was Murat Šećeragić, who later became the assistant *reis-ul-ulema,* the head of the Muslim religious community in Yugoslavia. My Nanna also attended. She studied alone, in a separate room from the men, wearing her veil. The teacher, an Austro-Hungarian officer, taught in both rooms, moving back and forth from one to the other, writing on the chalkboard in each of them.

The lower house, where Mother lived with Uncle Abid, was surrounded by green foliage. At the front of the house began Mujaga's and Arifaga's *baskije,* old plum tree orchards and fields, surrounded by wooden fences similar to those used today to demarcate mountain pastures. After them came the "Polimlje" sports club's playing field, with the clear Lim flowing like a tear just below it. The river encircled Polje in its bowlike course. On the opposite bank was the mouth of the Mileševka. In my day, this was an empty area, really the delta of the Mileševka, beyond which was the largest part of Prijepolje: the Center and Hamam.

Mother's house was built some time after 1900, when my grandfather divided the estate with his brothers, some deciding to emigrate to Turkey and others to stay in Polje. On the upper story were *kamrija* and three large rooms: Mother's, the guest room, and a parlor that looked out on the Lim. The latter was the first room flooded with sunlight each morning.

Grandmother used the spacious *kamrija* to entertain close members of the family, including her brother-in-law Arifaga, or cousin Mujaga, and others. They would sit on the wall seats near the window while she sat on a cushion near the small fireplace after making coffee to serve her guests. One of the younger women, usually one of my aunts, would bring the utensils for making the coffee from downstairs, then leave her to chat with the older people. Since my grandfather was no longer alive, his brother Arifaga had the right to enquire about the household and to give grandmother any advice he saw fit. In this way they oversaw Babba and the younger members of the family. Grandmother did not prohibit us children from occasionally listening in on the grown-ups' conversations. Our parents treated us the same way. It was like having a school at home, one in which we learned about life.

The first floor of the lower house was for living. In the winter kitchen, the women of the house would knead the dough for bread and pita or a savory filled pie. We stored the butter and cooked food in a deep wooden drawer. Unopened cans of butter, cheese, jam, and roasted meat were kept in the pantry.

The floor of the largest room in which the household sat was covered with an "everyday" *kilim,* a handmade woolen rug. On the window side were the wall seats, while the windows themselves faced the southwest for greater light. This room was the main gathering place, especially in winter. Along one wall there would be a loom with a *kilim* being woven by my Aunt Zubejda, who was a master rug weaver. The girls in the household, especially Arifaga's daughters, helped her. On the other side of the room stood the "Singer" machine on which Uncle Abid did his sewing. Aunt Zina, a skilled seamstress specializing in sewing men's suits, would use the machine when she came to visit. Beside the sewing machine there would be a tailor's long table, full of cloth cut and ready for sewing. Nearby were a metal *aršin* and a one-meter yardstick. The *aršin,* which was two-thirds of a meter, was still used. To calculate weight, our people used two forms of scales, one that used weights and measured in *oka's* (1.25 kilograms), and the other a regular scale that measured in kilograms.

At the end of the great room was a large, handmade sheet metal stove. We did not have one of the modern enameled iron stoves, which were already in use in some Serbian houses. This stove not only cooked our food in winter, it also heated the room. It used wood logs that were stored beneath it in order to dry them out completely, so they would burn more easily. This was the cat's favorite place. It would spread out on the logs at night after hunting for mice in the stables. We kept a supply of firewood in the lower courtyards, piled carefully in order to protect it from rain and snow. We bought wood from peasants by the *tovar,* which was the size of the load that one horse could carry. Beech and oak were the best wood for burning. At one side of the stove was a closed off *abdesluk,* a small bathroom/washroom in which we kept water used for the *abdest,* a ritual washing prior to prayer.

My Uncle Abid and his wife Zubejda gathered the youngsters in the family, either in the great room or upstairs in the parlor, since they themselves were considered young. Besides Muhamed, they had Hajrija and little Avdo (Abdullah), the heir to our grandfather's name. Murat and Paša had not yet been born. When a visitor dropped in at mealtime, he or she would be served at a *sofra* (a low table) with other members of the household. Winter breakfasts were separate, especially during grandmother's lifetime. Each morning before dawn, Babba and I would go down to the lower house to eat and pray the *sabah* (morning prayer). Then Babba and grandmother would discuss business. "Ćamil," she would say, "Our friend Čantra has guests—we ought to invite them to lunch or dinner." Or, "Jusufbeg has a new child—we ought to give it a gift." This meant that grandmother and her daughter-in-law would have to congratulate them and bring the child a gift. Or she would say: "We still haven't gone to express our sympathies to Mustafa over the death of his sister Rahima." After that they would discuss household business, such as the lack of Sjenica cheese, which meant that Babba would have to order a new can. Sometimes they would approach the subject of selling some land in a circuitous manner. In as much as the master of a household did not easily let go of land, such ideas would hover in the air as members of the household searched for faults in a particular field. For example, the property in Izbišnje had a snake, which was a good reason for selling it. On the other hand, if a really pressing need arose, such as paying for hospitalization costs or for sending someone away to school, then the master of the house had no other choice. On such occasions, they would even sell the household gold, whether in coins or jewelry.

My Aunt Zubejda would cook a breakfast of flat bread with baking soda, beef, and noodle soup. We would eat cold cuts that had been dried in the attic, as well as cheese and jam with sweet cream or honey. Sometimes neighbors would come to breakfast, and even guests from far away. The latter would usually spend the night with relatives or friends in Polje. As such visits usually had to do with business, breakfast was served in Mother's room. Sometimes such visits were kept secret because they involved decisions on sensitive family matters related to the division of the estate, a dowry, or the distribution of an inheritance. Especially secretive were transactions involving the selling of estates or houses, or the quest for a loan.

My Babba also took part in councils that protected the property of children whose parents had died. Other councils helped to maintain peace in families and prevent divorce. Families fought most often over the division of estates, or when a sister—at her husband's insistence—would try to get her dowry at an inappropriate time, such as immediately after the death of her father. Families sometimes did not communicate with one another for years after such incidents. This had a negative influence on marital harmony, because marital ties linked many families. Mediation, therefore, played an important role.

After we had breakfast, Babba would set out for the *čaršija* to open his shop. There, since the cloth was strong, he would sew on his heavy model

"Singer." In the shop he would give customers their tailored clothes, pay his suppliers, and wait for new customers.

The road from Polje to the *čaršija* was long, so in the summertime people would cross the Lim by boat at Bukovi, in the vicinity of our shack, where Uncle Abid sewed and on occasion transported people across the river. We had an extra "Singer," a manual in the shack, which could be carried home at night. We also had two boats on the banks of the Lim. On Saturdays, Uncle Abid would use the larger one to ferry peasants who were going to market, and on Sundays he took people who were attending soccer matches at the Polimlje field. The small boat was for the everyday use of members of the family and our neighbors.

At the head of Veselčić field, behind our shack and below "Banka," stood the branchy, noble Veselčić walnut tree. From Saint George's Day (May 6) on, swings were hung from its branches—a small one for the children and a large one for grown-ups. Early morning folk rituals were held beneath that tree on Saint George's Day. Our people from Polje gathered there—they came on other days as well—to sit by the water for a while in the shade of the walnut tree. We leased the Veselčić land and always planted the best quality corn and lima beans on it.

My mother's name was Fatima. Her family, on the side of her father, Ejupaga Kurtović, came from Belgrade, or "Bijograd," as our cousins used to call it. They told us stories about the women in that family, who wore long gowns when they visited Prijepolje. The men were merchants, having a branch of the family in Prijepolje, on the road to Saraj Bosna, today's Sarajevo. After the Turkish withdrawal from Belgrade, the family settled in the Hamam area of Prijepolje. Their workshops suffered heavy losses during a great fire at the end of the nineteenth century. They had great fertile lands at Kolovrat, where—during the Turkish period as well as under the Germans ("Schwabe")—there were found treasures of gold and jewelry dating from Roman times or the *kalu bela vakta,* as they used to say.

Nanna's mother, Dževahira, came from a local tribe of Malagić, which settled the village of Hisardžik—or "Fortress," in Turkish "Hisar"—above the monastery of Mileševa, which was built by Serbia's Nemanjić dynasty in 1237. The village is very old and is mentioned in the travel diary of Evliya Čelebi, a Turkish traveler from seventeenth century, as being located on the route leading from Raguza (Dubrovnik) and Salonika inland. Čelebi mentions a mosque carpeted with a white *kilim* brought from the Middle East. It still existed in my day, rolled up along the wall beneath the front windows. The mosque practically leaned against the citadel or fortress, which was built on the rocky cliff above the Mileševka River canyon. From the steep cliff of Mount Zlatar, on the other side of the canyon, the spring of Benića streams noisily downward, cascading into the Mileševka. Within the citadel itself there is a cave in the canyon's side with an almost inaccessible well known as "Sava's water." My mother used to tell me how, as a young girl, she would make her way along a goat path to this well, where, according to tradition, the thirteenth-century Serbian saint Sava Nemanjić, foregoing his monastery, used to sit in seclusion and meditate. Čelebi's travel diary also mentions a great, healthy pine tree opposite the mosque that is still in good condition and "doesn't allow itself to be cut down," as well as a large, barely perceptible Muslim graveyard of unknown origin.

The Malagić tribe had several educated members, of whom the most notable was Abdul Aziz, my grandmother Dževahira's brother, who died as a student in Istanbul. Among the families in the tribe there was a tradition of giving one son the name Abdullah, Servant of Allah, so my grandmother insisted that her first son be named Abdullah. This Abdullah was Nanna's eldest brother. He became a *hafiz,* one who knows the Qur'an by heart.

Life within Malagić's households suggested that the tribe was indeed descended from the ancient local aristocracy. The people were quiet and polite, showing exceptional respect to the head of the household, who had his own guest room and his *kitabs,* leather-bound books with pages inscribed with colorful arabesques. It was considered shameful to gossip about family business outside the house, regardless of whether it was to complain or to boast. The houses were spacious and clean, and the rooms lent themselves to privacy. Duties were shared according to rank, and seniority was quite clear, proceeding from the head of the family to his mother, to the oldest daughter-in-law or his eldest unmarried sister, down through the youngsters. My father's family had a similar hierarchy, and, as far as I know, one could find such a system among the Musabegović family in the hamlet of Zabuđe, as well as in the Galiza's homestead in the village of Peselje, from which came my father's first wife, Begzada.

In 1913, Nanna's younger brother, Bećir, who had studied in Pljevlje, went to Haydar Pasha Military Academy in Istanbul. While still a cadet, he was wounded at the battle of Čanakale in Turkey at the age of seventeen. He died in Haydar Pasha Hospital and was buried in the nearby military cemetery as a *gazija,* one who fell for his country. Mother's family got the news of his death a year later, when the academy sent them his personal effects: some letters and a French language textbook.

Nanna's eldest brother, whom she called Hafiz out of respect, remained in Hamam, which got its name from the public baths drawn from the thermal hot springs gushing forth at the bottom of Pušina Hill. He spent his time memorizing the Qur'an and was the imam, the priest who led the daily prayers in the Great Mosque. He also harvested the wheat, stacked the hay, and picked fruit from the orchards in Kolovrat. His wife, Arifehanma, was the daughter of Hafiz Ramiz Šabanić of Pljevlje, the head imam in the mosque at Moćevac. In ancient times, Moćevac was famous for its Miledbahča, and for the even more famous love song, *sevdalinka:* "Moćevac, little Stambul." Aunt Arifa was my wet nurse, and her influence on my Islamic education was almost as great as my Nanna's. She used no extra words and her voice was mild but convincing. She always left the choice up to you, which somehow made it even more binding. The names Muhamed and Murat were used in both my mother's and my father's families, so that I had two relatives with each of those names and was therefore forced to distinguish them according to whether they were from Polje or Hamam.

The importance of reading the Qur'an was passed down from the adults to the young in Nanna's family. Nanna used to tell me that when Bećir traveled to Turkey in 1913, he and some other travelers went on horseback via Sjenica and Novi Pazar in the direction of Salonika. Hafiz accompanied him to well beyond Hisardžik, where Bećir visited relatives and prayed in the mosque. The brothers said good-bye to each other on a rise near the hill called "Milošev Do." Bećir turned around several times to get a parting look at Hafiz. The last words to reach his brother's ears were: "Hafiz, don't forget the Qur'an!" The Qur'an was read in our home every day. During the World War II, when I stayed at Hafiz's home, I would spend several hours in the morning listening to him recite the Qur'an from memory. I would kneel at a small desk on which was set an open copy of the Qur'an, following his recitation line by line. Whenever he experienced some difficulty, I would prompt him with the correct word.

Muslims lived in large, two- and sometimes three-story houses with plenty of rooms. The houses were set back from the road, encircled by gardens and enclosed by walls or a fence made of long, thin boards so as to shield the inhabitants from outside view. They each had an upper and lower courtyard, and most had two entrances. One entered the upper courtyard through a wooden gate that hung on forged iron rings under a small overhang. The women planted flowers in the upper courtyards. Tiny daisies grew between the white cobblestones, so that the ground looked like a colorful rug. Water flowed in small ditches in some courtyards and gardens, cooling the air and the foodstuffs that were placed in them during heat spells, as in the dug wells. The lower courtyard had a work area that included the summer kitchen. Wood was chopped there and women did their laundry in wooden troughs.

Houses had a living room on the first floor, facing the sun, where people congregated. The rest of the rooms belonged to a particular person: the master's room, the elders' room, the parents' room, the guest room, and the maid's quarters. In the older houses, the downstairs rooms had thick walls, as in Zika's house. They were cool in summer and warm in winter. Winter flowers garnished the deeply set windowsills. Leafy basil filled almost an entire window, as if a plum tree with thick branches were growing there.

The living room had multiple functions. The stove was used for cooking in the wintertime. Some houses had green tile stoves with different recesses into which were placed various vessels for heating up prepared food and for cooking over a slow flame. Beside the stove were built-in, two-level wooden cupboards. Wood for fuel was stored in the lower level, and you could sit on the shelf of the upper level and warm up your feet when you came in from the cold. Some stoves were fed from an anteroom. No wood had to be brought into the main room when such was the case, and there was no problem with ashes, making such stoves easier to clean.

Broad wooden stairs led to the second-floor *kamrija* (main hallway). Rarely did one use the outside stairs to get to the upper story. Some *kamrijas* had a protruding section known as "the corner." It was completely glassed in, half-covered with finely carved jalousies through which came richly decorated curtains of silk. The other rooms seemed larger because there was little furniture. Cabinets for storing bed linens were built into the walls, and there were glass cabinets for keeping finer dishes, vases, glasses of jade, silver, and a family book. Thus, other elements in the rooms stood out: the cushioned wall seats, the built-in, hand-carved wooden shelves, the rugs, and the cushions for sitting. Members of the household sat on soft wall seats or on cushions on the floor. The younger people were not permitted to sit together with the older people on the wall seats—not even with their parents—unless they were invited. They kneeled along the wall, which was not difficult for those who had already learned to bow while offering their *namaz* (obligatory prayers). We were taught to sit modestly, out of respect for one's elders and for guests, and to enter a room saying *selam* (peace) and to exit while backing away, so as not to turn one's back to the guests. Good manners required that we close the door behind us softly.

In the guest rooms, where the more distinguished guests were put up, silken or velvet covers were stretched along the wall seats, over which was placed white chiffon embroidered on the edges. Stiff pillows in a variety of colors were arranged around the room, especially on the wall seats. They served as support when you sat. The pillow tops were covered with fine white cotton in order to keep them clean. The floors in each room were covered with rugs. The rugs on the lower level were typical, whereas those on the upper story floors were hand woven, sometimes with a long, soft woof and patterns that were mostly floral in design. The borders had motifs similar to those on the chiffon cloth on the wall seats. The wooden shelves were filled with tinned copper plates and engraved trays that were used to serve guests their food and sherbet in fancy glasses.

Larger windows having two sections were furnished with embroidered curtains that were either raised or pushed to the side in the daytime. Their cloth was woven from silk and cotton, and embroidered with various ancient patterns. Sometimes, women wove the finest textiles on which they embroidered old patterns with silk, silver, and red thread. The red thread was expensive. It was made from a very stable dye that came from algae. For everyday curtains, women bought printed cloth that already bore the outlines of the designs. Later on, the cross and the Toledo pattern came into use. Such embroidery was regarded as Christian.

The lower courtyards had small gates that led to another courtyard with sheds for the animals, or to other auxiliary buildings. Still further on was a garden in which vegetables were grown. Manure was thrown out through openings in the sheds to dry, then scattered about the gardens and fields in the spring.

Vegetable gardens stretched out behind the houses. Almost everything was grown there. We did not sell things from our garden. To do so was considered shameful. Instead, we sent food to those who temporarily did not have any, or to newcomers who had no land. Besides vegetable gardens, we had orchards full of plum, apple and pear trees. All kinds of plums could be found there: small, large, sweet, as well as tasty but not-yet-ripe white plums that were so sour no one but the children wanted to try them. They made our lips so tight we could not open them afterward.

Along the borders of the fields, which began behind the gardens and extended to the Lim, grew currants, raspberries, and miniature roses. Every house had at least one bush laden with fragrant, red May roses, and climbing roses that wound themselves around the windows grew in the upper courtyard. The roses yielded preserves and the rose-water extract used in making sherbet.

Other types of roses were planted in the flowerbeds surrounding the houses: sweetly scented ones with soft white petals, as well as pink roses; we also had the very rare blue rose. Carnations were another favorite flower—dark red, red, and mixed white—with a delightful fragrance, no matter what the species. Yellow, heavily scented African marigolds and ancient wallflowers filled the courtyards and gardens with their aroma. The strongly scented costmary (common tansy) that liked the shade at the end of the garden, and the houseleek that grew on the roof of the outdoor kitchen, protected the house from evil spells. Some houses had small flower gardens, thickly planted and separated from the courtyard by a low, carved wooden fence, where one ate breakfast or recited the Qur'an in the coolness of the freshly watered flowers. Here were planted colorful and white flowers, spring hyacinths, summer fragrant lilies, and autumn chrysanthemums. In May, the branches of white and violet lilac bushes began to bend downward under the weight of their blossoms, and somewhat later their scent would be replaced by that of white jasmine, which reached even into our rooms. From the windows of the rooms we could bend down the heavy branches of the trees and by the light of the moon pick a plum or an apple, while listening to the rustling of the Lim's cool waters, which made us sleepy. They used to say that the Lim did not always sound the same: on stormy nights, before it rained, the rustling became stronger, sometimes even explosive.

The houses in Polje did not have running water—only Azizehanma had a fountain in her courtyard. Drinking and cooking water was brought from wells, springs, or the public fountains (a system of piped water). We used the water from our brook, which was diverted through ditches to the small wooden fountains in the courtyards, for washing and other functions. Farther on, the water drained off into the vegetable gardens. Even though the Lim flowed nearby, there was invariably a water shortage during the summer droughts. There was neither the possibility nor sufficient will to set up an irrigation system using the river's water; instead, people looked to the sky and hoped for the best.

Two springs flowed from the foothills beyond our upper house. We got our drinking water from them, especially during the war, when there was no water in the fountain. In the early dawn, before the other people in Polje, Azizehanma and my mother would go for water. They used a washed pot, but they were not sure that everyone else did the same. Farther on, above Trnje (Thorns), in the meadow belonging to my mother's cousin, Ibrahim *aga* Veljović, there rose from an artesian well the water called Vuk (Wolf). During Ramadan, this water was brought home for the first meal after fasting all day.

Going for water was one of the first tasks one learned in childhood. We began with teapots, then with pitchers, and gradually progressed to larger vessels. The fountain on the road was a meeting place where people chatted while filling their vessels. Right next to it, an old apple tree planted by my grandfather Avdaga, extended its branches. They say that Avdaga was medium in height, had a light complexion, and was mild mannered. He loved to plant fruit trees. His nature and appearance were inherited by my first cousin Avdo, Uncle Abid's younger son. Our people believed that it was *sevap* (a good deed) to plant fruit trees. My grandfather had plenty of acquaintances in the countryside, and he, like my father, was an *abadžija.* It was never clear to me how such broad friendships developed in olden times, but even in my day I came across traces of them in my treks through the country villages. These friendships probably were a reflection of earlier, deeper connections.

Someone was always resting underneath the apple tree by the *mekteb,* an ancient religious school. It often was Serbs, returning from the city to distant villages like Toci and others farther down the Lim Valley. They would take out of their colorful woven bags a package containing rye or barley bread, a wooden canister of cheese, and a quarter liter of brandy with which to wash the food down. When they finished, they would get up and say, "Thanks be to God." Then, grasping the bridles of their horses, which had been left to graze on the *mekteb*'s lawn while they ate their lunch, they would move off toward their villages.

Every house had in its living room, and sometimes in another room, an *abdesluk* used for washing one's hands before and after meals, for ritual washing prior to prayer, and as a winter bathroom. Special guests were offered a light, copper washbowl over which water was sprinkled from a narrow-necked, slender pitcher onto the guests' hands. After that they were given a small hand towel to dry their hands. Water was kept in enameled tin pails or in large copper pitchers in the washroom. We sprinkled water on our hands and body. The wastewater was drained off by a trough into a ditch in the garden. Large houses had interior toilets at the end of a hallway or in protruding sections of the house facing the garden. Other houses had their toilets in outhouses set in a secluded corner of the yard. Their waste was directed into pits dug in far corners of the garden. Water was kept in clean, closed vessels, along with towels that were hung on nails and frequently washed in boiling water. The toilets themselves were cleaned with utensils kept there for that purpose.

Our people generally bathed only once a week, although women bathed more frequently on occasion. It was believed that too much soap would dry out the skin and hasten the aging process. Those who did *abdest* and used the water in the bathroom did not need to bathe every day. They thought that *abdest,* which amounted to massaging the face and hands several times a day with water of varying temperatures, was especially good for refreshing one's face and neck.

During the wintertime we bathed in the *abdesluk,* and when summer came the household would bathe in the summer kitchens, in sheltered sections of the gardens. For fun, men would bathe in the Lim, while women and children would wash in the river below Rakiće, a place overgrown with thickets, or at Bukovi, in a narrow section of the Lim where the women washed clothes. There were few people in this part of the Lim on workdays.

The children came next, after they had washed their clothes and laid them out to dry. Mothers washed them whether the children liked it or not: getting soap in one's eyes was no excuse for not washing. However, most of the children enjoyed it. Even now, I remember a great summer heat wave at Bukovi and bathing pleasantly in the Lim's clear, green waters while little fish darted here and there. They would gather in schools around the women and children, who would throw them little scraps of food. We would eat our lunch there on the banks of the Lim. The women would heat our food up on a fire set between two rocks. The little children would take their naps in hammocks in the shade of the willows and poplars. It was common belief that it was not healthy to place children on the ground because the dampness could lead to colds. We also had a hammock in one corner of the great room. Little children would sleep in it after they had outgrown their cribs.

Women did the laundry in wooden troughs in the lower courtyard. First, everything was soaped and scrubbed by hand in warm water. After washing, the bed linen was boiled in cauldrons of lye to whiten it. The women made soap once a year from fats that were collected during the course of the year. For a long time, Muslims refused to buy laundry soap in stores because they were afraid it might be made from fat of suspect origin, such as pig fat or the fat from other dead animals.

Older families and those in the countryside used oak lye rather than soap. The laundry was placed in deep cauldrons that had taps for draining the water. Oak or beech ash was then sprinkled on top. Water was poured in and heated to the boiling point after the cauldron's cover was put in place. A low fire under the cauldron kept the lye hot. At the end of the washing, the lye water was let out through the tap and the laundry was beaten with a battledore on a worn, flat rock beside the river or a villager's fountain. After being washed in this manner, and dried in winter in the frost and in summer on the sand by the river, or on the fences along the meadows, the laundry smelled naturally fresh.

Every house had its Qur'an, and some had old Islamic books of a semireligious character that explained the Qur'anic text and the Prophet's practice. They also had Ilmihal: elementary religious instruction for children. There were very few other books, if any. The old books handed down from generation to generation were leather-bound prayer books with richly decorated, colored initial letters. These were often kept in a trunk in the attic or some other hidden place. People used to bring them to my mother. She would examine them and call in the imams from the mosques to preserve some. The rest were buried in the countryside by village imams so that no one would harm them or use them as wrapping paper. Muslims and Serbs in Prijepolje believed that one should not use written texts containing prayers for inappropriate purposes, or throw them in places where they might be stepped on. If such material was no longer usable—for example, pages had been torn out—it had to be burned or buried in the ground. This was especially true of texts in which God's name or the names of God's messengers were mentioned, no matter what the religion.

Houses usually had a pad of paper and a pencil—or ink made from wood ash and a quill—for writing. People rarely wrote letters, unless it was to relatives in Turkey or to friends, usually the family of a daughter-in-law, typically around Bairam. They also wrote letters to express their sympathy if someone died, and to extend their best wishes to the remaining members of the family. The hodžas wrote special notes in ink: for healing, for success in business, and to counteract evil spells. These notes, called *hamajlija,* were worn around the neck in a special locket, or sewn into the inside pocket of a shirt, or braided into the hair. Sometimes they were soaked in water and drunk. Even Christians came to the hodžas for help, just as Muslims visited the monasteries for assistance, although to a lesser extent.

The household ate at *a sofra,* a traditional low round wooden table set for a meal. Bread was broken with the hands, while pita—in the Sandžak a type of savory, filled pie—and other food was served in copper or enameled dishes. Wooden vessels also were used, especially bowls. Bosnian specialties consisting of mixed meat and vegetables were baked in clay pots in the bakery's oven. Everyone ate with their hands, except for soup or cooked vegetables, which were eaten with wooden or metal spoons. Three meals were eaten in common: breakfast was taken before leaving the house; lunch was served around noon, after the men returned from the *čaršija* and the children from school; and supper was served after dark, when all the chores were done—the gardens watered, the cows milked, and the remaining domestic animals taken care of for the night. Meanwhile, the meal had been prepared in the outdoor kitchen. It was then that daily life moved from the backyard to the house.

In the wintertime almost everyone, especially the children and the elders, slept in the living room, where a fire burned all night. The upper rooms were rarely heated. If we had guests, we would put a bucket filled with hot coals in their room to take the chill out of the air. The coals were covered with ashes to prevent the release of carbon monoxide. During a cold wave, the small, thin metal stoves in the rooms were stoked with wood. The inhabitants of the house slept on wool mattresses that were taken up during the day and placed in built-in cabinets. Metal beds with yellow brass balls, as well as large, shiny, yellow-framed mirrors were already coming into fashion in the young people's bedrooms. To ward off evil spells—as well as for decoration—ritual towels embroidered with gold or silk thread were draped over the tops of the mirrors. Shaggy rugs with pleasing nature scenes in rose or green colors hung on the walls above the beds.

Households in town as well as in the countryside produced much of their own food. Our region was mountainous but sheltered, having a relatively mild climate in the valleys. This resulted in a long growing season for cereals, fruits, and vegetables. When the growing season finished in the valley, it shifted to the mountainous areas. For this reason, the people could count on good food and clean water through most of the year. Townspeople would sow their own fields in the nearby countryside and grow vegetables in gardens at home. They used to say that such families had their own wheat, which was a good status symbol. Those who did not have fields and meadows would buy their wheat and hay for their cows from farmers. It was not easy for them.

Natural fertilizer was used until after 1945, and the larger family farms prepared their own seed grain, had nurseries for vegetables, and grew shoots for fruit trees. The farm plots—we called them fields—in the mountain areas were smaller than those in the valley. The land was cultivated with a plow pulled by a horse or oxen. When keeping heavy stock became too expensive, the land was turned into meadows.

Peasants threshed their grain at a threshing floor, using horses that would trot around the pole in the center of the floor from dawn until afternoon, urged on by the whip of the farmer, who stood close by.

Barley, like buckwheat, prospered in the mountain fields. Oats, which were equally abundant in the mountains, were used for horses. Wheat, on the other hand, because of the short growing season, did not fare well in the highlands. For that reason, buckwheat and potatoes were an acceptable replacement. Different sorts of potatoes were grown everywhere, especially the "Russian" white potato, which spilled out of the skin when it was fully baked and was sweet when boiled. There was not a lot of income from grain, but, on the other hand, the cereals themselves—the wheat, rye, barley, oats, buckwheat, and corn—were of good quality. In the plateau areas and river valley, wheat, barley, and corn were planted because of their good yield. They fared well in rich soil with plenty of moisture, especially near watered areas and rivers like ours at Polje. People said the corn kernels on the cob were "as moist as milk" because they ripened beginning in August, when the nights were becoming longer and colder. The kernels thus were able to last longer in the cold, while during the day they suffered less from the heat.

In early spring, women popped wheat in a strainer over a fire in the yard as a treat for the children. In this manner, "popcorn" became a specialty—a substitute when the supply of apples and fruit preserves was running low toward the end of winter. Bread was baked every day. The wheat was milled in watermills, while the flour was sifted before being made into dough for bread and pita. A salted, heavy *kaša* was prepared from bran, grass, and vegetables—especially turnips—for milk cows, horses, and oxen.

Country households had their own earthen stoves in which they baked small loaves of bread—usually a two-week's supply. That bread was very tasty. During the summer, all food was prepared in summer kitchens that often had earthen floors and a fireplace. Pita was baked under an iron pan, while bread was prepared in earthenware dishes placed in the hot coals. The major part of the population made its bread from multigrains, including wheat, rye, buckwheat, and, to a lesser extent, corn. For variety, people sometimes made thin pancakes from buckwheat, or pita with cheese and cream. Even if they came out black or too doughy to be a "specialty," they still were a welcome substitute for bread. Fritters were cooked only for children, sometimes in oil. While the poor ate cornbread, those who were well off ate wheat bread or white bread. The latter was especially tasty because it was made from the finest flour, the same flour used to make expensive pita and cakes. Those households that could afford only cornbread suffered from tuberculosis in greater numbers than in homes that could afford a variety of breads. Sometimes it happened that whole families would die off.

In the summer, women would prepare light meals: vegetable stew—often meatless—stuffed peppers (some of them hot), and for supper pita, a savory pie made of spinach, pumpkin, and greens prepared with two or three eggs, young cheese, milk, and a little butter. In general, Muslims did not favor salads in their cuisine. They did, however, like fleshy, tasty tomatoes—lightly salted and eaten with bread and rich cheese for breakfast or supper. We ate supper in the late afternoon. Almost the only salad we ate in the summertime was a green one consisting of longish peppers, tomatoes, and cucumbers. There was no salad dressing, just a sprinkle of salt. Sometimes an onion would be sliced into it. Green onions would be diced fresh and mixed with cream and young cheese for breakfast. In the wintertime, people often ate salted and finely cut leek with cold cuts for breakfast. We also ate heavier food during the winter: cooked beans with smoked meat, *sarma*—a dish made of rice with lamb or mixed meats wrapped in grape or sour cabbage leaves—and *burek* with a meat filler. A pita made with potato and cheese inside was famous. There were also dishes made of dried plums and meat. These were specialties.

A variety of pickled foods were popular during the winter months, especially one that was a mixture of cabbage, green tomato, and peppers. People dried the plums, pears, and apples for which our region was well known and made compote from them in the wintertime.

In the fall, every household cooked plum jam. After picking, the kernels would be removed from them. Later that evening, while the plums were being sprayed with water and cooked in the courtyard, the young people would gather by the fire and tell stories amid much laughter. Jam was the winter food with the highest calories and most households consumed one hundred to two hundred kilograms of plum preserves. As they shrank, apples and pears were drained of their juice, which was allowed to thicken by cooking. It replaced sugar in winter and was sprinkled over pita. Mulberry jam was also used for this purpose. The thick juice was mixed with fresh cream and eaten with a flat, round bread made with baking powder instead of yeast. Sick people would drink the sour juice of wild apples diluted with water because it was touted as a medicine that would "put out the fire" (lower their temperatures).

Instead of water, we drank pickled juniper juice sweetened with honey. Small pears were preserved in wooden tubs. Their sour and bubbly juice was sometimes served as a dessert instead of sherbet. It was so sweet, and without sugar! Our people made use of various herbs for teas and medicinal purposes. These were gathered in the summertime and dried for the winter. Peasants had whole gardens of chamomile plants with yellow flowers that stood high on their stalks, a sure sign that they were healthy and growing in the proper kind of soil—not too moist, but rather more on the dry or sandy side. We also had yarrow, which the people knew by special names such as *hajdučica* because *haiduks* (renegades) used it to heal their wounds while hiding out in the forest. The small, sickle-shaped, greenish leaves that jut out at an angle from the stalk are full of juice that could be squeezed onto a bandage and applied to a wound. The yarrow's white flower was used for tea as well. The mixture was given to those suffering from illnesses causing inflammation of the lungs. Besides chamomile and yarrow, there were at least a dozen other medicinal herbs in our meadows. A household began each morning with tea—not coffee or milk. Only the children drank milk. Coffee was not served until about ten in the morning, when the women would take a break from their household chores, light up a cigarette if they smoked, and drink a cup of coffee. Alcohol was not kept in Muslim homes except, perhaps, for use as a medicine in case of a severe cold. Only a few individuals from the wealthier households "imbibed." The only thing said of such men was that "he drinks a bit." There were few drunks among the common people, and they almost always tormented their wives and children, spending all that they earned on their addiction. One could find drunks even in the finest houses, but they usually were people who lived by themselves. Their ranks included educated people who spoke Turkish and knew Arabic, of whom people said, "they grew up in silk and satin," meaning in great wealth. In the end, they would drink up their entire estate and find themselves sleeping on straw in stables. In contrast to their Muslim neighbors, Serbians served alcohol—usually strong or weak *rakija*—that they distilled themselves in their country places. However, they, too, had few drunks.

Marvelous preserves were made from plums, wild strawberries, and roses. These were served to guests as soon as they arrived. Serbs had the same custom, although they did not use roses. Muslims more often made sweet, oriental-style baklava, while the Serbian women were specialists in fine cookies and cakes. It was hard to find such delicious and sweet smelling cakes anywhere other than Vienna.

People in our region paid great attention to meat. They knew what meat was best for what dishes: beef for soup and stew, lamb for string beans and rice pilaf, mutton for baked dough. Mixed meats gave a special taste to *đuveč,* which consists of meat stew, vegetables, and rice baked in earthenware vessels in the oven. The best pita, *burek,* could not be made without leg of lamb.

The meat was cut with a *satara* (a small axe), thus keeping the juice inside. It was never ground with a machine. The bakeries in the *čaršija* used to make *ćevapčići:* small, rolled meat patties made of mixed beef, lamb, and ground onion, which they would grill and eat with pita bread. Men in the *čaršija* and children on their way to school would eat their *ćevapčići* on the run. They sometimes were doused with cream and smothered in baked peppers that were a little on the hot side. They were not eaten later in the day, or in the evening. *Ćevapčići* was a special Bosnian Muslim dish and had no connection to Turkey or Greece, which had a similar food, but in name only: kebab.

Baked lamb served "hot off the fire" was perhaps our most famous dish! The lamb was baked in a baker's furnace—just like bread or pita—over a wood fire, then cut while still on the smoldering fire and sold fresh and hot.

Lamb was prepared on a spit in household gardens or in glades in the woods when people went on picnics. Households planned their slaughter in view of winter. Sheep, goat, and beef meats were dried in the attic. The meat would be fully dried by November, at which point it could be served for breakfast, sliced or cooked. There was less use of fresh meat in the wintertime. Just as today, *pršuta*—a dried, thin, boneless beef—was cooked, as were dried slices of sheep and goat meat. Sausages made of ground meat mixed with black pepper but without any additives were dried in the attic and then smoked gently over a low flame.

The best-known cereal dish was *keške.* It was made with *bungur* (cracked wheat) and either lamb or chicken. Cooked with very little water, it was steamed over a slow fire the entire day. At weddings, a whole lamb or sheep of two years or less was used. At the end of the cooking process, the *keške* was stirred slowly to even it out and to retrieve the bones. Then the cereal was steamed with melted butter. Cooked in this way to the end, it was everyone's favorite because of its special taste.

Chicken was eaten less often, and then only one's own. It was used in the famous "cotton" stew, which got its name from its texture—nice and soft, like cotton on the skin. Serbian families prepared light, clear soups for their first dish at lunch. These consisted of cooked meat and a bunch of vegetables, including carrots, parsley, and parsnips. Sometimes these soups were fortified with dumplings, dropped eggs, and groats. Muslim women did not cook carrots. Instead, their children ate them raw, right out of the garden.

We used to make rice with chicken—again as a specialty—baked in the stove to lose all its water so that every grain of rice could be separated. Chicken was truly delicious then, unlike today. Our fried eggs, cooked in our own butter, were known far and wide. They were so good that they were served to women who had recently given birth to straighten out their digestive system and to give them strength.

Fish was also a specialty. The Lim was famous for its trout, which often attained considerable weight. It was fried in oil. There were no special fish dishes—they were just fried in small amounts of oil.

We had cheese every day, mainly for breakfast and inside pita. We did not eat cheese in the evening. All kinds of white cheeses were consumed: young, rich cheese, and lean (lenten) ones. Best of all was the fatty sheep's cheese from Sjenica and Pljevlje.

Rich pitas needed even richer sheep, goat, or cow cheeses to bring out their fine taste. Zeljanica, a pita made of greens or spinach, was served with young cheese, milk, and two or three eggs. As a rule, only small quantities of each item were used, so as not to detract from the pita's light, edible taste. To overload a pita with lots of other rich ingredients just for show was considered bad taste. Pita usually was prepared with a little dough in thin layers and with butter. However, pita made from rolled dough could not do without a heavy cheese and *kajmak,* a rich cream from which not a single drop of milk could be drained. Such a cream came from the village of Babine on the Jabuka Plateau. Kajmak, by the way, was a specialty made only in the Sandžak, Montenegro, Serbia, and Bosnia. It was unknown in the western regions of the former Yugoslavia.

In addition to cheese, other dairy products were consumed daily: fresh milk straight from the cow, *varenika* (boiled milk), and yogurt, as well as a kind of diluted buttermilk. Fresh milk was poured into shallow wooden or enameled troughs. Copper vessels were never used. The milk troughs were lined up in a cool place in the pantry until they began to turn sour. This process would last a few days. When a skin of sour cream appeared on the surface, the sour milk would be poured into a churn and churned. One had to be a master in order to know just how much warm water to add while beating just enough to separate the fat from the milk. People would drink the refreshing liquid thus obtained instead of milk, especially in the summertime. It had fewer calories and was tasty, like the Turkish *ayran.* Fresh butter scraped off the surface was the best spread for children's bread at suppertime. From melted butter came the pure yellow, translucent butter—clear as a teardrop, and with a sweet scent and taste that was not too strong.

You could not buy milk in the *čaršija.* On market day we would get yogurt made from sheep's or goat's milk in the mountain villages only. It was so thick that you could cut it. Otherwise, goat's milk and cheese were never expensive; nor was the meat.

Goat's tallow had many applications, both as food and medicinally. For example, in making "potato pita," a goat's dried peritoneum would be cut up in pieces or strips and mixed with diced potatoes and onion, plus black pepper. The mixture would then be wrapped in a fine crust of dough. The pita had to be eaten while it was hot, so that the tallow did not have time to cool. It was unusually tasty, a gourmet's delight. Tallow was used in cooking fried meat that had been stored for the winter in wooden tubs. The tallow kept the meat from contact with the air while it was being stored. Tubs holding from ten to twenty kilos could be transported or sent as a present to relatives in other towns, or to provide food relief to those who had suffered from some natural disaster like a flood or a fire.

An open wound would be cauterized and a salve containing lots of pine pitch placed on the burn. Tallow would then be rubbed over the wound site. People also used eggs for healing wounds. An egg's white would be emptied out onto tallow put in a spoon prior to heating it white hot. The concoction was then transferred to a bandage and, when it cooled, the bandage placed on the open wound. The same was done if the white part of a person's eye was injured. Such wounds were not uncommon, especially with children at play or watching the flocks, or grown-ups cultivating the land or fixing the house. People rarely called for a doctor. If the situation were urgent, they would bring in a folk healer, a woman or man who was experienced at healing. The same approach was used for ailing livestock.

There were very few fat people, partly from fasting, but more so because of the strenuous lifestyle.

Houses were proud of their estate or property, which included domestic animals in addition to their shop and land. In my day, houses in town had at least one cow in a barn or, in a few cases, in a cellar on the ground floor.

The animals were kept to feed the family. Larger households had horses as well, and Mujaga had oxen to till the soil. I remember Smailbeg riding to Dušmaniće wearing a turban, and Mehmedbeg's son Adem, who used to lead well-groomed horses to the brook to drink. They would stamp in the water until they found a quiet spot and then would drink their fill. There was a time when we pastured our cows, sheep, and goats in the country to fatten them up, or for *kurban,* the ritual slaughter for the celebration of Bairam.

Every courtyard had its chickens. The egg-laying hens would be "implanted" sometime in the spring, either in the nearby underbrush or in some other hidden corner of the garden. We would lose track of them for about twenty days, after which they would suddenly appear one day in the courtyard, clucking and leading their new brood of chicks. We welcomed them with joy and made special places for the chicks. As soon as they were settled, the hens would take over, clucking continually and attacking anyone—especially the cat—coming too close to the chicks. Houses were proud of their roosters when they crowed the loudest and most dependably before dawn. Their early morning song informed us it was time for *sabah.* Events were sometimes remembered in relation to the cocks' crowing. For example, it might be said that something happened "when the first roosters had not yet crowed."

Houses also had cats that roamed everywhere freely. During winter cold spells—when it used to be said, "tonight the cat will sleep with the mice"—we would call the cats in when it got dark, if they were not already inside. They would curl up on the wood stacked under the stove or sleep with us children under our blankets. We would make room for them, even if our hands ached from holding up the blanket so "they wouldn't stifle from lack of air."

Some people kept hunting dogs for the sake of prestige. They were well looked after and special food was prepared for them. Our imaginations were stimulated as, huddling close to our elders, we used to listen at parties as Mehmedbeg recounted some hunting adventure or other. Aunt Zina's husband, Fehimbeg, was also a hunter. Whenever he visited us, he would bring his catch with him: usually rabbits and pheasants. Uncle Abid would prepare the meat and then meat-filled pastries would be served to those who dropped in to see the guest and to chat.

However, the most important animals in every household were its cows. They had their own names and temperaments. For a long period, our two cows were Zlatulja and Blagulja. They were spoiled: they mooed in the evening before milking, looking for their hot, thick *kaša* of cooked bran or wheat served with sliced turnips, pumpkins, or grass—whatever was available. When it was time for them to go to pasture, they would bellow, so that we would have to come back early from swimming—just when it was best. We got up before sunrise in the summertime to let them graze before the sun got too hot and the flies and hornets began to bite. Then we would drive them home to shelter in the coolness of the barn.

I had my own cow, Cura ("Girl"), which I had cared for from the time Zlatulja gave birth to her. Cura was pretty, well formed, ruddy, and had a beautiful coat. When I groomed her, her shoulders would sag with pleasure—I could hang from her neck or crawl under her stomach and she would never kick me. She would put her head in my lap and look for a turnip, nudging me. My Cura got plenty of milk as a calf, for we waited a long time before weaning her from her mother. The Chetniks took her from me during the war and slaughtered her.

In general, we taught our animals to follow certain rules. For example, we showed our cats—while they were still kittens—where to eat, how to play with each other, and what not to touch. We would throw them little pieces of rope, which the kittens would seize and chew, thus sharpening their teeth. They would jump at our raised hands, wrap themselves around them in a ball, and nibble at them, never biting—they knew how far they could go! We loved them, too, treating them gently so as not to frighten them.

The richer houses had hired men to care for the cattle and help with the heavier fieldwork. They were usually young country lads who were hired for long periods of time. Some men worked for the same families for years. In some cases they married into the family, thus becoming co-owners of the estate. The hired men most often ate at the same *sofra* as family members, and in the summertime they slept on the hay in the barns or in their own area in an outbuilding. In addition to caring for the cattle, they helped the family to get ready for winter. They would cut and stack wood, fill the barns with hay, and gather and thresh the wheat and store it in barns. They also harvested corn, placing it on racks to dry. In the summertime, we hired shepherds—usually older children from the village—to watch their cows. At the end of their hire, they were given a newly tailored suit as part of their pay. Besides the shepherds, our own older children took care of the cows, going with the shepherd boys to learn the ropes. I liked to graze the goats and sheep most of all. They were much more interesting company than cows. There was always something going on: they would rush somewhere to find better branches to browse on, or a herd of them would follow the shepherd if he called to them while holding something they liked to eat in his hands, especially salt. We would drive the cows through the nearby forests toward Zalug—to graze on the stubble of the harvested wheat fields—or into our own garden, which we did not like because it kept us from being with the other children. Easiest of all was minding our cows down below the Lim or in Rakiće, a thick willow underbrush area between the fields and the Lim. We children loved to congregate there.

Fall was always delightful. We could graze the cows anywhere we wanted, once the corn had been picked, and would gather around a fire and tell stories. We baked leftover corncobs over a fire and potatoes in hot coals. We would pull from the hedges thorny branches bearing wild berries softened by the first morning frosts and then draw them through the fire to kill their bitterness and to diminish their dryness.

On cold, rainy days, the fire was everything to us; life was empty without it. We strove to keep it burning in the tree stumps as long as we could, banking the embers deeply inside before setting out for home. If it went out, we would light it again, rubbing two sharp stones together by a piece of dry peat or dried humus fiber. We never had matches—or the money to buy them—unless someone stole some at home. By transferring a fire from one stump to another before it burned itself out, we were able to keep it going for more than a month.

In the summertime, after we had driven the cows back home, we looked around the house to see what chores needed to be done before going down the path to play. We waded at the ford in the Lim, feeling with our feet for the shallows to avoid getting our clothes wet. We raided the fields for watermelons, which, generally speaking, did not prosper in our area. Walnut trees were our favorites. Our first choice was two of the Veselčić family's walnut trees that were on opposite ends of Polje. They were full at the top and had branches that reached down into the cornfield. We loved to hide under them, stretching out on the ground in order to escape the heat when we grew tired of swimming. We would drink in the intoxicating, heavy scent of the leaves. In the fall we would crack the not-fully-ripened nuts, preferring them to the ripe ones that came later. The Veselčić family rarely visited their estate. They never said anything when they saw us, so we treated their walnut trees as our own.

It was shameful to steal like that, but it was a challenge. We always observed a certain ethic: we did not tear up plants or break branches. Since we were familiar with each fruit tree—even loved them—we could do them no harm. During a drought we would haul water to them from the Lim.

There were a number of fruit trees we would have liked to have had in our own garden: Mujaga's apricots and peaches, for example, or the cultivated strawberries we saw for the first time in Prota Šiljak's garden. Šiljak was an Orthodox priest, the equivalent of a monsignor. That fruit was a novelty, but in Mujaga's case one could say that he led everyone else. He had everything in his garden and cultivated it himself. We were ashamed to steal anything from him and usually waited for him to bestow his fruit on us. Nevertheless, the challenge was sometimes too great to resist.

Polje was both our playland and our freedom, tying us to nature and its world for the rest of our lives.

3 Customs and Schooling before the War

The Muslim woman's place was in the home, and there was no chore in the home that she did not do. She raised the young children and cared for the elderly. She saw to all the work that had to be done inside the house: the cooking, the sewing, and the washing. There were times when she even wove cloth, spun wool, and knitted socks and sweaters and other articles of clothing. The garden was another of her concerns. She was the one who planted the vegetables and watered them, boiled the jam, and made the preserves. She also did the canning, put up pickled fruits and vegetables, rolled out and cut homemade pasta, and churned soup noodles. The cows in the barn also fell in her domain. She was the one who milked them, spread their litter, prepared their feed, watered them, and sometimes even cleaned the stalls. She was also the one who fed the cats and chickens. With all of that to do, she was housebound.

Girls were expected to rise at dawn, before the rest of the household, and not to lie lazily in bed. In those days, industry and cleanliness rather than beauty were the qualities most highly valued in a girl. A man expected the girl he married to embrace his house as her own.

When I was young, girls were allowed to use the parlor to entertain prospective suitors. Fathers would pretend they did not notice the young men who came and stood outside beneath the windows of their homes, chatting with their daughters—as long as the fellows were decent and well intentioned. In reality, few fathers ever saw the young men. Fathers would enter their houses by the front door and would not even peek into the lower courtyards or gardens, which were the women's area. Worthy young men would come to the garden or the courtyard door on horseback. This was a sign that a closer tie already existed between the young man and the object of his affection. Such courting did not obligate the suitor to make an offer, but it was not allowed to go on too long as the young man, too, could lose his good reputation. In the early stages of courtship, the girl did not even show herself, but instead sent a maid to stand at the window and relay to the young man the girl's whispered replies. Such conversations usually were lighthearted in tone, but girls endeavored to answer intelligently and cleverly and otherwise tried to show that they were not easy to get. Sometimes there were jalousies over the windows, so that the girl could see the young man clearly but he saw only her silhouette.

Young men would come courting in the evening or late afternoon, when a girl's father and brothers were at the *čaršija* or having their coffee. Sometimes a young man would throw the girl an apple or candy or a sweet pastry from the bakery, but the girl would not eat any of these treats if she was not sure of the young man. Girls were afraid of *sihir,* they feared that the young men had cast a spell on their gifts hoping to deprive them of their reason. So the girls would give the presents away to children. Young men from other parts of town would come on Fridays to personally verify in what houses there were girls and to see the houses. All dressed up, they would approach along the path, making loud comments that the girls could hardly miss. Meanwhile, the girls would find a way to appear, perhaps by going down to the garden to draw water from the well or to water the flowers. Then a young man might say, "A flower comes to the flowers," and the girl would smile shyly.

Young girls who went to school usually finished grade school and then stayed at home until they married. They learned housekeeping chores from the older women and made other preparations for marriage, usually between the ages of seventeen and twenty. Beyond age twenty they were considered "a bit old," and those over twenty-five were "rather old." Women who remained unmarried beyond the age of thirty were "past their prime" or "getting on."

A suitor went to the father, brother, or another relative to ask for a girl's hand in marriage. In the event permission was withheld because the groom or his family was not thought to be suitable, a persistent suitor might "steal" his prospective bride. It was said in such cases that the girl had been "lured away." Sometimes girls were "stolen" in order to reduce the cost of a wedding.

My sisters were given in marriage according to proper custom. In 1937, Šehza went off at age seventeen to Sjenica. The groom's house was full of the members of his household: father-in-law, mother-in-law, brother-in-law, two sisters-in-law, and—by the time the family resettled in Turkey in 1941—two sons of her own: Enver, who took after our side of the family, and Hamdija, who took after theirs. Ferida married at the age of nineteen and went off to Nova Varoš in 1942. I recall when Ferida's hand was sought. Before the wedding party arrived, Babba called her in to recite the obligations she would have in the new family toward Mustafa, the groom, his mother, and the others. I loitered outside the room's partly open door so I could hear what Babba told her. I was sorry to see Ferida go. Young girls went off with a firm resolve to survive whatever came and build their family.

In the early evening, the maidens from Polje would take us along on their strolls along the split-rail fences of the plum orchards down to the River Lim. They went unveiled because no outsiders ever passed there. The girls mostly talked about their future life, about preparing their hope chests, and about things they had made by hand, such as embroidery and bed linens. The custom was for them to take to their future mothers-in-law and grooms kerchiefs embroidered with gold that were both beautiful and valuable. They would visit an aunt in Prijepolje so that they could look out the window. Usually this would be a house in the *čaršija* or on the Meydan Square near the bridge on the Mileševka in Vakuf where the Gajret, the Muslim cultural and educational association, was located. They wanted to catch at least a few of the whispered sounds of the *tamburitza* that reached them from behind the lowered blinds of the Gajret's poorly lighted room. The *tamburitza* is a stringed instrument resembling a guitar in shape and a mandolin in its sound. Young men, usually artisans who were not yet married or were newlyweds, went to the Gajret to have a good time or to practice for the sunrise picnic on the Ravne Plateau above town on Saint George's Day. Even then it would be on the rare occasion, with the host's permission, and sometimes thanks to an arrangement made by mothers, aunts, or grandmothers who sympathized with girls. That is why it was important for them to go down to the Lim to gaze across the water at the town and perhaps spot someone descending steep Prlo Bluff toward Hašimbegović Polje. The maidens would return not long after to milk the cows, prepare the house for the night, fetch water, and help the women prepare supper.

There was something festive about early evening. When fires were lighted in summer kitchens, savory smells of supper would perfume the air. There was a hum and constant murmur as the herders brought the cows in from the pasture and our men came back from the *čaršija* right at *akšam*. I would wait for Babba, leaning with my forehead against the window glass, trying to catch his first appearance, especially during a winter blizzard. He would carry the wooden basket containing things to be sewn, but also groceries. Sometimes there would be a cream puff for me and meat for the cat. The cat always waited for him and would spring out before me to greet him. I would never ask if he had brought me a present; we were taught that it was impolite to do so. When the light became dim outside and a pie was being baked, light wood torches were lit if there was no moon. Later, during the war, lanterns came into use. They were "much easier, less trouble."

Muslim women wore Bosnian dress, which consisted of a *mintan* (long-sleeved blouse) and *dimije* (baggy pantaloons). A kerchief knotted at the back of the neck, beneath which their hair was done in braids, covered their heads. Young married women would distinguish themselves from the maidens with a dangle of bobbed hair beside their ear. For festive occasions and to go visiting, the blouses and pantaloons would be sewn from expensive fabrics in pastel colors, light and heavy silks, and Lahore woolens brought back from Mecca and Turkey.

The women took pains to look attractive. While they were dolling themselves up, we would wait on them, bringing them articles of their makeup just to hold them in our hands, even if only for a moment. They would rouge their cheeks, but they did not wear lipstick. They liked mild, very expensive perfumes, and they would curl a bit of their hair in front for festive occasions, weddings, or when visiting new mothers during their forty-day confinement after childbirth. After that the new mothers would come out in public with their mothers-in-law and child, visiting first those dearest to them: usually a family with a flock of healthy children who were advanced for their age. The newborn infant again would be given a small present: an embroidered kerchief wrapped around fresh eggs was almost obligatory. A child born in the family or to very close friends were presented gifts of gold immediately after birth.

Sometimes young girls would have their hair bobbed instead of braided and would wear little ankle-length dresses. When they reached the age twelve, they were taught to cover themselves. When Muslim women left the house, they wore a *zar* (a long, hooded overdress), and a veil over their faces. Only a few who were more modern or lived in Bosnia or somewhere else with husbands in the civil service wore mantles with a special kind of cap.

Muslim women did not go to the *čaršija.* Even when they set off on a visit, they would take the back way—"below the Lim." If they wanted to buy calico or other fabrics, the shop would send them a pattern book from which to pick. Apprentices would then deliver the order and the man of the house would later pay for it. It was rare for Muslim women to deal with money before the war—something the older women never did. Their obligations stopped at the gate. If visitors happened by, they would send a child with a message asking them to go to the *čaršija* or to come back when the men were home. They never did any job alone that required going out or making a purchase. The exception was when the household responsibilities fell entirely on a woman's shoulders because the man of the house had died. Even then, it would only be for a short time: just until a guardian, brother-in-law, brother, or son could take over.

In those days, conversation was a means of finding out news. After dinner, men from Polje would set out for the mosque at Šarampov, and then go to the nearby coffeehouse. The shops in the *čaršija* and the coffeehouses were the places where business people gathered. But they only went to the coffee-houses in the evening. Anyone who sat in such a place during the day was not considered to be a good householder. One could find out what was happening in the state by going to the coffee places. Radios were rare, even though some people—like our neighbor Nedžibeg—had them before the war. Otherwise, people learned what was going on in the news from the *telal* (town crier). When the town council wanted to make an announcement, it would send the *telal.* He would go from neighborhood to neighborhood, reaching all the quarters very quickly if people did not pester him with questions. There were town criers even after 1945. In Polje, the *telal* would climb onto the pedestal of the fountain and, while banging a drum, cry out: "People, hear me and listen!" Then he would recite to us, and later read to us, the latest council ruling: for example, that the fountain's water was being shut off until further notice due to trouble with the pipes; or that children needed to be taken for their vaccinations. They would call the people to preelection gatherings of the various parties that had candidates for the national assembly. I remember when our women went in 1939 to a meeting at the head of the *čaršija,* where Muhamed Hašimbegović, a Muslim candidate for the Yugoslav National Assembly, appeared. There was a huge crowd around the Great Mosque and Nanna held my hand tightly. I remember only that some people said you should not believe what politicians said—something that amazed me, since I saw no reason for their coming to hear them in the first place if that was the case.

Of course, there were town criers in Turkish times. The *telal* used to announce important news from the sultan at Meydan Square in Vakuf. When people were called to serve in the army, before leaving Prijepolje they would first go to pray at the public prayer place near Meydan, called the Musalla. For some, this was a prayer for forgiveness, addressed to their homeland, in case they did not return from battle. To all of them, it was an encouragement that they would win in battle. The Musalla was a very old space near the main road surrounded by a low, barely visible, wall. The imam stood in an indentation at the head of the walled space when he led the prayer. To the side was a stone platform where a dead person's coffin would be placed while they said the funeral prayers. Meydan used to be the largest square in town and it had its own clock tower, which was still functioning. On Friday at Meydan the Turkish army used to give out food to the poor: usually *pilav* (rice cooked with lamb), with halvah (nougat pastries) for dessert. They would bring it in large copper canisters.

My family used to go on outings lasting from one day to several days to some spring or stream. Planning for one such outing—to Mioče, near Rudo in today's Bosnia—required a whole year. There was a fair there that served as a great gathering of people in that border area. Outings to a hamlet like Taševo or Staro (the Old Place) were local. We had some distant relatives in Staro, a very old settlement on a plateau above Župa, in the Lim Valley, toward Bijelo Polje. I remember that they used to say that the people there prayed only during Ramadan. They evidently would tell the *hodža,* an Islamic teacher whom they invited to come to pray the *teravija,* that they did not have time to pray at other times because they had to be constantly on their guard from attacks on the village by Montenegrin bandits. The *teravija* is an evening prayer during Ramadan. To make their point—Uncle Abid said—they would organize pursuits on horseback, with loud shouting and calling back and forth against supposed cattle thieves whom they would chase until dawn. After coming back home, they complained to the *hodža:* "So, *hodža,* you see how we spend whole nights, and there is not any time for us to sleep, never mind to say our prayers."

Muslims liked to visit. Whole families, especially in the wintertime, would go visiting for a day. It was a special occasion when townspeople went to visit a village. If their relatives and friends lived far off, the guests would stay for several days. Usually mothers, aunts, or older sisters-in-law would visit their daughter or sister when she had a baby. They brought her the *babine* (birthing gifts), which were especially rich when it was a first child: a gold piece of jewelry or a gold coin for the child, silk for dresses, bedding, or an item used in bathing. The mother-in-law, father-in-law, husband, and residents of the house all were given gifts called *bohčaluci.* The *babine* were carefully assembled over an entire year in anticipation of a child's birth and were displayed to everyone who came to welcome the guests.

Members of the household called a newly wed woman *odiva.* Her first visit home after marriage was called going *uprviče* ("for the first time"). She usually came with her mother-in-law after she had her first child. This was meant to show that she had tightly bonded with those in her new home. If she came from afar, a male member of the household—for example, her best man, usually her husband's youngest brother—would accompany the *odiva.* After they visited for a day or so, the mother-in-law and the best man left her to stay on with her family for a longer period, sometimes for as much as a month or two. It was believed that this contributed to her health and recovery after giving birth, and it was understood that she should be separated from her husband during this period.

If, on the other hand, the bride's house was very strict regarding such matters, the visits were shorter, usually lasting only about two weeks. In such cases, the mother-in-law would remain with her.

It was customary to invite other people's guests to visit. The relatives of a host invited his guests to their homes for lunch, dinner, or—if they were not close relatives—to breakfast or for an afternoon visit. The host, too, would be invited, and some of the friends, but not in excessive numbers. The guests did not bring presents, except for a few small things. Fine dishes were prepared for the dinners, not the usual fare. There usually were ten or more courses, beginning with a *sarma* made of lamb and rice. Then came Bosnian stew made of lamb and beef and vegetables, followed by cheese and meat pastries. After that, baklava, an oriental sweet pastry was served, while for less formal occasions small cookies were offered. Finally, light dishes were placed on the *sofra*— for example, a *pilav* of homemade noodles, tapioca, and sweet and sour *hošaf* (a sour-sweet compote).

In addition, people visited their neighbors. Women used to visit one another in the morning, after they had done their chores, or after lunch. They would gather for coffee at someone's house, exchanging local gossip. Sometimes they had larger gatherings if they lived in town. Besides coffee, they were served Turkish delight and juniper berry juice, or perhaps some candies, and nothing more. While visiting, the women would do some handwork. They would weave fine laces and embroider scarves and handkerchiefs because they often did not have much time for these things after finishing their housework.

When the men came from the *čaršija* in the evening, families would gather in someone's home. Usually, they visited houses where the women were not veiled. This meant the homes of relatives and close friends. Such visits were more frequent in the wintertime because the day's work was finished earlier and people could sit around for a long time. The young men would go skating or sledding down our neighborhood path, which had been frozen into a fine crust with the aid of sprinkled water. The path belonged to the children in the daytime. However, we enjoyed the general gaiety, when the lads would squeeze us into their handmade sleds and we would hurtle downhill at breakneck speed. We also took rides with them down the main road that led from above Polje to Dušmaniće, on the route to Babine and other distant villages.

I remember the house parties at Mehmedbeg's most of all because of the hunting tales. I loved his wife Vaha, as she was called. We would come to their house bearing lit brands of pine from which emanated the smell of pine tar. The flickering shadows they created around us made us draw closer to our elders for security. Vaha was a great prankster. She always brought dried fruits and bowls of sweet-scented apples and nuts from their estate in Begluci.

We used to go to house parties at Kuna and Ahmet's. They had no children and lived peacefully and comfortably. Ahmet was a policeman, and Kuna was a great friend of animals, with whom she could converse. Kuna's cows knew her: they would amble toward her as soon as they noticed that she had entered the meadow where they grazed, and it was difficult to restrain them from following her when she left. I learned from her how to talk to my cow Cura. She also taught me to feed stray dogs and cats by trickling a thin stream of milk down my finger into their mouths while they learned to suck, if they were unlucky enough to have no mother. In order to get them to take the milk from my finger I had to do a lot of stroking, holding them in my hands and coaxing them. Our joy was endless when the doggies began to expand like barrels and would stumble around us, wagging their little tails excitedly.

Gatherings at our Mujaga's house were something different altogether. The children did not attend—or if they did bring us, we would sit in another room. Sometimes we were given permission to be with the elders, kneeling alongside one wall. We did not dare to speak until someone asked us something. We were, however, able to listen and to talk quietly among ourselves. Mujaga, who was a few years older than Babba, was his first cousin. He had a wife, the quiet and dignified Emina, and five children. He was tall, blue eyed, straight, with an easy gait; in my childhood his close-cropped hair was already gray. As befitted one advanced in years, he wore the traditional Bosnian dress: a men's *mintan* a blouse of cotton with a narrow collar and *čakšire,* men's baggy pants, together with a vest and a red belt around the waist. On his head he wore a red fez that was of smooth cloth and had a little tassel. Mujaga was strict. He began the day's work with the Bismillah ("In the name of Allah"), and his garden and estate stood out. You could see cleanly pruned fruit trees, full of new shoots and of miniature pears and apples that our people did not like because they regarded them as a novelty that would upset nature's established order. Mujaga was the first to adopt anything new: he introduced light into his house and the auxiliary buildings, including the stable. He was a true opposite to our lower house, in which something was always going on: presents were being given, money was being spent, and people were being received at all hours of the day. There was no need to let Uncle Abid know of your coming in advance because every day was like a holiday. My mother and Mujaga were very much alike: they did not make small talk because they were always doing something, such as taking care of the gardens. Both had a work schedule and money. No one knew how much, but people would come to them for a loan: "Give me a loan, sister-in-law, and you'll get it back—something unexpected has come up." Mujaga, before agreeing to make a loan, would say: "Well, let me see," which meant that you should wait a minute or two. He usually consulted with our Aunt Suleima—

his middle-aged, unmarried sister—on business matters. They would call each other *Burazer* (brother). The younger family members did not attend discussions of business and family matters between Mujaga and Babba, who called him Mujo. Aunt Suleima apparently did not attend them either, but people knew that such conversations took place.

Not to be forgotten are the evening gatherings that took place in our upper house. Babba sat by the lamp during the long winter nights and hand sewed the baggy pants and vests of blue and black cloth. We would sit around the room, waiting for the storytelling to begin. I realized long afterward that they were from "The Thousand and One Nights." He knew how to tell a story so that everyone would listen. The stories had been handed down orally. My Uncle Ibrahim was the first to bring a small booklet with some of these stories in it, when he came with his family in 1941, after having left the *šerijat* service in Macedonia, following the fall of the First Yugoslavia.

When the storytelling came to a halt, the grownups would pray the *jacija,* the last night prayer, and we would eat a light evening meal of boiled or baked potato with cheese and dried meats, boiled corn, and sour apples we brought from the village of Zalug. They drank coffee, using Turkish delight in place of sugar, and sweetened juniper berries were also served. An evening gathering would last until about four o'clock *a la turka*—the time set according to the lunar calendar, or roughly until about midnight. After the evening gathering, the room was cleaned up and aired. A piece of wood was shoved into the stove for the night, and mattresses and pillows were spread out on the floor. Because the winters were so severe in those days (the windows often were covered with ice by noontime), we all slept in the same, well-heated room. Blankets were placed over the curtains, helping to make it warmer and also so the light could not be seen outside. Our night activity thus was kept hidden from view. There was always the chance that a peasant returning drunk from the city, especially from a fair, might shoot through the windows.

We know from various documents that Muslims were in Prijepolje from the beginning of the sixteenth century. An important region through which Ottoman imperial routes had passed, it had several mosques and neighborhood *mektebs* (religious elementary schools), one secondary theological school (*medresa*) and several *tekkes* (Dervish houses/lodges). All of these institutions educated the Muslim people mainly in religion. Modern secular education did not begin until toward the middle of the nineteenth century. Since then, Muslim children have studied in so-called *iptidaija, ruždija,* and *idadija,* respectively, using Turkish books written in Arabic letters. This education lasted twelve years in all. Serbian children studied separately, because beginning in the mid-nineteenth century they had their own grade school supported by the Serbian community, rich Serbian merchants, and even donations from Russia.

In Šarampov, next to the mosque, stood the *medresa,* which the students called *talebe.* Only boys entered after they had finished *iptidaija* and *ruždija.* It was there that Nanna's Hafiz and Murat *hodža* Melić had studied. Prior to the Young Turks' Reform of 1909, the Turkish government had tried to introduce Latin letters into the schools, but it met with determined resistance.

Musabeg, Smailbeg's oldest son, told me that members of influential families were not in favor of the change requiring that writing instruction employ Latin letters. They went to the principal of the *medresa* hoping to get him to use his influence. He responded by waving his hands, regarding such demands from powerful families as "the devil's work" and finding support for his position in the Qur'anic chapter Iqraa (Read! or Proclaim!).

In Pljevlje, the residence of *pasha,* higher education was carried on in the secular mode. Not only did one study Turkish in the military academy, but other foreign languages as well, including French.

The dual educational system was removed in 1912, immediately after the Serbian government was established. In Prijepolje, a four-year primary school was opened for all children, as well as a lower gymnasium of four grades corresponding to a junior high school. Around 1920 a full gymnasium with eight grades was opened in Pljevlje and Novi Pazar. Muslim teachers were integrated into the system, so Nanna was able to continue teaching.

Muslim children, especially girls, did not always finish primary school. This was primarily because their parents and other relatives did not want them to learn to write using "infidel" letters. Male children had a difficult time passing the entrance examination for the gymnasium. As a result, many of them took up trades, becoming tailors, barbers, bakers, and shoemakers. Few finished junior high school, and even fewer went on to higher education. Some young men were educated in *medresas* or universities in major centers like Sarajevo, Istanbul, and Cairo. The *mektebs* attached to the mosques received no support from the state, and the impoverished Muslim society was incapable of maintaining them in sufficient number. The Muslim charitable foundation Vakuf helped as much as it could, but the Agrarian Reform program had weakened it.

Children learned the most fundamental things in the *mektebs*—like how to pray, to do the ritual washing, and to memorize some of the shorter *sura* (chapters) in the Qur'an. Fewer and fewer people knew how to recite from the Qur'an and to write in Arabic letters. More often, imams and *hodžas* who had no formal education taught the children. Rarely could one of these religion teachers translate from the Qur'an, even in part. They would translate the more important Qur'anic sentences according to their sense, or they would point out words the children already knew because they had been assimilated into our language. These words had been radically changed in our local dialect. For example, *kuja,* which in our language means a well dug in the ground and covered with a board. In the Qur'an, we find that word in the expression *fi džennatin ve ujun* (the gardens and the spring waters).

As part of educational reform conducted in 1929, the government reduced the number of hours of religious instruction and allowed only teachers who had finished pedagogical school to assume this responsibility. The number of Muslim teachers thus fell even further, and Nanna lost her job. There were few Muslim teachers, especially teachers who had fulfilled the pedagogical requirement. Before the war, a teacher named Aiša had come to Prijepolje from somewhere in Bosnia. She wore a veil and would walk through the *čaršija* with an umbrella in her hand. Nanna used to visit her. She lived in a room in the Salihbegović house near the Great Mosque. It seemed unusual to us children to see such a woman, alone, without a house or family.

In an issue of the *Herald of the Islamic Religious Association,* the number of pre–World War II students from our region in the Sarajevo *medresa* and advanced *šerijat* law school is given as ten.

The King Aleksandar *medresa* opened in Skopje during this period. It got its name from King Aleksandar Karađorđević, who was king during the First Yugoslavia. Its students received scholarships and free lodging. The *medresa* apparently was established in order to pacify negative Muslim feelings toward the government, as well as in response to Turkish pressure. Yugoslavia tried hard to maintain good relations with Turkey, especially after Ataturk came to power. This school played a meaningful role in the emancipation of Muslims. Its best students were later active Partisans, and those who survived the war later played important roles in the government. This was a Muslim intelligentsia that had been educated in the European manner, its graduates continuing their education in Belgrade, Zagreb, and other European universities. They distinguished themselves by their fine general education and understanding of Islam, of eastern languages, and of Arabic, Persian, and Turkish literature.

In spite of the widespread illiteracy still prevalent in those parts, there circulated among our Muslim houses booklets containing tales written in *bosančica,* the Bosnian vernacular language in Arabic letters. Someone received the magazine *Behar* (*Blossom*), in which were published stories, songs, and accounts of historical events, including stories of famous Bosniaks, Muslims of Slavic origin. Before World War II, Čaušević's translation of the Qur'an was published.

I was not yet six years old when I started attending the *mekteb,* an elementary religious school, with Bilal *efendija,* imam of the Ibrahim Pasha's Mosque in Šarampov. It is the oldest mosque in Prijepolje, built in the sixteenth century. Muhamed escorted me to the *mekteb.* I carried my *Ilmihal,* the Arabic primer, in a black cloth satchel slung over one shoulder. Nanna saw us off, spilling water behind us from the cup so that my schoolwork would "flow like water if God so grant." We jumped over the threshold of the gate with our right foot forward as we said the Bismillah, in the name of Allah.

The *mekteb* in Šarampov was in the Vakuf building, which had previously housed the *medresa.* There were some fifteen of us girls in a spacious classroom that previously had held many more than that. My classmates included Alibeg Avdagić's granddaughters Fatma—who was pretty and proud of her origin, then married young and went off to Sarajevo—and the nimble Ata—a bit older, who later married Zaim Kadribašić, a legendary hero of the 3d Sandžak Partisan Brigade in World War II. There were also boys in the *mekteb:* our own Muhamed from Polje, Mahmut, Mehmed, and Abdullah, sons of Hasan *efendija* Veljović, a merchant, and my Nanna's very wealthy first cousin Hatidžehanma from Hamam.

I spent less than a full year at the *mekteb,* and then in 1940 I entered the first grade of the elementary school at the upper end of the *čaršija* kept by the young teacher Lepa Minić. The Minićs lived in a three-story house of their own on the bank of the Lim, just opposite our boathouse and Bukovi. They were regarded as a well-off Serbian family who had come recently and included three teachers: Radmila, who married and went off to Montenegro and was widowed early, Bosa, who was Muhamed's teacher, and Lepa, who was mine. Bosa and Lepa came to a tragic end: Chetniks killed them during World War II. Both of them left children behind who were raised by Radmila and their grandmother.

Uncle Abid found Lepa's husband, a Montenegrin Partisan, in 1943 in some bushes beneath a stump in Rakiće. He had lain there wounded, at the coldest time of the year, after having swum the Lim during the sixth German offensive and the famous battle of Prijepolje. Uncle Abid brought him warm milk and dry clothes, pretending that he had gone out with his pruning hook to get wood in the event he encountered German patrols. Later, he shouted over the swollen Lim to Adem Hašimbegović to get word to the Minićs. They came to get him with a German permit for the hospital. I cannot remember whether he died in the hospital or if the Chetniks killed him or if he died in battle. They left behind a young son who after the war was taken in by his father's relatives in Montenegro. I felt I had to tell this story about the fate of Lepa Minić out of respect for the teacher who taught me my first letters, but it has taken me away from my starting school on the eve of World War II.

We would line up by twos when the school attendant rang the bell. Inside, we would stand up when the teacher entered as a form of greeting. The first thing we did was to recite the anthem "God Save Us, God Defend Us," after which the Serbian children would cross themselves, and we would stand with our hands at our sides. We finished the first semester in late December, when we received little booklets with a picture of Petar Karađorđević on the first inside page and this written on the next: "The palace is built stone by stone, the loaf is made grain by grain." Then came pages for "grades: native language—Serbian, arithmetic, nature, handwriting." A girl from Polje went with me. We spent all of January on vacation because that is when the Serbian holidays came: Christmas, New Year's, and Saint Sava's Day, which was a festive occasion in the school.

The classes began to be irregular when the second semester started. The teacher would go off somewhere, leaving us alone in the class. One morning in late March, 1941, we saw a large crowd in the *čaršija* in front of the town hall. The same thing happened the next day. Crowding together around the windows in our upper-story classroom we saw Bosa Minić leading a crowd of people in the Serbian national dance, the *kolo,* through the *čaršija.* They seemed to have forgotten us. At some point our teacher came in and explained to us that young Petar II Karađorđević had been crowned king, and the people were celebrating. We were finally sent home. I could hardly make my way through the crowd of dancers, which wound through the entire *čaršija* from the town hall to the bridge over the brook near the Minićs's house. We went to school for a few more days at someone's house in Vakuf after saboteurs demolished the town hall. Then, in early April, we received little booklets saying we had completed the first grade.

Part II: The War and Liberation

Occupation

4

Rumors of war had already begun in 1939. People from Polje used to gather on the green lawn next to our fountain to chat. We children hovered around them, listening fearfully as they spoke of a war coming in which many people would be killed. When the war was over, people said, there would be "many caps, but few heads to wear them." They said that Germany, which had attacked Poland—I remember the word Poland because it reminded me of Polje— would invade Yugoslavia.

"The Germans are coming." We did not know why they called them "Nijemci"—we thought it was because they were "mute" and fear gripped us even more. Namely, German—Nijemac—and "mute"—*nijem*—have the same root in the Slavic language. People were drafted into the army. My father, who was forty-five years old, was chosen for the reserves and stationed at the barracks next to the police station. He also received a military uniform that reeked of mothballs. Muhamed had already begun to take me to father's shop. We would carry home clothes so that the finishing touches could be put on them there. One day, Babba gave us his uniform and we carried it home, too. I could not even look at it. "Is Babba really going somewhere?"

The trip to the shop was about two kilometers long. On our side of the Lim we passed above the Luka and the cemetery where non-Muslim outsiders were buried. The native Serb families had the smaller cemetery on the meadow below the Jusufagić houses in Čair. Walking from Luka, we would pass the Catholic church, the police station, and the gymnasium before crossing the Lim bridge in Šarampov. This bridge was Serbia's main link via the Lim Valley to Montenegro. Then we would go in the opposite direction down the Lim, past "Gypsy Forges." On our right, toward the mountain, stretched two big Muslim graveyards that were still in use for burials. In the second of them, on a gentle hill in the middle, there was an oval, dome-shaped *turbe,* a small mausoleum of white stone open on all four sides crowned by a small, tile-covered cupola. According to some of the older people, the *turbe* had been built on a site where martyrs had perished in the Turkish-Serbian wars of the previous century. It symbolized the Earth, the four sides of the world, and the souls of the dead that are all around us, spreading their *nur* (light), which is visible only to good people.

The government destroyed the cemetery and the *turbe* after World War II and in their place constructed buildings without a single indication of what had existed there before. Further on, we would come to the big, dilapidated Hadži Petrović *han* (inn). Next we passed the Hotel Polimlje, a small bit of modernity in an old setting, and finally, Babba's store. One day, we saw trucks with crates and soldiers in the *čaršija.* They were moving toward the bridge in the direction of Montenegro. It was rumored that the king had abandoned the country and taken the state's gold to England. Fast planes soon appeared and began bombing the troops. It was the first time we had seen several planes together—formerly, we had known only the mail plane, which flew over Prijepolje en route from Belgrade to Podgorica, the capital of Montenegro.

Smailbeg once told us that the people in Prijepolje saw their first plane around 1910. They remembered it because that was the year the border crossings were closed, Austria having annexed Bosnia two years earlier. Moreover, because the new border ran close to the Muslim cemetery in Šarampov, Smailbeg's first wife was buried in the garden of his house on the road to Zalug so that passersby could recite the *fatiha,* the opening chapter in the Qur'an, for her. According to Smailbeg, the plane appeared in the sky overhead while the men were doing the *dženaza* (burial ceremony). I still have childhood memories of seeing her grave in the garden.

Now, thirty years later, German aircraft had returned. They were attempting to bomb the army barracks at the post on the hill above the Lim Valley and the bridge over the Lim. However, instead of hitting them, they struck the houses next to the Catholic church, killing Mujaginca, one of the earlier refugees from Herzegovina. She was the second war casualty, following Kadribeg Hašimbegović, who was killed when the town hall was blown up just before the war. People claimed that this was done in order to destroy the deeds to Muslim property and the Ottoman archives.

We were so surprised by the first bombing attack that we did not even try to hide. We ran out of our homes and watched the bombs falling toward Šarampov and the bridge. On subsequent days, when the planes came in sight, we ran to the nearest gardens to hide behind the trees, or to the brook between the stones, not realizing that this was the deadliest place of all, because of the nearby bridge and the soldiers' barracks. After several days, we began to hear that Yugoslavia was going to fall and that the army was retreating in the direction of Montenegro. Some troops actually did pass through town, miserable in their long military coats; they offered only token greetings to the people watching them go by. Military warehouses were opened in order to ration out food to the people. Babba was one of the quartermasters. We received two sacks of white flour, a sack of rice, and a smaller bag of salt—rations for two households—just as everyone else did. The next morning, after the rations had been handed out, we heard several short, powerful explosions from the direction of the police station. It had already been blocked off. Babba arrived home a little later and told us that the fuel stores had been set on fire. The explosions destroyed the police station and the gymnasium. My father was demobilized, but some of the younger reserve military officers ended up as German war prisoners, working as forced labor in Germany until the end of the war.

Soon after the army's departure, we heard that Yugoslavia had capitulated. I remember that some young lads brought the news to our fountain, and from there it went from house to house. The word *capitulation* was new to us, but people understood what it meant: Yugoslavia had finally collapsed. The Muslim population was not particularly saddened by the news, just as one would not be grieved by the news that a person who had not done any good in his lifetime had died. While not celebrating, one was not likely to feel sorry for him. In his passing, there would be seen, above all, a sign that everything has its end, that everything ends up the way it's supposed to.

Muslims' feelings toward the First Yugoslavia were complicated. It is difficult for me even now to find the exact words to describe it. It was a feeling of nonfreedom that was transmitted to us children in the land where we were born. In order to understand that simultaneous feeling of belonging and alienation, one needs to know certain facts about Muslims' status in the First Yugoslavia.

Among the Muslims, the last days of the Turkish administration were described as not worthy of regret. The government was often in the hands of influential but corrupt Muslim families. Bribery flourished, and the estates and the old way of life were marked by decadence. Only a few families tried to march in step with the times. Others cultivated their illusions about their grandeur. The *begs* and *agas* would say that their sons would not have to suffer because they had enough resources for even their great grandchildren to live and enjoy life. They generally did not work, but instead lived off the income from their estates, on which Serbian peasants did most of the planting. In fact, that later was one of the reasons given for the land confiscation under the Agrarian Reform program. People were illiterate and found it difficult to adapt to school. Mother told me that she often had disciplinary problems in school with the children of the better-off families. They dressed lavishly and refused to do their homework or to sit at the same desk with poor children, meanwhile relying on their parents' power. Teachers were frightened of the possibility of parental intervention.

The disproportion between the former power of families and their present way of life was very great, and it was not rare to see men from such families acting as servants, or engaging in small businesses and old trades. Many young men did nothing, as even those trades were unavailable. In my day, one could still see in the Prijepolje *čaršija* a number of *ćepenci:* shops whose fronts opened out, thus serving both as entrances and storage space. The shops themselves were old and the smell of dampness came from their storerooms, where goods were once kept. There was a string of closed *ćepenci* throughout the *čaršija,* because families had died out or had been left without a male heir to carry on the business, or because the younger men had emigrated. At the far end of the *čaršija,* some of the houses were "eyesores" in which only one or two rooms were still used. Their windows were covered with paper because there was no money to buy glass, and in the few cases where there was a little money, no one had the will to find someone to replace it: people just hemmed and hawed to the end. There was hardly a house that had a piece of paper on which you could write a note. Perhaps an unsharpened pencil might be found with which to write, if there was someone around who knew how to write in the first place.

When a letter came from far away—and everything that was not a part of everyday life seemed be from far away—people would seek out a literate person and ask that he read it to them. Afterward, there would be a lot of talk about what was in the letter. Hadžije (pilgrims) brought the chief news from Muslim lands, but their numbers grew smaller and smaller. The rare young men who went abroad to study in Istanbul and Cairo generally did not return, and over time they lost contact with their homeland.

It was under such conditions that in 1912 the local Ottoman government was replaced by Serbian rule. Serbia "entered" the Sandžak. The Muslims were not able to force their lips to say that Serbia "liberated" the Sandžak, as the Serbian people described the event. Old people have told me that this was the greatest shock Muslims had to bear: to witness the disappearance of the Turkish period and the arrival of the enemies of the faith, who would be their masters from that time on. According to their account, the Serbian army, coming from the direction of Sjenica and Nova Varoš, entered the town peacefully early one evening. They passed through the *čaršija* in the direction of the former Turkish barracks. Some of the units installed themselves there, while others went farther up the Lim Valley toward Montenegro. The Muslim people watched them secretly, through the gardens' fence cracks, not from the windows.

Our Sandžak, such as it was, was lost. The situation of the Muslim people went from bad to worse. After the Serbian and Montenegrin armies entered the Sandžak, local violence became a daily thing. Massacres in the villages and smaller towns—especially on the Montenegrin side of the Sandžak—drove away entire families. People who successfully fled and reached Turkey or some other place with a Muslim population were lucky, despite leaving behind their houses, estates, and cattle. In Prijepolje, Serbian children would plot to kill a Muslim male child, especially one from a well-known family, thus wiping out the family line. Or drunken peasants or someone else would kill an *aga* or some peace-loving men. Beyond our house, in the direction of Zalug, was the grave of our cousin, Ahmed Čuturić, who was killed in this way while working in the fields. Sporadic killings were a way to frighten people into leaving or into selling their estates for next to nothing.

The Agrarian Reform program was unjustly carried out after the formation of Yugoslavia in 1918. Muslims were deprived of their best land, in some cases without being left enough land on which to live. Compensation for the confiscated land was paid yearly in small allotments. I remember that in 1940, Babba bought two blue copper water pails and some cotton with his yearly allotment, so that Nanna could weave cloth for our household needs. It seemed as though nothing new was being created. A new factor was the banks, which lent money while placing mortgages on property. Unfortunately, the mortgages could not be repaid because of the shortage of cash, so people fell deeper and deeper into debt.

Muslims had religious autonomy in the First Yugoslavia, and as citizens they had "the same rights as everyone else." The autonomy consisted of the following: people could freely confess their faith and have *mektebs, medresas,* and charitable foundations. Religion was taught in grade school. Babba told us that they had military imams for religious services and that they ate their meals separately in the army. Muslims followed *šerijat* law in questions of property and marital relations.

Our societies lived together for centuries, or at least side-by-side. There were mutual influences, passing from one side to the other. The old families of Muslims and Serbs in Prijepolje and elsewhere in the Sandžak lived in peace. Nanna used to visit with women teachers from prominent Serbian families. Like my grandfather, Babba was held in great respect and esteem by Serbian families, such as the Hadži Petrović and Veselčić, as well as by many Serbs in the villages. It was the same with other Muslims.

Yet, the idea that this was a Serbian land, and that Muslims were Islamicized Serbs, was the state's raison d'être. Muslims put up with it only because they had no other choice. In trying to explain this phenomenon, one could say that the First Yugoslavia was not taught to accept variety, because being a young state it just did not manage to do so. That would be the easier explanation—one that held out hope for the possibility of a common existence. But there exists another possibility, one that is much worse. I do not know whether it was the leitmotiv of all those who ran the country that the Muslims should be uprooted and driven away.

The Church magnified the Serbs, it bemoaned and wailed over their fate, and when there was nothing else to do, it stirred up the people and aroused baser passions against the Muslims. This was the well from which the Chetniks, Serbian nationalist fighters, drew their inspiration, as well as the source of ordinary Serbian hostility toward the Muslims or "Turks," as they liked to call us. The state was the creator of a great and continuous ambiguity, which it brazenly promoted without admitting it. Muslims served in the army, but they could not become officers; they worked and paid taxes, but they could not fill administrative positions; they went to school, but they never learned anything about themselves; they were scolded for having large families, but at the same time their young people's work was exploited.

The Serbs and Croats knew nothing about the Muslims, their history, or origins. There was almost nothing that showed that the founder of Novi Pazar, in 1416, was a Turkish governor of Bosnia, Isak Beg Ishaković, who also founded Sarajevo in 1454. Almost all the teachers were Serbs, the school programs made no mention of Muslims, and the courts were unjust. I remember my father's trip to Belgrade just before the war. He went to the Superior Court to defend Polje's rights to the water in our brook that the Serbs from Dušmanići had completely diverted, leaving us without a drop of water during the summer drought. He returned without accomplishing his task, since the court ruled in favor of the Serbs. Such treatment of Muslims as a nonexistent society, as well as the combined efforts of the Serbian and Croatian ideologists to assimilate them while taking over their values was what turned Muslims against the First Yugoslavia, a state in which they no longer saw any future.

After news about the fall of Yugoslavia reached us, Prijepolje was cloaked in a veil of uncertainty. The people waited in anticipation of what would come next. A certain calm had set in, even though the town was now without a government. People claimed that the Germans had already entered Priboj and that "they were on their way here." We anxiously left our houses, expecting to see them as they came from Prlo Hill on the other side of the Lim. Though it was still far away, we were able to view the German army as it approached. First came helmeted soldiers on motorcycles, with automatic rifles slung across their backs; next came trucks with soldiers and their equipment, followed by more motorcyclists. They entered Vakuf, heading toward the center of town.

It shocked me so deeply that, years later, while working at my laboratory in Vinča, as I heard the buses moving out of the garage to take us home at three in the afternoon, I would again visualize that scene. The discreet revving up of the motors and the arrival of the column of buses before the path where we were waiting, reminded me of the entrance of the Germans. The army did not come to Polje itself. We saw our first German soldiers when they occupied the repaired police station and we began to go to town over the Lim bridge, which was being guarded by soldiers walking back and forth in front of their guard posts. The Germans did not talk to the people, so they remained strangers. But we began to hear stories that they were "cleansing" the town, which meant that they were arresting, segregating, and killing the insane and the simpleminded, as well as Gypsies and Jews, although we really did not have any Jews to speak of since they had fled. Thus, there disappeared from the *čaršija* the very people who had given it its uniqueness and over whom people exercised a certain care, even though they made the usual exaggerated jokes about them. Our family was worried about Zika and Nedžiba, but perhaps because they were descended from distinguished houses, nothing happened to them. On the other hand, some unfortunates who used to spend the night in deserted huts along the Lim were victims of the "cleansing." They neither knew nor understood anything about the situation, but they nevertheless paid with their lives.

After we had adjusted to the country's capitulation, our situation became more difficult, for we did not know what would happen from one day to the next. That summer, the Ustaše, Croatian nationalists, came to Prijepolje and moved into the former police station, even though there were already Germans in the town. It seems that the Sandžak was to be included in the newly formed Independent State of Croatia (known by its Croatian acronym as the NDH), which had also absorbed Bosnia, whose Muslims had been declared "Croats."

The Ustaše rounded up whatever communists they could find and sent them in the direction of Sarajevo. I remember that people were afraid of the Ustaše. I also remember that some blonde women came with them. They bathed shamelessly in the Lim, which was unusual for us. Above Luka, near the Catholic church, they laughed, shrieked, and screamed, splashing Ustaše standing on the riverbank. Muslim men passed along the road, avoiding them as much as possible, fearing that they might attract the attention of those licentious women.

Not much time passed, however, before it was decided that the Sandžak really belonged to Italy and that the Germans and Ustaše had to withdraw. Thus it was that the Italians came to Prijepolje. Below the Serbian graveyard at Luka they built some fifteen barracks for their soldiers, as well as storehouses for food and weapons. The entire Luka field, as well as Miledbahča, was filled with troops. The Italians took the upper floor of our lower house for their officer's mess. In the guest room, where they had placed a long table, they painted an eagle on one of the walls. Sometimes, when we would go up there, they would give us caramels. Soldiers brought prepared meals from the military kitchen in Luka. Waiters set the table for sixteen officers, then started them off with glass bowls full of plum compote of a rosy hue. Since our women had never made such a compote—even though we had plenty of plums—we children were surprised at their beautiful color. We were also amazed when we saw them going out into the meadows to pick various "grasses" for salads, like garden orache, sorrel, and dandelions in springtime—stuff that we thought fit only for cows. After lunch, the officers would pick up their guitars. They would play and sing, and so we learned a few of their songs. I remember that one of them was called "La Campagnola Bella."

The Italians loved children and would laugh when we took the rustling caramel wrappers and straightened them out to save them; or when, prior to entering the house, we cleaned our feet with sand in the brook. Some of them thought that we did not know what soap was, so they would bring us various soaps and show us what each was for: fine soap for the face, a coarser kind for the feet. We had always played with homemade toys, gathering up pieces of broken coffee cups, or manually making toys from the strings and scraps left over from sewing. So the colored caramel wrappers were our first encounter with something that was "factory made." Later, we gave the Italians peppers and tomatoes from the garden in exchange for bonbons. We could see from their looks that they were surprised that we preferred bonbons to vegetables. The Italian soldiers—unlike the Germans—were sociable and seemed less disciplined. Over time, there developed a small trade—a kind of barter—between us. They used to give us shirts and other clothing in exchange for food supplies. We received rock salt and regular salt from them. In their stores were sacks upon sacks of dried vegetables, which were a little bitter to the taste and had to be soaked before cooking. "What do they need that dried stuff for?" we pondered. "Don't they have more than enough string beans, peppers, and cabbages like us, who even have to throw it away?" We gradually came to understand that the reason they dried them was to escape the frost. "But how do they do that?" we puzzled—until our elders told us that they had a "factory" that did it.

The soldiers liked our corn flour, so they would make a fire between two stones, either at "Banka" or Miledbahča, and they would cook polenta in their sooty covered pots. The polenta would burn when the Italians stirred it. Our women explained to us that polenta had to be boiled slowly in covered pots and not stirred while cooking. The Italians ate sparrows, shooting them from the branches of apple trees with slingshots, which seemed wrong to us. They would bake them in hot coals and crunch their bones. Our people told us that the Italians normally ate cats, frogs, snails, and salamanders. We would never touch or bother such creatures and would even help one, if, for example, a bird broke its wing. Black salamanders with yellow stripes appeared around the verges of fields after a rainfall. It was believed that if they walked over a girl's hand she would be a good worker. We thus forced ourselves to put a hand in their way and to endure the cold contact. Our Aunt Suleima used to pick up various little animals and salamanders fearlessly, and for that reason I thought she was skilled in everything.

It was a great experience for us children when one day we were able to see a plane up close. It landed in Polje's field. The soldiers did not let us get very close, but it was exciting enough just seeing the Italians carry their wounded into what appeared to be some kind of large room. "Is an airplane really that common looking—just a heap of scrap metal that flies?" we wondered, somewhat disillusioned. We expected a plane to look more like a bird—as it seemed to be in the air.

There were some mean-spirited Italians as well. Sometimes they would come to our fountain and set their dogs after our cat, which would run and climb up the willow tree in the brook.

They would throw stones at it while the dogs barked, trying to force it to come down. We watched all this from the window, fearing that they might get a gun. But at a certain moment, the cat jumped from the top of the tree and flew like lightning into the brook. We relaxed. Our little domestic cat knew the terrain! The Italians went on their way, laughing.

They also liked our girls. Our people forbade the girls to show themselves, so that their houses would not be noted. Parents saw to it that their daughters were married off as soon as possible, finding them "shepherds," or husbands. My mother also had a narrow escape when she threw hot coals on an Italian who was peering through our fence. The soldier returned to our house with a rifle, and if it had not been for the children's warning cry from the path he would certainly have killed her. Nanna ran and hid in the far end of the hay barn, while Ferida went out the side gate to the brook. The Italian checked everywhere, even poking his bayonet into a haystack. Fortunately, Uncle Abid appeared at that moment and told him there was a crazy woman living in the house who had escaped. After that, we lived in the lower house until the Italian unit left Luka. The Italians ultimately succeeded in making contact with the girls, however. They would call to us children to deliver chocolates and letters to the girls and would give us something as a reward for doing so. A few girls married them. Rada, the daughter of our Serbian neighbor, Jovan, married an Italian in the middle of the war. He sent her off to Italy right after the wedding. Theirs turned out to be a happy and lasting marriage. Occasionally, even a Muslim girl married an Italian. Such marriages were harbingers of the postwar mixed Muslim and Christian marriages.

The Italians reached an agreement to turn the administration of Montenegro over to the Chetniks. They also entrusted them with the temporary administration of eastern Bosnia, where it bordered the NDH. The Chetniks were also supposed to organize the people's defense against the Ustaše. The Muslims thus found themselves caught in between as each side tried to turn them against the other. In the winter of 1941–42, the Chetniks, claiming that Muslims were collaborating with the Ustaše, carried out cruel massacres in the towns of Čajniče, Foča, Višegrad, and Rudo, and in the villages around Priboj. People fled in all directions, even to us at Polje. Local councils were set up to provide housing, as rooms were crammed to the doors with women and children. No one had more than a few feet of space and there was no room anywhere to put them. The scenes of overcrowding impressed themselves deeply on our memory as we carried food to them. Meho and Asim, from Potok, a village in the Priboj area, entered our household at this time. Local Chetniks had killed their wives and children: four from each family. The men were away from their homes at the time, and thus escaped the massacre. I have not forgotten the events and scenes from those times, nor have I ever believed that they would not be repeated.

In Višegrad, the Chetniks killed and wiped out the Osmanagićs, the family of my friend Vasvija. The Osmanagićs had a factory. Only Edhem, Vasvija's uncle, and Enisa, the daughter of another uncle, were saved. Edhem had come to Nedžibeg's house in Polje and remained there when the war broke out, not returning to Višegrad. He had horses that he groomed and he taught Vasvija and me how to do it. "Cows like to be brushed down," he would tell us. We would groom them and they would bend so low that their stomachs almost touched the ground. "I'm going to groom my Blackie," Vasvija would say, grabbing her dog—which had droopy ears, was round like a barrel, and close to the ground. He would follow us everywhere, running around the cows. But Blackie did not want to be groomed and would run into the bushes at the front of the garden.

Soon, those hardy people were stricken with an outbreak of typhus. A considerable number died from it, and not just refugees. For example, the mother of my friend Fikreta was a victim. She left behind four children. When the epidemic began, mosque councils in the various quarters of town quarantined the area. The illness died off after one or two months. That same year, both Hamida—Vasvija's older sister—and I came down with typhoid fever. Our grownups, ignorant of the fact that the illness comes from contaminated water, said we got it from eating "too many plums and unripe fruit." We barely survived. For days we had high temperatures, were delirious, and could not eat. An Italian military doctor named Giorgio looked after us. It was the first time we ever took any medicine. We were in bed for a long time, but in the end we recovered.

The Italians waged war with the Partisans in the outlying areas, as well as in the direction of Montenegro—especially in the Jabuka highlands on the road to Pljevlje. They restored the Catholic church there for that reason and brought their dead to it. They would line up the flag-draped coffins under a tall tree in the little park in front of the church. Priests in red chasubles and white robes served the funeral mass near a unit of soldiers, who fired a rifle salute at the end. The dead were buried in a military graveyard terraced into the mountainside above the road. In two years' time, the graveyard was almost completely filled. Its area was the equal of a fair-sized garden. We children used to go there to read the names of the soldiers from the wooden crosses and where they were from, as well as to see their photographs.

The Italians would take their revenge at night, using mortars emplaced at Polje to shell the remote mountain villages on the road to Pljevlje, as well as farther down the Lim Valley. I remember the attack on Babine and Toce. Whenever there was unexpected gunfire, we would run for the cellar, open a trap door in the floor, and go down the steps to a hidden room that was separated from the cow shed by bales of straw and hay. We would bring along warm blankets and sit out the attack, which sometimes lasted until dawn. Amazed by their accuracy at first, we quickly grew accustomed to the fact that they could hit objects several kilometers away without moving out of their encampments. Previously, our conception of distance had been formed by hours of hard walking to reach those villages. How many times did I look through my window on a winter morning as peasants shuffled toward the marketplace alongside oxcarts loaded with bags of grain and crates of foodstuffs? Inhabitants of high mountain villages, they were wrapped in black sheepskin coats with red shawls around their heads, and wore turned-up peasant shoes and wool stockings encrusted with snow and ice. They returned in the evening, reaching their villages long after nightfall. I was not indifferent to such a hard life, which I had come to realize could be destroyed in a second, while I, tired and cold, listened to the shells and worried that one of them would hit us. After the firing ended, troops would set out for the villages. We peered at them fearfully through peepholes in our cellar hideout. The tall alpine troops, who wore green feathers in their hats and were accompanied by angry mules, were more dangerous than the almost peace-loving infantrymen whose ranks were filled with average-sized, dark-skinned soldiers.

The soldiers usually returned the next day, their mules loaded with all sorts of things, mostly food and woolen clothing they took from vacant houses before setting fire to them. The people had already fled into the woods before the attack began. Sometimes, the slow-paced column would take hours to pass, soldier after soldier, rifles slung from their shoulders, accompanied by heavily laden mules. The columns included prisoners: relatives of the Partisans who were kept in a special wing at the police station. When I went to the store, I would see women in the prison courtyard, which was surrounded by barbed wire. They were the wives of men who had joined the Partisans, mainly Serbs from the Stiković clan in Toce. In addition to this evidently transient jail, which filled and emptied, there was another jail in town that was worse. People were led from the latter jail to their execution, or they were shipped off to Montenegro or Dalmatia. Ahmo Šehović was kept there in 1942, when the Muslim militia handed him over to the Italians. From there he was taken to a prison camp in Cetinje. The families of condemned Partisans used to find out when they were being taken away and would come with bundles to the bridge over the Lim, where they would greet them and pass food and warm clothing to them for their trip. Amazingly, such leave taking was not prohibited.

The German and Italian commands shot communists sentenced to death on the other side of the Lim, in Purić's Brook above Hašimbegović's Field. In 1942, they shot the sons of Murat Šećeragić and Musabeg as well as Mujaga Veljović. The latter was a hostage for his three sons and a grandson, all of whom were Partisans. The sound of the rifle fire, sometimes accompanied by a scream, would reach us quite clearly at Polje. The military patrol even took away my Aunt Šaćira, Ahmo's wife, to shoot her. The soldiers came to the house in the morning to get her. Someone gave me her son Sakib to take down to the path. While they were leading Aunt Šaćira down the road, the two of us waded in our brook. Sakib would turn around, trying to catch sight of his mother. Evidently, someone intervened on Šaćira's behalf at the place of execution—a spot near Sjenica — because she was separated from the others and led away to prison. The mother of my schoolmate Dobrila survived a firing squad as, wounded, she crawled to a nearby village. Her two sons were fighters, one with the Partisans and the other with the Chetniks. I remember that when the Partisans took over Prijepolje, her son Mile, a Partisan, sat on the little bridge before their house. Earlier, when the Italian's were in control, her Chetnik son—who died later in the war—had also sat on the same bridge.

The Chetniks did not succeed in getting control of the Sandžak from the Italians. So, after the installation of the Italian administration, the Italians chose a distant relative of my father, Alefendija Aginčić as mayor. The Italian army controlled exits from the town, especially via the Lim bridge. Grownups received "permese," personal documents containing a picture that they were to show the guards at the bridge. They also took away our boats, so that our freedom of movement from Polje and nearby villages was diminished. In the town itself, besides the Italians, there were the Muslim militia and the local Chetniks, each side looking after its own people. The most famous militia commander was Hodža Pačariz, who had come to our region from Montenegro before the war. Farther up the Lim, in the direction of Gračanica and Brodarevo, there was the militia of Husein Rovčanin. The militias generally cooperated with the Italians and Germans against the Partisans, although sometimes, if the situation warranted it, they would enter into tacit agreements with Partisans. The main objection that the militias had against the Partisans was that they were atheists and opposed to the holding of private property.

Local Chetniks cooperated with the Montenegrin Chetniks. I remember Montenegrin Chetnik officers with long beards, cockade badges on their caps, and bandoleers across their chests as they came to our town to visit Prota Šiljak and other important Serbs.

The people always regarded coexistence between the Muslim militia, Chetniks, and Italians as unstable. For that reason, individual towns organized their own defenses. Especially successful were the villages in the direction of Bijelo Polje and Sjenica, where the famous militia of Hasan Zvizdić held sway. The militia made a camp for the whole village at the citadel of Hisardžik, one that could be easily defended. At one point, the people organized a reconnaissance group that kept watch during the night against sudden Chetnik attacks. It seems to me that the commander of that activity was Ahmet *efendija* Salihbegović, whom the Partisans shot after the war. I do not know what happened to all the militias, but they disappeared after the Italians capitulated and the town faced a serious threat from the Chetniks.

The Italians had intended to remain in the Sandžak permanently, since their plan was to join the Sandžak, Montenegro, and Albania to Italy. As a result, they devoted special attention to children. In Prijepolje, on the meadow below Zika's house, they founded "Kolonija" a kind of children's camp, supposedly with the intention of improving children's nutrition during wartime. When it came turn for the children in Polje to go, my parents forced me, even though I had no desire to go. Each one-month cycle involved a hundred children. We arrived at the camp in the morning and stayed until twilight. For breakfast and supper we received milk, tea, and a slice of fresh bread with marmalade, which we had never tasted before and which we found to be tastier than our native jam. They served us lunch under a tent. Usually, it consisted of tomato and rice soup—I can still recall the smell—and cooked vegetables with meat, as well as salad and a piece of cake. Pork was never used. We took a nap after lunch, with separate tents for boys and girls. In the morning and after lunch we did exercises. We practiced for the rally at the end of our cycle, as well as for special performances when Italian officers visited our town. A grandstand had already been erected for such occasions on top of Miledbahča. I still remember the guests on the platform: there were Italian officers in dress uniform with all their medals, as well as the mayor, Alefendija Aginčić. Also present were his wife Esmehanma and daughter Aiša, both dressed in expensive outfits, wearing gloves and veils and carrying large handbags. The brief sojourns of high-ranking Italian officers in the town, or even their passing through town, were exploited in an effort to save communists, Partisans, and their sympathizers. Since there was no hotel, these officers stayed in the homes of rich or distinguished local residents. The house of the Džandžanović family was in the center of town and at that time the most appropriate for this purpose. The rooms were furnished with modern furniture and had bathrooms with running water. Sometimes, the Italian officers were given expensive rugs (*kilims*). The master of the house, Abdurahman, called Manjo, was a peaceful and industrious man who had a large estate in Polje, right behind our gardens. Parties with plenty of food and music were held in the early evening in that estate's gardens for the heads of the Muslim militia in the hope of freeing the members of leading families from jail or the Italian prison camps in Montenegro.

The sisters of Derić and Prota Šiljak's granddaughters conducted most of the training for the girls at the camp. We wore gymnastic costumes and our rallies were really well prepared. Prijepolje did not see activities on such a scale again until the 1960s, during the Sandžak Games. I did not like the exercises or the camp or the discipline, nor was I especially good at gymnastics. I preferred to play freely on the playground below our fields, where there was another grandstand on which an Italian band practiced military marches most mornings. When they left around noon, the grandstand and the playground were all ours, and we played hide-and-go-seek or ran along the fine sand on the banks of the River Lim, resting in the shade of walnut and poplar trees, without giving a thought to the time.

Local Muslim councils opened *mektebs.* A *mekteb* was formed in our house in Polje with Nanna as the religion teacher. Each morning, the neighborhood children would arrive, carrying with them their primers—called the *Ilmihal,* and the *Amesufara.* We learned how to pray, to read the Arabic alphabet, and to recite the Qur'an. A few of the better students completed the *hatma,* that is, they recited the whole Qur'an. The first recitation of a *hatma* was celebrated before the whole family. The girls received silk kerchiefs to cover their heads. For this occasion, it was necessary to look for silk in the hope chests, because it was impossible to buy it anywhere.

Nanna insisted that we learn to write Arabic letters and read other Arabic texts besides the Qur'an. I remember that we came across a Bosnian novel written in *bosančica.* I read that text quite fluently, even though it did not have the usual diacritical marks over and under the Arabic letters. We drank in the words of the Qur'an and endeavored to identify them in the text we were studying at the time. Thus, we were able to connect our household *kitabs* with the books mentioned in the Qur'an: for example, *Ya Ahlul-Kitabi* ("O People of the Book!"). It means Jews and Christians. The children were frightened by the words *Kullu nefsin thaikatul mavt* ("Every soul shall have a taste of death"), connecting them with our elders who had passed on, or with those who were mortally ill, for whom there was no cure. I still remember the story of "Hudhud," the bird with whom Suleiman/Solomon, God's messenger, conversed. In the evening, Nanna would not allow us to put apple cores in the fire in order to give our room a pleasant smell, because that smell was "Hudhud's food" and it would awaken him, since he was still alive. I later learned that this was the bird that brought Solomon the news about the Queen of Sheba.

The government reopened the schools in early 1943. From Polje, Ahmo's son Sakib entered the first grade and I went into the second. We had classes in various places: at first it was in the former post office at the head of the *čaršija;* then it was down by the Lim, in sheltered sections of the garden behind the church; later still, it was held in a summerhouse on Ravne Plateau above Prijepolje. There were plenty of children. We studied counting, spelling, and geography, and then we had an orientation, both according to a map and outdoors. We also learned to write in Latin letters, which was part of the program for the second grade. Strangely, we had no classes in Italian. Our education was irregular in that enemy bombing was always a possibility.

One Friday, Sakib and I set out for the afternoon session. Above Luka, we met the men from Polje as they returned from their prayers at the mosque. Babba tried to persuade us not to go to school, but we continued on. Then, just as we neared the school, airplanes appeared and began to drop bombs. I ran back through the *čaršija,* headed straight for home, while Sakib continued on to school. In order to shorten my journey and to avoid the bridge over the Lim, I set out over the pontoon bridge erected below Luka, which the Italians sometimes allowed us to cross. When I reached the bridge I saw Italian soldiers, crouching with weapons in hand, running toward their nearby encampments. There was shooting nearby, probably from the antiaircraft unit the Italians had emplaced near the bridge. Paying no attention to them, I continued to run. Within moments, a second wave of bombing attacks began.

Bombs were falling above the barracks on the Serbian landlord Tapo's hills and pieces of metal began flying around me. I thought at first they were slivers of marble from gravestones in the nearby graveyard, but I kept on running between the barracks. At that point, a soldier caught up with me and knocked me to the ground. He lay there next to me and did not let me up until the planes had flown away. When things quieted down, I continued my run homeward, book bag and sweater in hand. I found Nanna praying the *ićindija,* the midafternoon prayer. She sent me to Ibrahim *aga* Veljović's meadow, where I found Babba. He had just taken water from the Vuk fountain and had sat down with several other men beneath the plum trees. They were in such bloom that you could not see more than a few feet beyond them. The scent of the blossoms filtered through the garden, while the quiet buzzing of the bees informed us that they were busily sucking nectar from the pink flowers. What a contrast to the sounds of shrapnel that had earlier been whizzing around me!

Several days later, the town council closed the school and I received my certificate for having finished the second grade. School did not open again until after the war. Meanwhile, the airplanes "visited" us several more times. Nor did we always know whose they were. Thus, in the summer of 1943, there appeared above Prijepolje squadrons that people said were "allied planes" heading for Germany. At about seven o'clock in the morning we would hear a muffled roar that got louder and louder. Soon we spotted the planes, which were flying from the direction of Nova Varoš and Sjenica. Clusters of aircraft would appear in the clear blue sky. Each group had three lead planes, followed by five more, and then two in the rear. The planes covered a good part of the sky as they moved slowly northwest before disappearing in the direction of Pljevlje. They would return in the same formation at about five o'clock in the afternoon. We became so used to these squadrons that we could tell the time by their passing overhead. But we never knew when they might hit us, too. In truth, Prijepolje was bombed once more that summer, but the planes hit the Hamam section and the center of town that time. I will never forget seeing pieces of bodies scattered among the stones near the Mileševka River's confluence with the Lim. I remember one piece that, I was told, was a spinal column. It was sticking up in the blood-covered dust. Further on lay a woman's arm, covered with a colorful chintz sleeve. People were searching the area in the hope that they might be able to identify one of their own. Not far away, in the gardens of Hadžagić, some bombs hit a trench, killing more than twenty people from the neighborhood, most of them women and children.

The Germans occupied Prijepolje for a time following Italy's capitulation in 1943. Soon after they arrived we learned that they were going to withdraw and surrender the town to the Chetniks. They withdrew in the direction of Pljevlje, and quite a few local young men went with them, loaded in their trucks. Their departure from Polje took two or three days—enough time to destroy the Italian barracks before they left. This was the most terrible time of all for us. Men swarmed around the German trucks at the gathering place around our fountain, taking the weapons being handed down as the air around them was rent more and more frequently by stray bullets. The Chetniks were firing on the Germans from the surrounding hills, initiating a firefight as they waited to enter the town. The Germans finally left in the early evening, torching the Italian barracks in the field along the Lim known as Luka. Everyone who was left was looking for a safe place to spend the night. We took shelter in a trench dug under an open shed at our upper house. As the barracks went up in flames, the sky was blood red and filled with hunks of metal from the explosion of weapons and munitions as far as our eyes could see from the trench. Because we were in the immediate vicinity, most of the debris flew right over us and fell in the gardens and fields around Polje. It was during Ramadan, but no one ate the evening feast. Nanna and Babba knelt in prayer for the *akšam* at sunset and *jacija* in the evening. Crouching in the trench, we could see the Chetniks gathered around their fires on Srijeteže Hill and occasionally could even recognize their songs through the roar of the explosions.

Even now I have a clear recollection of that trench, of the moist black earth and its heavy smell, and of a vast sense of hopelessness. As I remember it, that was our most difficult moment in the war. People never feared death as much as Chetnik savagery and the destruction of their very humanity. People were not so mobile that they could flee, and there was hardly anywhere to go. In the past, they had gone in the direction of Novi Pazar and Kosovo, so that some among us spent as much as a year there. It was then that I first heard of Đakovica and Peć, places in Kosovo where Muslims from our area had found refuge among the Albanians. But for the majority, to go even to Kosovo was difficult—they had no money, and the Albanians were a different nationality who spoke a different language. Thus, people preferred to stay in their homes, hoping that because they were peaceable and had not done anything bad to anyone they would not be killed.

Just before dawn, the explosions quieted down somewhat and Babba went to the house to get milk to begin the new day's fast and to see if the cows in the cellar were all right. We entered the house about noon. The next day—since nothing was happening—people felt free to move about a bit. Babba went off to the *čaršija*. There were Chetniks in town, but I did not know which Chetniks. Supposedly they had given guarantees that they would not do anything to the local population.

For days, Serbs from nearby villages would come with their oxcarts to haul goods away from the Italian garrisons, which continued to smolder for more than a month with occasional small explosions. It never occurred to any of the Muslims to take anything. The children would visit the smoldering ruins, poke at the flames, sift through the ashes, and view the layers of Italian uniforms—still starched and clean. Pear-shaped artillery shells, some of them twenty centimeters long, and grenades were scattered everywhere around the flattened garrisons. Some could even be activated, as we learned while playing war games in the midst of that horror.

Not long after they entered the city, the Chetniks came to both our houses. I was the first to spot the group of some fifteen soldiers with beards and cockades, all festooned with crisscrossed ammunition belts. "There they are," I told Nanna. Babba was still in the *čaršija,* as it was not quite evening. Hidden behind the food chest in the pantry was a gun we had taken from a German truck. Nanna grabbed it, carried it quickly across the yard, and hid it in the brook. A moment later, the Chetniks entered the yard through the main gate. They made a superficial search of the house and went away. Most of the grownups thought that someone had informed on us about the weapon, but there were other theories. Babba, for example, thought that they were preparing to take the men away, as they had done in Foča before the slaughter.

After the Chetnik search, our people began thinking every day about how they could flee. It would soon be Bairam, which came in the fall that year. There was increasing talk that the Chetniks were preparing a slaughter for Bairam. There were no Chetniks in Polje itself, so the people began communicating with "the woods" (the Partisans). Someone said couriers had come with secret news that the Partisans would liberate us just before Bairam. That was when we learned that there were couriers and contacts with the Partisans. We did not know who they were, but it was said that Pero, our neighbor Jovan's son, Arifaga's Iza, Hadžira, Nadira, and Smailbeg's Akča were somehow involved with them. Others in the Partisan ranks were Ahmo, who had been in since the beginning of the war, Arifaga's son Hanefija, and Smailbeg's sons Musabeg, Juso, and Haso, who were in the 3d Sandžak Brigade, commanded by Halil Hadžimurtezić from Nova Varoš. Our access to this information meant that the Chetnik lid was not on very tight and that the general situation was no longer as strict as it had been at the beginning of the war.

We all gathered together in Jakup-aga's house—that is, in the upper part of Zika's house—to be more secure together and so the thick walls would give us some protection if there was fighting. On the third night of our wait, sometime after midnight, from Srijeteže Hill, in the direction of Nova Varoš, we began to hear gunfire and shouts: "Forward 3rd Sandžak Brigade, forward Halil, hurrah!" The Partisans entered the town and Prijepolje was liberated by dawn without much shooting or fighting.

It was two in the afternoon before we learned that the Partisans were in Polje, in the garden of Anica and Mićo Pajević, close by the hill. We children ran off to get a look at them. We saw little tents set up and soldiers hurrying in the garden, evidently preparing to move out. In fact, they went away the next day. That was when I saw my first woman Partisan: Safa Lotrić from Vakuf. She wore a uniform consisting of a skirt and short, olive drab jacket made of English wool, a Partisan cap with the red star on the front, and high boots. She carried a pistol in a leather holster strapped at her waist. Someone said it was the standard uniform the Partisans had been getting from the English. The Partisans remained in Prijepolje until December. They set up their own government, called people's committees. They also taught young people to read and write, and they put on performances and arranged other entertainment. Their relaxed attitude later got them into trouble. In December, the Germans launched their sixth offensive. The attackers destroyed the Partisan hospital, where soldiers from the proletarian brigades, newly arrived from battles in Serbia, were recovering from their wounds. They also retook the town.

5 The Battles and Flight to Zalug

Many Partisans were stationed in town when sudden firing erupted near our houses on December 4, 1943. The snow had recently melted and the River Lim was swollen. We fled through our trapdoor when we heard the shooting and hid out in the cellar room. No one knew what was happening. The Germans, dressed in white ski outfits, had managed to enter Šarampov undetected after wiping out the Partisan lookouts posted on the Sokolica Cliffs. Later, the Partisans blamed Hasan Zvizdić's militia troops in Sjenica for showing the Germans a way to get into town from an unexpected direction.

Once they entered Šarampov, the Germans quickly took the Lim bridge before unleashing a full-scale barrage of fire. By seizing the bridge, the Germans were able to keep the Partisans from retreating across the Lim or defending the hospital, which was just over the bridge on the road to Bijelo Polje. Because of the swollen river's width, which had reached an extraordinarily high level as a result of runoff from the melting snow, only those who were good swimmers and who knew the terrain were able to make it safely across the Lim. The Partisans lost more than five hundred soldiers killed that day, including almost all of the wounded in the hospital—most of them from crack proletarian units. The Germans battered the building with shells from tanks positioned on the bridge, until by evening they had crushed the resistance of the wounded and their guards.

The guards probably had hoped that at least some of them would be able to escape by withdrawing into the mountains under the cover of darkness. Only a few managed to get away, however. The mountains began right behind the hospital, rising upward to the Gradina Cliffs, which, together with Sokolica on the other side, formed a ravine. It was impossible for fleeing soldiers to remain undetected as they fled up the naked mountainside, their every step dogged by the machine guns mounted on the German tanks. The only choice left to the Partisans encircled in other parts of town was to reach the river's left bank and retreat in the direction of Pljevlje or Priboj. Unfortunately, the Germans who had crossed the bridge and taken Polje were waiting for them. Partisans in our area were generally able to escape. They knew the terrain and where to find the narrower spots in the Lim where it was possible to swim across. They also sought shelter in friendly homes, a dangerous practice for both them and their hosts.

After the battle, the Germans took over our upper house and turned it into a military hospital. Fearing German revenge, we again went to Jakub *aga*'s house. Others had also fled there. In the darkness, some people brought in a badly wounded Partisan they had found in "Banka." Our hosts set out a mattress for him next to a stove. He had many wounds and did not talk. In the dim light of the fire from the stove, we silently gazed at the Partisan, afraid to approach him. Our men looked for Partisan insignia, hoping to hide them and to be able to tell the Germans that he was a conscript, forced by the Partisans to carry food and ammunition. He told them that he had no such insignia. A little later, a German patrol arrived and, while conducting a search, found the wounded Partisan's cap with its red star. After the patrol left, a German doctor came and dressed the man's wounds. The doctor visited him regularly after that night.

When we saw that the Germans did not do anything to people, and that the doctor had taken care of Vlada—which we learned was the wounded Partisan's name—we felt free to go outside, even though it was late in the evening. The fighting had stopped completely and the army had moved off toward Zalug. Above Banka we came upon three members of the Communist Youth, Pero Koković, Arifaga's daughter, Hadžira, and Kusin Čelebić of Šarampov with a Partisan woman who had managed to escape. They were talking softly and waiting for a signal that it was safe to lead her toward the village of Dušmaniće, which was outside the German encirclement. We hovered around the three locals and the Partisan fighter, listening to their promise that the Partisans would be victorious. On parting, they sang softly and defiantly, "I rode my horse over the mountain of Konjuh, the wind blows and whines, the leaves sing mournful songs." How many times, after the war, did we hear that popular song? It seemed especially appropriate at that moment, in the dusky twilight that hid so many dead and wounded who were dying in the fields down below by the Lim. Pero and Kusin, who himself died in battle later on, moved with the woman Partisan through the gardens above our brook, heading for the mountains as we turned homeward.

The next day, Vlada opened up a bit in the friendly atmosphere of Jakub *aga*'s house. He told us he was a Serb from the 1st Proletarian Brigade, formed by Marshal Tito in the small Bosnian town of Rudo (near Priboj) on December 22, 1941. That date subsequently was acknowledged as the birthday of the Yugoslav People's Army (JNA). Vlada became especially close to the children. He would call us over to his bed in order to get some news about the dead along the Lim. From our descriptions, he tried to identify his dead comrades in the fields who had not yet been gathered up. Some dead Partisans even lay in the brook from which we drew our water.

We returned to our house several days later and the field hospital also moved. Vlada was sheltered in a side room in Banka. We visited and fed him daily and, since there were no more doctors, our people bandaged his eighteen wounds. He stayed in that room for about a month and was on his way to recovery, when, to our consternation, the military command moved him to prison. We watched his transfer from somewhat of a distance, while our grownups looked furtively out the windows. A German soldier and a local boy from Prijepolje who was a member of the German SS unit came for him. They put him on a barrow used for removing the rubbish from Zika's yard and wheeled him to the car. An SS trooper removed the worn sheepskin coat that the women had thrown around him and replaced it with a torn overcoat, in spite of the fact that it was the middle of winter and he was weak. His wounds prevented him from putting it on by himself. I do not know what happened to him. People said that Partisan activists with connections rescued Vlada from jail. He did not come back after the war—not even on July 7, the day of Serbia's insurrection, when a service honoring those who died in the hospital attack was held. The hospital's ruins were preserved after the war and the area around it was made into a memorial park.

Life moved on. In the spring of 1944 we went to Zalug for the summer. After Polje, I most liked this village, which was located about four kilometers down the Lim Valley from us. The village had consisted of about ten houses divided between the Beganović and Turković families since ancient times. The Mekić family lived farther outside the village, surrounded by their gardens and fields. After the war, a lot of those people emigrated to Turkey.

The houses in the village were on a plateau from which foothills and forests continued upward. Below the houses were the fields. A brook separated Zalug from the few houses at the beginning of Izbišnje and Toce villages that were already in the forests and mountains in the direction of Priboj. On the Zalug plain itself, and all the way down to the Lim, were spread the fields and meadows of numerous old Prijepolje families. A major part of these estates belonged to the Čuturić family from Hamam and its Hadžišehović branch from Polje. Serbian families acquired the land that joins Polje and Zalug in a variety of ways, but mainly through Agrarian Reform or by purchasing it cheaply from members of our families who had emigrated to Turkey. Many of the Muslims in town became impoverished or lost the will to cultivate the land themselves, reluctant to do rural work after having become accustomed to the indoor urban life. The village of Zalug thus became a small Muslim oasis in a Serbian environment. Nevertheless, the spacious meadows of the Zalug Plain gave witness to the former life of Muslims in the town. Here could be found thick and branchy fruit and walnut trees. The meadows all had their own springs and wells, each with its own name.

We often fled toward Zalug and the meadows along the Lim during the war. We spent even more time in the village itself, at the house of Nina, the mistress of the Beganović family. Above the village, where a brook ran down the mountainside, there spread a beech forest. The Jarčište estate was established on the peak, framed by groves into which Nina and I went to pick medicinal herbs. Nina told me the name of each one and its medicinal use. Then she would sit down for a rest and after she rolled a little tobacco in a cigarette paper, she would light a cigarette. She did not like manufactured cigarettes, just as she did not like coffee unless it was brewed with pure spring water, even though they had a deep well with cold, potable water in their garden. While she was smoking, I would ask her about the surrounding area. "That place in the distance is Merica Cliff on top of Mount Zlatar in Kosatica village, from behind which the sun first moves when it lights up Polje. Farther on," Nina would continue, "in the direction of Sjenica, above the red ravine that is barely visible, you can see the outlines of the Dundore estates above the village of Hisardžik, where your mother used to spend the summer with her relatives." I already knew from my mother that those were the fields of Avdaga Malagić, her first cousin. The places Nina pointed out were enveloped in a bluish haze, looking like another world from which we used to be aroused by golden pheasants that would suddenly appear beside us in the silence, without sensing our closeness. We would return home slowly, arriving just as the cattle came down the path from their pasture, led by their most warlike member, who wore a large bell slung under his neck. Aunt Nina also worked with bees. She kept hives in a garden full of tansy bushes, so that no one could cast a spell that would keep the bees from producing a lot of honey. She removed the honeycomb—which she claimed was healthy to eat right away while leaving the bees their part, which is probably why they did not sting her.

The Saint George's Day celebration was observed early in the morning in the countryside and in town according to the ancient customs. Even though Saint George's Day was a Serbian holiday and a household saint's day, it was significant for others as well. Usually in the week before and after Saint George's Day, people planted early vegetables such as string beans and onions in their gardens, and peas and white beans in the fields. Shepherds could no longer pasture their flocks freely in our fields after that day, and houses hired temporary labor from Saint George's Day to Saint Demetrius's Day. Saint Demetrius's Day, another important Serbian holiday, was observed on November 7. From that day on, the fields and meadows were once again open to everybody, and flocks were allowed to pasture freely.

On the eve of Saint George's Day, as the sun was setting, the women, children, and maidens of Zalug went into the dark groves or by some body of water seeking herbs and a rare flower. Many girls would go with milk pails to scoop up the water swirling within a small space and at a great depth, called *tavnik.* On their way home, they would pick flowers and herbs along the Lim, dampening them in the water. While picking the herbs and sprinkling them with water, a girl would confide to them her heart's wish. The herbs that they gathered were supposed to act like a magnet, drawing the destined young man into their dreams. They hoped that from their dreams, as well as from the position of the herbs in the milk pail and their freshness, they would be able to divine their future beloved's name and their own happiness. But if girls already had a beloved, they would recite incantations to make his head swirl, as the water swirled in a deep river pool or a mountain stream. Childless women hoped to learn whether they would have children.

After these rituals, people gathered at daybreak for the outing near the water, in the gardens. Swings were placed in the walnut trees, fires lit, and meat roasted on spits. Music and singing continued until early evening. Even though families would choose in advance with whom they wanted to share the accordion playing, singing, and good food—anyone was welcome to join them in the afternoon. There was no alcohol.

People would disband before evening, tired but happy. The men would lug the heavier things, while the women carried the sleeping babies. If the picnic was held far from town, the older folks left for home in a wagon pulled by oxen, carrying with them the children and party stuff. Riding in a wagon hitched to fast horses was even better. The big swings made from heavy ropes were taken down from the walnut trees, where they usually were hung. The smaller swings were left for the children.

The summer of 1944 was a time of abundance. In the village of Zalug, women cooked jams and thick apple syrup; they also prepared dried pasta for winter. Blackberries and dogberries were gathered along the forest paths and their syrup was extracted for storage. We especially loved the wild service tree that grew in the brook. It had a tiny fruit that we picked while it was still green and left in the straw in the stable to ripen. My mother also prepared a large stock of winter stores to take with us to Polje at the end of September, planning to use them during the winter.

In October, however, long columns of Germans and Chetniks began to turn up from the direction of Sjenica, headed for Priboj in the direction of Sarajevo. The Germans were retreating from the south, from Greece and

Yugoslavia. People said they were going back to their homeland. Polje was filled with Chetniks, while the Germans avoided the population. There were about forty Chetniks in our upper house. They usually stayed for a few days and moved on.

Soon, the people from Zalug swarmed into our crowded Polje. They had a sad story to tell. A column made up of Russian Nazis attached to German units, plus some Bulgarian detachments, turned up in Zalug. After crossing the pontoon bridge in Zalug Field, they separated from the main force headed toward Priboj and killed everyone in their path. First they killed fifteen members of the Sekulić family; then they slaughtered the Čović family, along with their mistress, Nasta. I remember seeing Nasta in her yard with a great bundle of keys dangling at her waist. The Čović family was numerous and she was always busy. Of those two large Serbian families, only two of the smaller children survived. They had gone after the cattle in the grove above the house. The children saw everything that happened. The oldest son in the Sekulić family also survived. He was in the Partisans, but his wife and four children were killed. A third Serbian family, the Čarkilovićs, had gone to join the Partisans, so the soldiers burned their buildings.

In Zalug, the soldiers came upon the separate houses of the Mekić family. In one house, they killed the mother and wife of Ćamil Mekić, as well as his five children. Ćamil himself was a Partisan. In a second, they killed the women and girls, five in all. Little Šefka, who lost an eye, survived the shooting, as did her younger brother, whom the sisters drew under them as they were falling. Seeing the killing, the Zalug people gathered in front of Aunt Nina's house. Entering the village itself, the soldiers killed Nurčo Turković's mother on the threshold of their house. She was the oldest woman in Zalug. Then, evidently deciding to spend the night there, they drove the gathered inhabitants from the village and led them to the pontoon bridge. Their guards kept the people there for several hours, their submachine guns trained on them all the while. At the last moment, members of the local SS units who accidentally passed by the pontoon bridge with the German units headed for Priboj, saved the Zalug villagers. Unable to return to the village, they came to Polje.

Among the Chetniks in our house there happened to be an officer of the former Yugoslav Royal Army. Sometimes he and my father would smoke and converse. This officer knew that the Partisans were making headway and he did not expect the king to come back. Nor did he believe that the planes passing over Polje at night were being sent by the English to save them.

The crowd of Chetniks and soldiers swarmed around Polje, as in a beehive. The Chetniks would light fires at night near the path and the road, using them for warming themselves and cooking. The local inhabitants feared the fires might attract planes, but no one dared mention that prospect to the Chetniks. On November 6, the day before Saint Demetrius's Day, Allied planes began a full-scale bombing attack on Prijepolje at about eleven in the morning. Everyone was at work either in the garden or in the house: people were preparing winter food supplies, cutting wood into small logs, and storing leek in covered pits. It was a cool but sunny day, and the children were playing that they were airplanes around the fountain and near the apple tree on the road.

When the heavy bombers appeared in the distance and began to separate, some heading for Sjenica and Pljevlje while others began to circle overhead, we knew what was about to happen. I ran home. Nanna stayed behind, as usual, while Babba and I set out for Zalug, moving through a group of gathering people and Chetniks who would not let us run—for fear we would create a panic—because, they said, "those are allied planes." They did not know the "prehistory" of the planes as we did, or what it meant when they started to circle over a town. Moving quickly, we had already distanced ourselves from them when the first bombs began to fall. We ran to a zigzag military trench above the road on the slopes of Tijana's meadow. There were about twenty of us, including that Chetnik officer who stayed at our house. Bombs fell even on the slopes and on the gardens down below—there was a rattling sound everywhere. Beneath the deafening roar of the planes came the penetrating sound of the bombs whistling through the air, followed by deafening explosions, and then a maelstrom of stone, metal, and earth that lifted from the soil and flew over our trench. I quickly took all that in when I lifted my head for a moment to peek.

After the first wave of aircraft departed, we got up from the trench and continued to run toward Zalug. By the time the second wave of bombers arrived, we were already at the spring in Topčić's field. We lay down again, but were already safe. Babba and the officer sat up and lit cigarettes. After the second attack ended we continued on to Zalug and the Chetnik officer returned to Polje. The planes had already flown off.

We reached the charred ruins of the Čarkilović's houses and the burned grapevines in their yard. I still recall them outside those abandoned buildings. Babba had no water, so he did a symbolic washing, rubbing his face and hands with earth, as he prayed the *ićindija* on a toppled beam below the road. Other fugitives began to arrive at that point, but they were afraid to go on to Zalug, so they began to swarm around in the field and in the bare forest above it. Uncle Abid came with his family, but there was no word of Nanna. New fugitives told us that our upper house had been destroyed as they signaled to Babba that Nanna had died. Someone reported that Hodža *hanuma,* a woman teacher, had died. Babba decided to return home and, since I did not want to remain there, he took me along. We set out through people who were fleeing through the fields and forests toward Zalug, carrying with them various tales. We had just passed the bend below the neighboring houses when we spotted Nanna in a black dress without a veil over her face. She was carrying a large pot full of meat and cooked vegetables that had been cooking on the stove when the bombing began. She talked quickly in Turkish to Babba, but I was able to understand that the upper house had been partially destroyed. It appeared that our cow, Zlatulja, had survived in the basement stall. Nanna had given her some water and hay before setting out to find us. We turned back toward the Čarkilovićs's houses. Uncle Abid, noticing Nanna—whom he had already saved from the irate Italian the time she spilled hot coals on him—shouted: "My goodness, where have you been, sister-in-law?" We spread a cloth on the ground so we could eat, for no one had eaten all day. The food that Nanna brought was very welcome indeed!

My mother rarely fled from the house. She believed that if it was her time to die, nothing she did could prevent it from happening. She would pray, read the Qur'an, and then do her household chores. This time, too, she had remained at home. However, when bombs began to fall all around, damaging the house, she managed to escape through the dust of the explosions since she knew her way. Nanna went out through the small side gate and followed the brook up toward the Trnje bushes. After somehow reaching a plateau in Ibrahim *aga* Veljović's meadow she was able to watch the streams of bombs shining in the bright sunlight as they fell on Hamam, where her brother Hafiz used to live. Nanna decided not to go any farther but to pray the *ićindija* right there on the grass, where she could still see the rose bushes that had been tended by her dead Aunt Đula, Ibrahim *aga*'s mother. Before she finished the prayer, Nanna heard someone call out from the slope of Trnje, where the brook ran down. She finished her prayer as quickly as she could and turned toward the voice of a suffering, moaning man. It was a wounded Chetnik. Nanna hesitated to move to help him, but his words, "Sister-in-God, please help me!" drew her toward him. She descended to the brook and began to pull him out to the path, after trying to stop his bleeding with a piece of her scarf, as he instructed her to do. Suddenly another Chetnik appeared above them, whom the wounded man called to: "Where are you when the wounded need to be rescued?" He cursed the man's god, at which Nanna said "Neuzubillah" ("God save us!"). After his friend drew near, the wounded man thanked Nanna for her help. She returned homeward, passing several dead Chetniks lying by the brook and around the house. Almost none of the locals had fled in that direction. They knew better.

We returned to an empty Polje shortly before evening. The Chetniks had left town as soon as they finished gathering up their dead. There were bomb craters all around. You could put a house inside one if you turned it upside down. Returning with groups of people, we passed the trench where we had first taken cover. Off to the side, we saw a number of dead people. Among them was the wife of Jevđen from Zalug, a Serb. Farther on lay their dead teenage son. Their youngest daughter, Rada, who was my age, was with us. The women took Rada's hands and led her, shielding her from the sight of her dead mother and brother. Jevđen survived the war, along with his oldest son, who was a Partisan. Jevđen was well known throughout the area for his healing abilities, as he had set many a broken leg or arm. He even could restore flexibility to people whose neck or back had stiffened.

After we arrived home, we stopped at the upper house to salvage some things and to get the cow. We got Nanna's Singer sewing machine, some books, and the Čarkilović family's girls marriage gifts and embroideries that they had left with us for safekeeping when they went off to join the Partisans. I found our neighbor Jovan's son Nikola lying dead beneath a garden window. We had played together that morning. He was about fifteen and was lying on his back, as though resting. A small trail of blood ran from one ear to his mouth. Now he, too, would have to be buried. Nikola's mother, Sofia, was left completely alone with her little daughter Branka. Jovan had already died, their eldest son Pero was in the Partisans, daughter Rada had married an Italian soldier and gone off to live in Italy, and the beautiful Nada had fled toward Belgrade to escape a local Chetnik named Sima. When she refused his offer to marry him, he shot at their house during the night. She married an English officer in 1945 and went to London.

It was already dark when the men went with Sofia to the nearby graveyard to find a grave for Nikola. They sent for Vojin Dosković so that there would not be just Muslims at the burial. Our neighbors dug a shallow grave because it was getting close to midnight and there was no time to dig deeper. There was not even time for Sofia to cry: she had to think about saving little Branka as well as burying Nikola deep enough so that the abandoned German dogs in the area could not get to him. Babba and Uncle Abid returned to our lower house. There we gathered close to the stove and lay down with our clothes on, after first covering the windows with sheets. Our black cat lay on our things like a guard. It, too, was a refugee.

We set out for Zalug once more the next morning. Mujaga stayed behind to repair the roofs of his houses. Like Nanna, he did not flee, but he did make sure that his family went to the village of Mijoska.

When we got as far as the Čarkilovićs's houses, we turned off into the woods when we heard the dull roar of planes as they got louder and louder. The aircraft appeared at about ten o'clock—earlier than the day before—and began their bombing run. We lay down beneath the oak trees next to a clearing. The earth shook from the powerful detonations and the leaves of the young oaks rustled, but none landed near enough to us to cause harm. This raid was heavier than the previous day's, but it was directed more at the town and the roads used by troops moving along the other side of the Lim.

We spent the day in the forest. Returning homeward before evening, however, we again spotted bloody stones near the fountain and the impressions left by bodies thrown against the walls of the houses by bombs exploding in the brook and near the bridge over the Lim. The Chetniks who had come into Polje during the night had also left. They must have disposed of their dead while we were returning. "But where?" people wondered. The fresh bloody traces testified to the fact that they had suffered casualties, too. Perhaps they had thrown them into the Lim. That certainly would have been the quickest way. Witnesses had earlier told us that the Germans had thrown the bodies of all those who died in the battle for the Partisan hospital into the Lim.

6 Liberation and the Partisans

It got so that we were fleeing every morning. We used to take cover in the forest, passing the rainy days in shelters fashioned from tree branches. We kept our ears tuned for the dull roar of the bombers and learned to distinguish it from the hum of trucks carrying troops along the Prijepolje–Priboj road on the other side of the Lim. We did not dare light fires, yet it was getting colder and colder as the rain drizzled down on us day after day. Lots of people decided to flee even farther, to the villages on the way to Sjenica and Župa. Uncle Abid and his family went to Mijoska to stay with a friend named Mehonić. Mujaga stayed behind to guard the house. My parents decided to go to Hisardžik to join the Malagić family, where Nanna expected to hear about the fate of her brother, Hafiz.

One quiet, rainy, early morning around November 15, we loaded Zlatulja with small bags of articles, including Nanna's very valuable embroideries, and headed off toward the Lim bridge. We passed by our upper house, of which there remained only the lower wall and nothing else. We came upon an empty, destroyed Prijepolje. There was no one from whom we could learn the fate of our friends and neighbors. The soldiers were gone, too. They had exited through Vakuf, heading down the Lim Valley. Nanna stopped for a short while to recite a few prayers above the Kurtovićs's houses in Hamam, which had simply collapsed, and then we continued on through the less-destroyed Vakuf section in the direction of the Mileševa monastery. German troops were concentrated near the monastery with their trucks, weapons, and antiaircraft batteries. It was their main stopping-off point, besides the one in Zalug Field next to the pontoon bridge. We avoided the army by traveling on a side route used by peasants, but we came upon an armed Chetnik who stopped Babba and began to interrogate him about something. Babba motioned for us to keep going. We breathed a sigh of relief when he finally caught up with us after the Chetnik released him and headed back toward the monastery.

At the entrance to Hisardžik, we stopped at the home of Nanna's relative, Ema Inajetović. There we found Hafiz with his family. They had fled their houses before the bombing, losing everything—even the women's fezzes with their ducats—as well as other jewelry. The village was full of refugees from Vakuf and the center of Prijepolje. We continued on to the house of Avdaga Malagić at the very top of the village, below his estate of Dundore. I had gazed at Dundore that summer from Jarčište Field above Zalug, never suspecting that I would get to see it up close so soon.

The danger from planes and soldiers never ceased. Even here, smaller fighter planes would appear unexpectedly and strafe the Germans near the monastery. Since the monastery was sheltered beneath the slopes of Mount Zlatar and Titerovac Cliff, and also because of the German antiaircraft fire itself, the planes did not dare to fly low. Perhaps they did not want to destroy the monastery, which was an ancient religious site, and thus dropped their bombs on the slopes near Hisardžik. We used to escape into the cellars, and sometimes we ran as far as the Dundore estate, which I finally reached at last.

Those fields truly seemed otherworldly to me. The spacious, black cultivated land was full of potatoes that the peasants had not been able to dig up in wartime. While we were waiting for it to turn dark so we could go back to the house, we baked some of them in hot coals, popping off the burned skins to get at the white core, which spilled out like flour. All around us there was an almost heavenly silence. Because Dundore was on a high plateau, my face tingled in the cold air. I could see far away, as far as the dark forests of the mountain massif above Nova Varoš.

Down below, next to the monastery, were elements of the German army, the ruts from their trucks and weapons carriers visible when the fog lifted. Everything seemed tiny, as though the soldiers were puppets in slow motion on a field. So, the time had finally come for the Germans, who, while they did not mix with people as the Italians did, wanted to rule them instead. "Eh, their time has come to go," people said. Where were they going to go—where were their houses, finally? Who was waiting for them? Who worried about their whereabouts, as we waited for Babba and others to return, praying that nothing had happened to them?

Darkness quickly fell on Dundore, and since the village was not nearby, we returned completely frozen, moving easily in our wool stockings with the leather soles, but otherwise lightly dressed. We warmed ourselves by the fire at the hearth, where supper was set out for us. The household ate by the light of the fire and of twig torches. The smoke wavered as it moved toward the chimney because there was no ceiling in the anterooms of peasant houses.

I took Zlatulja out to pasture on quiet days, even when it was cold. All kinds of fruit trees were full of unpicked fruit, including pears and the chestnuts for which Hisardžik was famous. Everything had taken on a glassy sheen in the cold, wintry sun. The ground underneath the trees was heaped with fallen fruit. However, there was nothing good there for a cow to eat. It was not safe for people in the village to go out at night. Sometimes soldiers would leave the road, break into houses, take the men to carry ammunition, and seize their horses. Some people disappeared forever. Plenty of young people fled to the Partisans, who became more and more popular as the war drew toward its end, and it was commonly assumed that the communists were not really as much against religion as people used to say they were at the beginning of the war. There were constant fights between the Germans and the Partisans on the road from Sjenica to Prijepolje. Many others, among them collaborationists, also departed with the Germans, fearing Partisan revenge.

A small number of the local population fled with the Germans. Our people were immobile. As ancient settlers in the area, they guarded the threshold of their houses no matter what befell them. Some thought that there was no reason for them to flee, much to their later regret. The Chetnik leaders and ideologists fled, as did the Muslim militias, the soldiers who served in German SS units (mainly Muslims), and military suppliers and merchants. However, the majority of them were captured throughout Bosnia and shot after a quick trial. There were young Chetniks and sympathizers who succeeded in reaching Belgrade, where they lived out their lives. They neither dared nor wished to return to the Sandžak. The wounds remained fresh there for a long time afterward, because the occupiers of the Sandžak towns had shot plenty of young people from Partisan families, both Serb and Muslim. The Muslims fled toward Bosnia and Sarajevo. The luckier ones among the leadership found safety in Turkey, as did, for example, Hasan Zvizdić, who was the chief military commander of Muslims in Sjenica. Serbs in the Sjenica region had their own commander, too.

Babba left for Polje toward the end of November, hoping to visit Mujaga and reestablish connections with his relatives. He found Polje full of Germans, even in Mujaga's house. They stayed for only a short time, sometimes just for the night, the darkness lit by their carbide lamps. People said that they had softened a bit, although they were still disciplined. The soldiers would accept the bit of food that Mujaga, in light of their skimpy military rations of zwieback and cold bitter coffee, would offer them. By the beginning of December, there were no more Germans passing through.

After he left Mujaga, Babba continued southward to the village of Oborce, where his sister Hanka had fled with her family. When we received a message from him saying that it was all right for us to come, one of Nanna's relatives led us there. We chose a circuitous route that took us along forest trails and over the Dvorište Plateau, the frozen snow making for easier going. We took Zlatulja with us as well. We had to cross over the dangerous Sjenica–Prijepolje road at one point in order to descend to the Lim Valley. On the road we saw the burned out wrecks of vehicles and weapons discarded in the brush, but the road was clear of both German soldiers and Partisans. It may be that the Partisans had moved farther down the Lim Valley in order to follow the Germans moving toward Sarajevo.

By nightfall, we found ourselves above Oborce at last. Below, on the far side of the Lim, we could make out the fertile Župa Plain and the road from Prijepolje to Bijelo Polje, while on our side of the river we could see the village of Ivanje. What a view we had from those heights of the cultivated land below! It was like we were looking down on them from an airplane. We could see the parcels of well-marked-off land, the green winter wheat, the tile-roofed houses, and two school buildings at the far end of the field, right by the Lim. It was there that I was to finish grammar school after the liberation.

The Rondić tribe inhabited the village. We moved into a small room in Mujaga's house. It was not bad, and Babba was able to return to his trade, doing sewing in the villages behind Oborce for Serbian landowners who had sewing machines in their houses. He carried his scissors and tape measure with him, and I went along to help. He was paid with flour, dairy products, and honey since there was no such thing as money. This serves as a good example of how valuable it is to have a trade—we never lacked for anything. There remain in my memory the pickled yellow peppers and the rich, almost ceremonial luncheons the hosts prepared for us, because it was the custom to receive people who came to your house in that manner.

Yet even in Oborce there was no peace. From the road along the Lim small, ragtag units of soldiers of every allegiance except German attacked the villages, plundering as they retreated. We would spot them when they appeared below Crna Stijena (Black Cliff) at the entrance to Ivanje and go hide in the forest in two big caves above the village. One of them, Šupljača, was said to be endless. The troops never climbed to Oborce, probably because they already had their fill of plunder in rich and level Ivanje. Not far from Ivanje, situated on a low mountain range, was the Partisan village of Divci. Perhaps that was the reason none of the marauders penetrated the region more deeply. The important thing was that they did not kill anybody.

Nighttime was the most insecure. The sky high above us was red from the gunfire on the road to Priboj. People said that a tobacco factory in Sarajevo had been set ablaze. At night, we used to put our heads to the ground to hear the thunder of the shelling in the distance. We had already learned to do that when we were in Zalug in 1943. We hoped in that way to pick up the trembling of the ground from the firing of the Russian *katushas.* We had just heard about them for the first time.

Village life followed its own rhythm. In the wintertime, it was the custom to eat twice a day. In the morning, we would eat clumpy polenta set before us on the table. We would eat it unseasoned, instead of bread. In the center of the table were placed honeycomb and copper dishes of cheese, sour cream, yellow pickled peppers, and yogurt. We ate with our fingers or with wooden spoons. Breakfast was preceded by the invocation to the Almighty, the Bismillah, and ended with a prayer. Around noontime, a dish of peas and dried meat was set to cook in a copper pot hanging from chains in the outside kitchen. A fire was laid using dry branches from which the cattle had already munched the leaves.

In summertime, big branches from oak and beech trees, called "leaves," were cut in the forest with a pruning knife and placed in a cone-shaped stack to dry. Sometimes, a branch with plums on it was secreted in the stack to serve as a dessert in the middle of winter. The leaves were brought in as cattle fodder by sleigh two or three times a week, thus saving on hay.

About midafternoon, the girls began to mix the peas and meat slowly, and before evening it was garnished with butterfat and served as the main dish. Women baked wheat bread, as well as wheat mixed with buckwheat and rye. At the table, we all ate from enamel or wooden bowls. In the evening, we would pray *akšam* at sundown in Mujaga's room, and then we would retire to our own small room to sit near the fire until it was time for the *jacija,* a night prayer. Sometimes we would make little lights from pieces of cloth, dipping them in tallow at the bottom of a little copper vessel.

Toward the end of December, the first Partisans entered the village. They were Albanians from Macedonia and Kosovo who had taken part in the liberation of Skopje. These soldiers stayed only a short time. Many of them were apparently sick with typhoid. These were placed in separate houses and later taken elsewhere, most likely to a hospital. We were amazed that, together with their food, they slurped water loaded with salt. Moreover, because they also loved cabbage brine, we would pour them whole bowls of it. The Albanians went off to the west, to the Srem front, where the Partisans launched large-scale frontal attacks against the Germans.

As winter drew to a close, we learned that there was an epidemic of grip in Hisardžik and that Nanna's Hafiz had become ill at the very end of it—after everyone else in his family had recovered. Babba went to visit him and pray the Friday noon prayer, *džuma,* in the Hisardžik mosque. He took me along to show him the route. We went by a short cut over the frozen snow, passing through unsecured forests where, for a long time after the war, people would come across the so-called *komita* or guerrilla bands that lived in caves. We crossed the Sjenica–Prijepolje road, which was still blocked with burned out vehicles and overturned tanks, but there was a feeling of freedom in the air. We entered the village of Dvorište before noon. Babba stopped at the house of a friend, where he was informed that Hafiz had already passed away and that he was going to be buried after the *džuma.* He left me in the village and set out with some of the peasants to attend the funeral service in Hisardžik as well as to visit Aunt Arifa, Hafiz's wife, in order to wish her and their children well.

He returned in midafternoon and we began our return trip to Oborce. Tired of waiting, Nanna had gone out into the fields to meet us. She saw us through the dusk and ran up to us: "How is my Hafiz," she asked anxiously. "May you be well, but Hafiz has exchanged this World for the Hereafter," said Babba. He informed her that the men had said the burial prayers for him after the *džuma* and that he was buried in the graveyard to the right of the entrance to the mosque, just below its windows. He was next to the grave of Murat *hodža* Melić. "Your sister-in-law, Arifa, sends you the message not to be upset, but to accept God's will, and to be reconciled with it." Nanna turned, burst into tears, and only said: "Allah's Mercy, my Hafiz." We entered the house and she did *abdest* and began to recite "Yasin," the chapter on death from the Qur'an.

Thus, her second brother died while a refugee in his sixty-second year. Bećir, her youngest brother, had died in faraway Istanbul, and Hafiz in old Hisardžik, where he was buried among his relatives.

Hafiz *efendija* and Murat *hodža,* of whom people used to say that he was so good you could see the *nur* (light) over his shoulders, were *talebe* of the Prijepolje *medresa* and were friends during a lifetime of faith spent with the people they taught. They died in time to announce the departure of the old era and the arrival of the new in our parts.

The Partisans entered Prijepolje in early December, 1944. We did not intend to return just yet, because our house needed some repairs. My parents began to send me to Šarampov to Aunt Hanka's house to buy something in the *čaršija* or to find out what was going on.

At first, I was afraid to traverse those few kilometers alone—a snowbound route with scattered houses that looked as though they were asleep. With time, I learned to shake off my fear and examine my surroundings carefully. I was able to spot some chance passerby and discern his intentions from the distance.

During one such trip I found our cat. I recognized her one day at a place not far from Hanka's, where I noticed her looking at me. Subsequently, every time I turned up at that spot, the cat would be there, too. She had a familiar mark under her neck, as well as a chewed ear. It was the latter more than anything else that told me she was our cat. I carried her to Oborce in my arms—she did not resist—and when anyone came near us she would bury her head in my sweater. How she made her way from Polje across the Lim to

Šarampov, only she knew. When I brought her home, she did not leave the room for days, until she felt completely acclimated. Later she went back to Polje with us, returning to her old hearth.

On the whole, the new government established itself rather quickly. People brought back stories of crowds of people at night at the head of the *čaršija* in Prijepolje, which was a great novelty when compared to the poorly lit, empty *čaršija* of prewar days. We heard that the young people were arranging performances, which amazed the people in the countryside. Muslim women were not wearing their veils, they said, and everyone was mixing with everyone else, regardless of religion.

They opened an office in Ivanje for the local council, and the Partisans—I think it was the 5th Montenegrin Brigade—were billeted in private homes and schools. Polje, too, was full of Partisans from other brigades. The newly organized militia began to scour the terrain for Chetniks, who would leave their underground positions and hideouts at night to kill government representatives and discourage people from accepting the new regime.

When the weather turned warm, columns of people began passing through Ivanje on their way to *meetings.* That was another word we learned. They were mainly from Serbian Partisan villages above the Lim Valley, especially from Divci. It was there that Tito was welcomed after the fall of the Užice Republic at the end of 1941, as he crossed the Lim in his retreat from Serbia to Bosnia during the Germans' first offensive in Yugoslavia. The Užice Republic was the Partisan's free territory at the juncture of Serbia, Bosnia, and Sandžak. Long lines of people were carrying signs and singing songs like: "Comrade, Tito, we swear to you that we will not veer from your path!" The slogans "Death to Fascism, Freedom to the People!" and "Down with Traitors!" on the signs—something new for us—denounced fascism and local quislings. There were also signs calling for reconstruction: "Everyone Rebuild the Country!" Others anticipated the kind of government that would be formed: "Long Live the Soviet Union, the First Country of Socialism!" Finally, there was the cherished slogan that encouraged the people of Yugoslavia: "Long live Brotherhood and Unity!"

The peasants of Oborce lived mainly as before. No one could imagine that Muslim women would ever leave the house unveiled, stand in line with strangers, or appear in public. On the day Germany capitulated (May 9), there were especially massive meetings, with crowds streaming toward Prijepolje beginning at dawn. It was a bright, sunny day and I was minding the cow in the cellar stall as the women in the house wondered at such large crowds and where they were going. Then the news that Germany had capitulated was heard throughout the village. We had not seen any Germans since the beginning of winter and had almost forgotten about them. "Where have they been up to now?" we wondered. "Did it really take them this long to surrender?"

Immediately afterward, we were called back to the school alongside the Lim, facing Župa Plain on the opposite bank, with the well laid-out houses of the large Muslim Kozica family.

There were two teachers in the school: my instructor, Dana Varagić, a student of architecture, and Finka Kijanović, an older teacher. Several classes studied in the same room, so each pupil had to work on his own separate assignment. We took up reading and writing again, and had free activities, including picking medicinal herbs, composition writing, and organizing wall newspapers. A Pioneer (scouting) organization was formed in the school and we were given kerchiefs to wear, as well as posters to carry, when we visited other Pioneers in the town in column formation.

Our classes were finished in July and I received a handwritten certificate stating that I had finished primary school. The column for nationality was left blank and I received a five (excellent) for my "maternal" language.

Besides school, I minded our cow, grazing it in the forest. We were suffering through an intensive drought—there was very little fresh grass—and our cow would return from pasture hungry. She would moo during the night, but we had nothing to give her. Babba had to entreat the peasants who had fields in Ivanje to give us a little grass. There, where the ground was firmer, the grass held up better near the slopes and in among the wheat. Without thinking twice, I would pull up the grass just so Zlatulja would not go hungry. During that period, we had an influx of foxes that would raid our chickens at night, as well as wild dogs abandoned by the German army. Joining with the wolves in the forest, they would roam through the village.

The heat was so terrible that while we were going through all this we had to sleep at night in the courtyard, under the branches of tall, thick oaks and elm trees. At night it would get ready to rain: the sky would cloud over and there would be lightning on the horizon, but without thunder, and the rain did not come. The Serbian peasants' response to the drought was to hold their traditional "processions." Led by the village priest and children with crosses in their hands, they toured the fields and prayed for rain. The Muslims had not yet made up their minds to go down to the water's edge—to the rivers and streams—and pray, for "Allah knows best," but in the end they went, too. The drought lasted a long time. In the village itself, there were three large, reinforced fountains from which spring water flowed continuously in thick streams. The cows would run to them on their own initiative. That's how I lost Zlatulja. Once, in the forest, I looked everywhere, even going into dangerous, out-of-the-way ravines and isolated places. There was no sign of her until—after two hours of searching—I met a peasant who told me he had seen her by the fountain at the head of the village. I found her there, grazing on tiny, sparse grass that could barely be pulled from the ground.

Unlike the forest—where I used to have shepherds for company— I was on my own in the place called Grobnice (graveyard). It had been a burial ground in Roman times. I would drive out the cow at about four in the afternoon, as the heat began to die down. I usually wore a blouse and *dimije* made of tent canvas that rustled when I walked, because the material was stiff until washed. On my feet I wore *opanci* and long woolen stockings that protected me from the common vipers that inhabited the rocky ground, because Grobnice was located in a sunny spot, warmed by the sun as soon as it rose. A little farther down in the foothills, there stretched oak forests full of acorns. Usually, I sat on the edge of some clearing, playing jacks or examining the moss on the rocks, trying to figure out in which light it grew best. Sometimes, I would look for fox tracks in the mud.

Bored from being by myself, I would go deeper into the hazel forest to pick the still-green hazel nuts. I was hoping that it would not begin to thunder on Alđun. According to peasant lore, if it did thunder, the green hazel nuts would fall from the trees. Alđun or Christian's Ilindan or Saint Elias's Day is on August 2.

When I was in Grobnice, I most feared the protracted rustling of the dried leaves on the ground, as though a log were being dragged along. That was a sign of the passing of snakes, which sometimes made clicking noises as well. The peasants claimed they did this when they were with their young. I saw enough of them myself, but never with their offspring. It was not easy to distinguish the barely visible stripes on the shoulders of the common viper from the dry branch I would pick up for a walking stick.

The women in Oborce taught me how to milk goats and sheep, to harvest wheat and collect it in stacks for threshing, and to spin balls of wool and linen into thin, uniform threads that Babba tried to substitute for regular thread. There was not much to buy in the Prijepolje.

Sometimes, I even went to the mill in Zabuđe hamlet, descending through the forests and steep valleys to the Lim Valley above Ivanje. Nanna would give me a small bag woven from goat's hair and filled with wheat to be ground into flour. Peasants would collect their goat's hair to have bags made for holding grain. Such bags lasted a long time and were highly prized. While I was waiting for the grain to be ground and for the miller to take his share, I would spend some time in one of the Musabegović houses, a branch of which had lived there since time immemorial, sealed off as in a medieval citadel. Their younger people had been in the Partisans and had remained in the town.

Meanwhile, conditions had stabilized in Prijepolje—it was time for us to return home from Oborce.

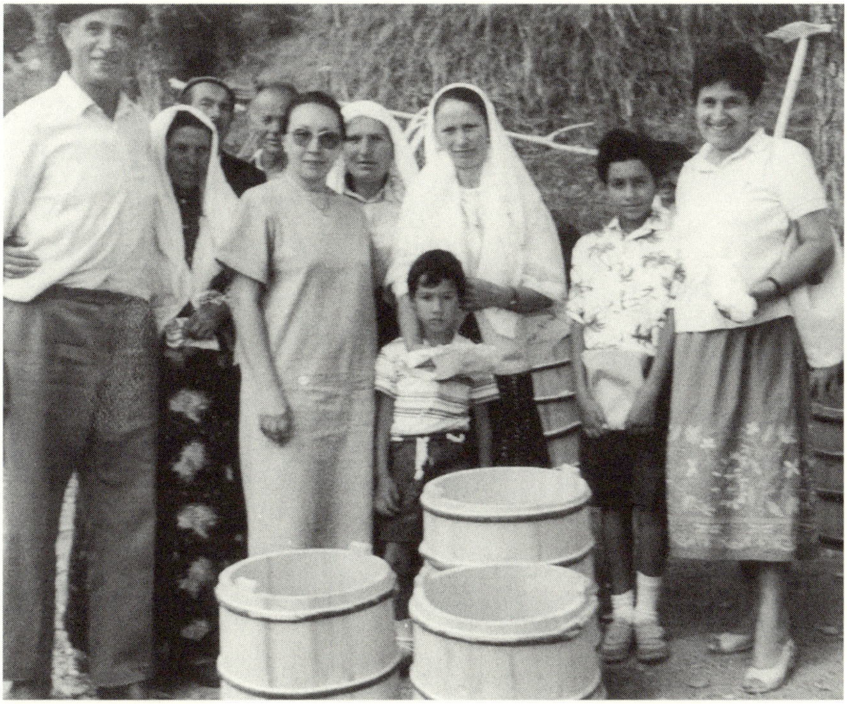

Muslim peasants on market day at the Duga Polijana village en route from Sjenica to Novi Pazar. My friend, Vera Marković (third from left), Dr. Kamal Buraei's wife, stands with her two sons and me. The eldest son, Zafir, is now doing his doctorate in molecular biology in the United States.

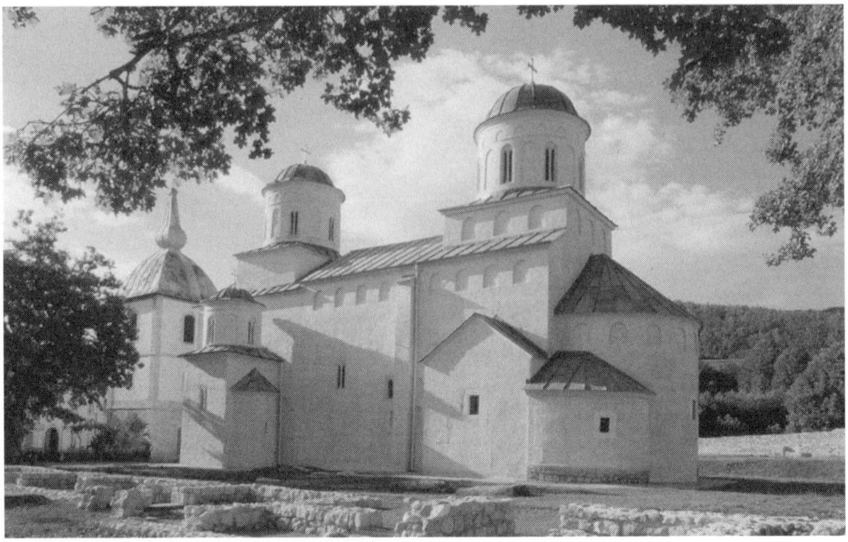

Mileševa monastery near Prijepolje, built in 1237 by King Vladislav of the Nemanjić dynasty. The Nemanjić dynasty ruled the independent medieval Serbian state.

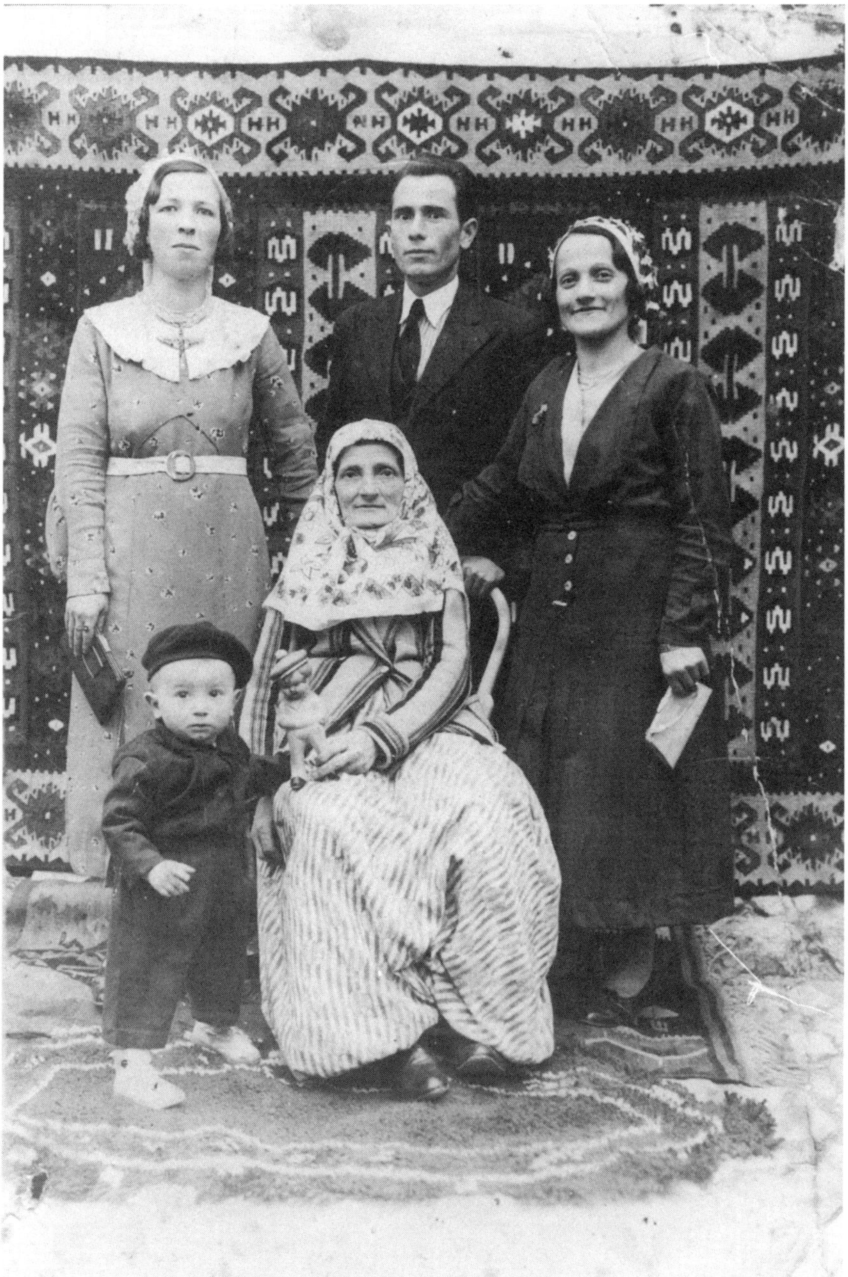

Ahmo Šehović family. Ahmo's mother is in Bosnian dress and Ahmo's son, Sakib, is to her left. Standing from left to right in rear is Ahmo's wife, Šaćira, Ahmo, and sister, Emina. Hanging behind them is a Bosnian hand-made woolen *kilim* (rug). The photo was taken in Polje, 1939.

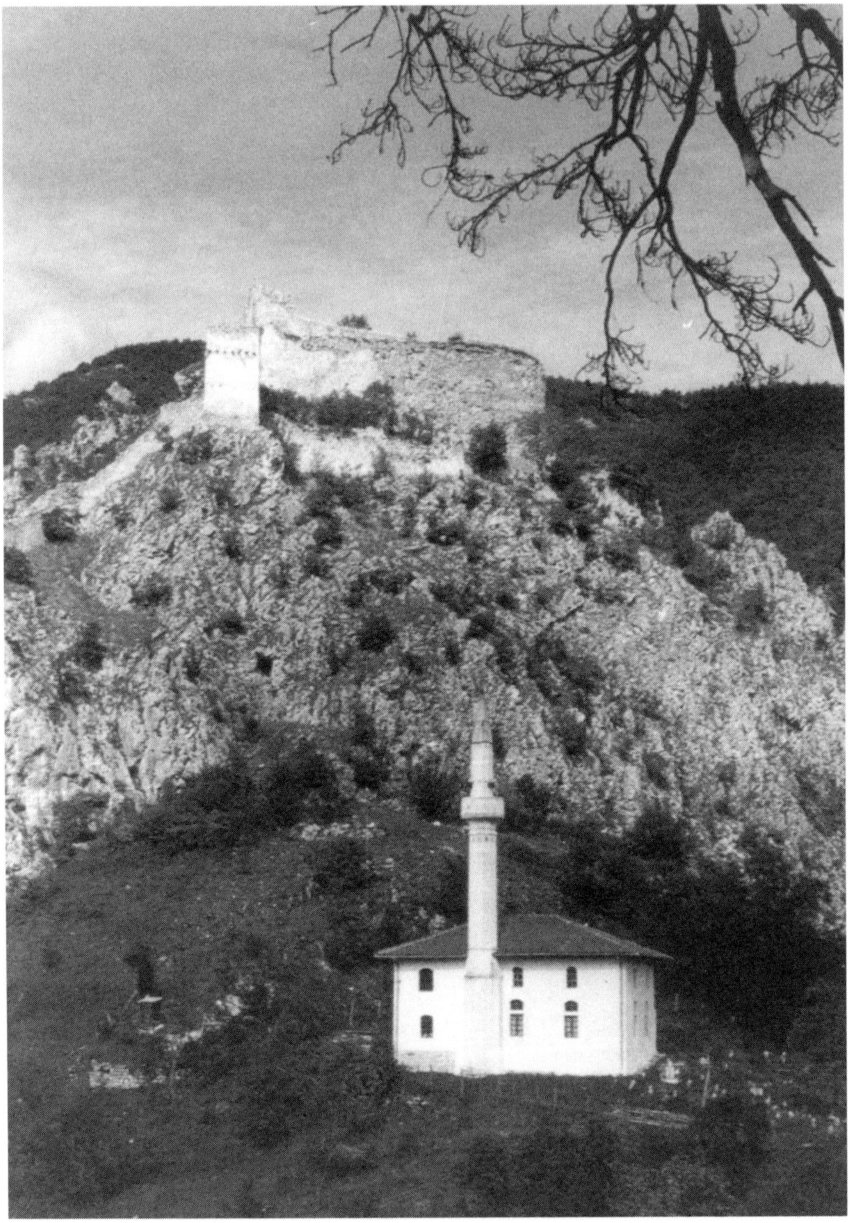

A citadel and a mosque below it in the village of Hisardžik. In Turkish, *hisar* means "fortress."

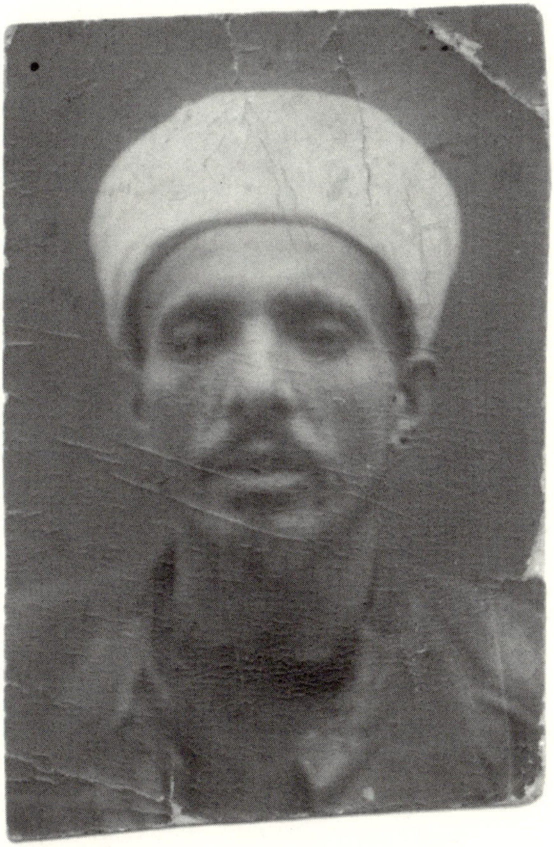

My mother's eldest brother, Hafiz, as a student in Prijepolje's *medresa,* circa 1905. *Medresa* is an Islamic theological school.

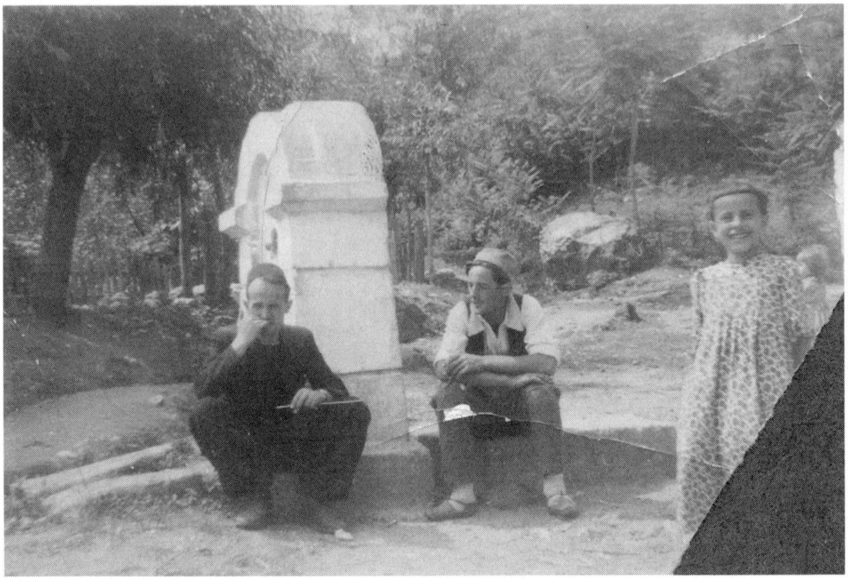

Polje fountain, 1942. From left to right is our neighbor Šahin (a Muslim), Vojin Dosković's son, Živko (a Serb), and me. Polje brook runs behind us.

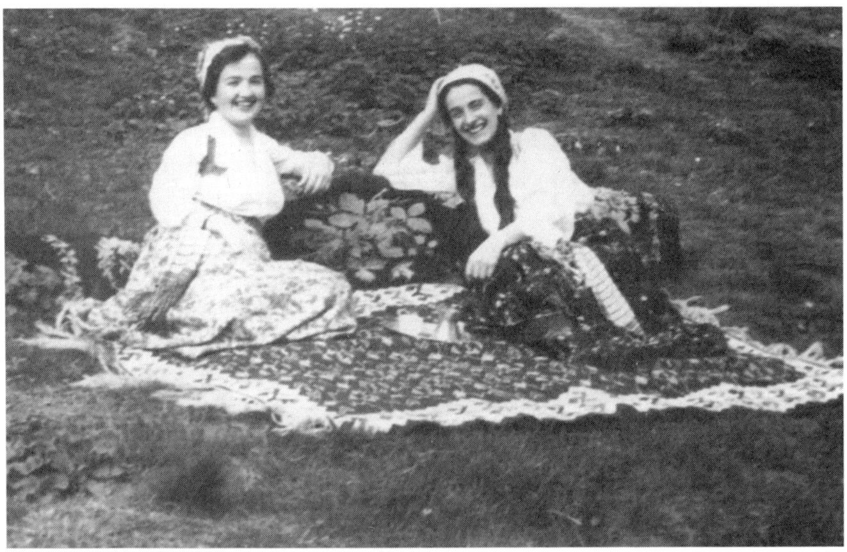

My cousin and me in Bosnian clothes.

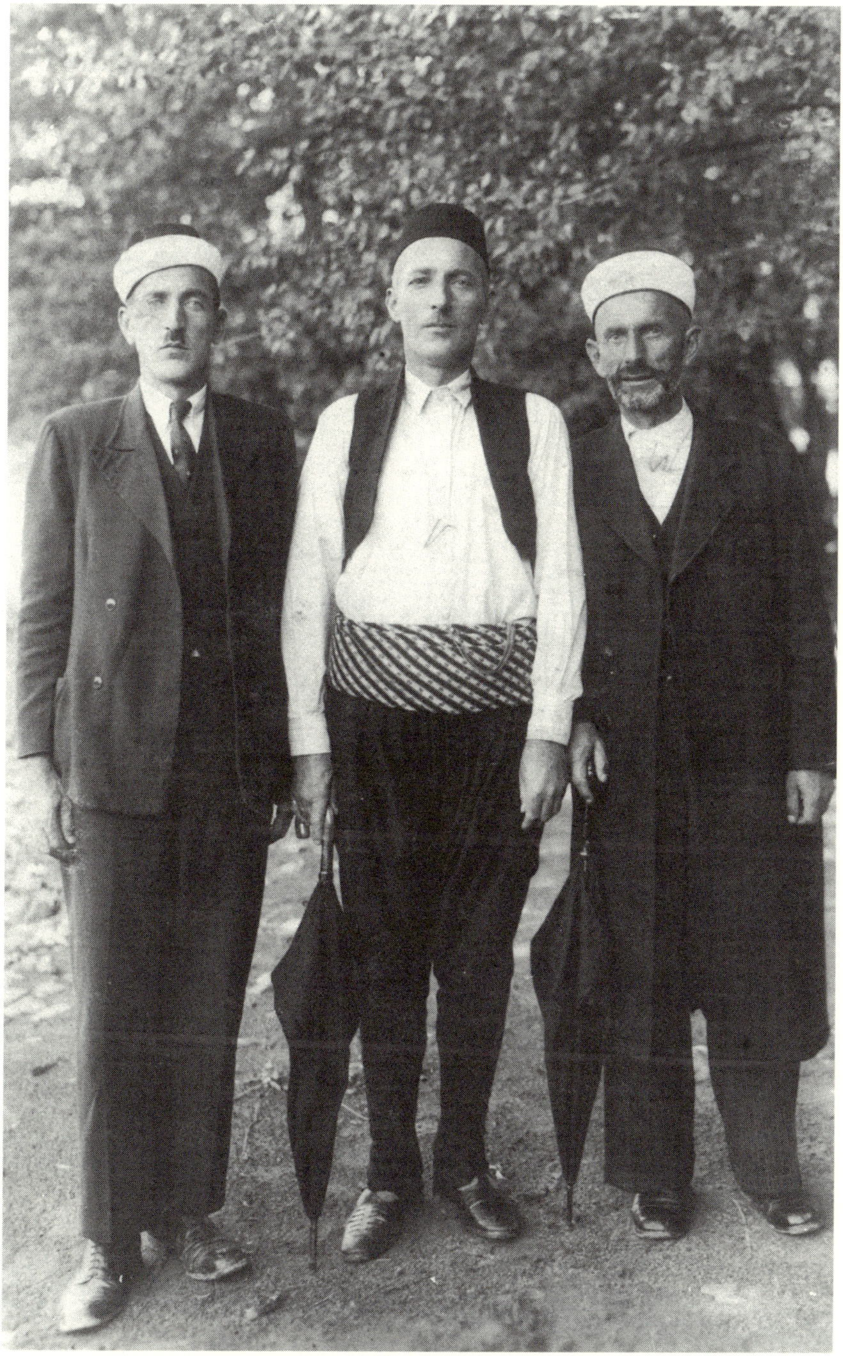

Some men from Prijepolje before World War II. The man on the right is the *imam* (main priest) of the Ibrahim Pasha Mosque in Šarampov.

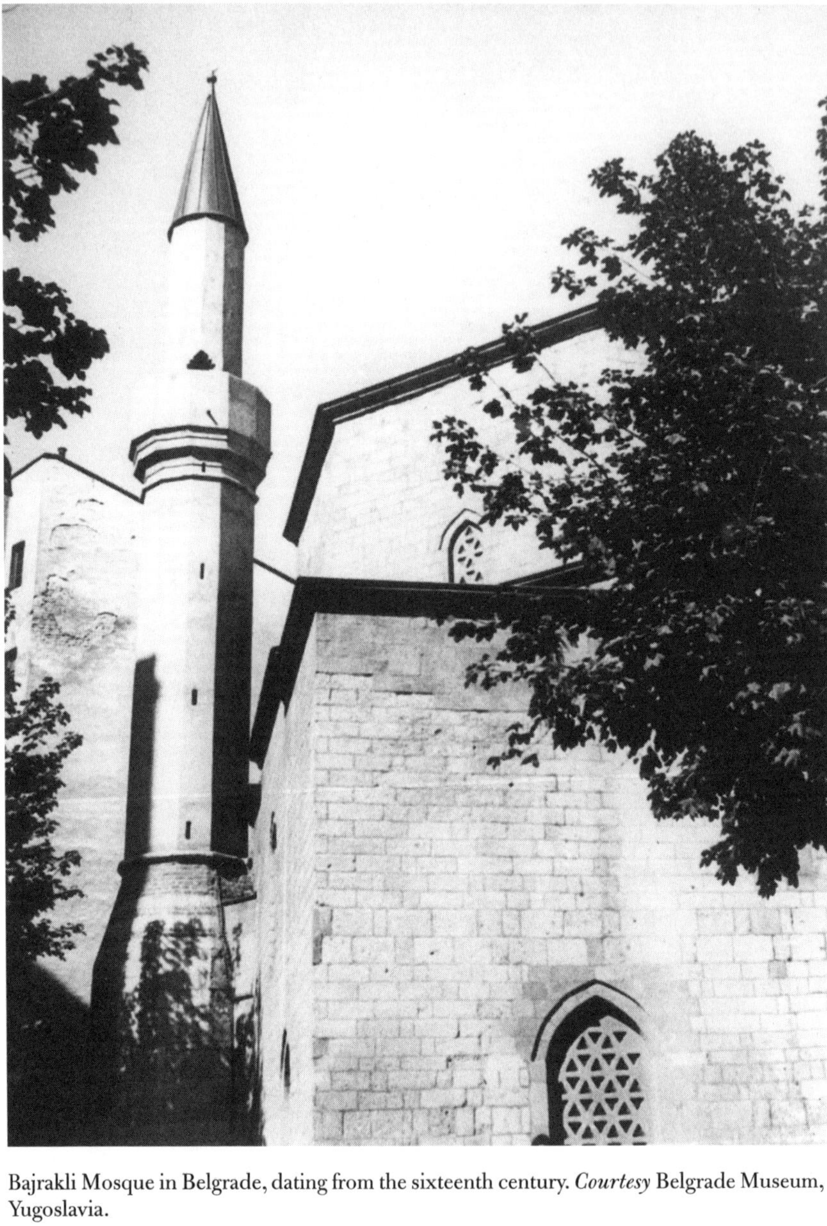

Bajrakli Mosque in Belgrade, dating from the sixteenth century. *Courtesy* Belgrade Museum, Yugoslavia.

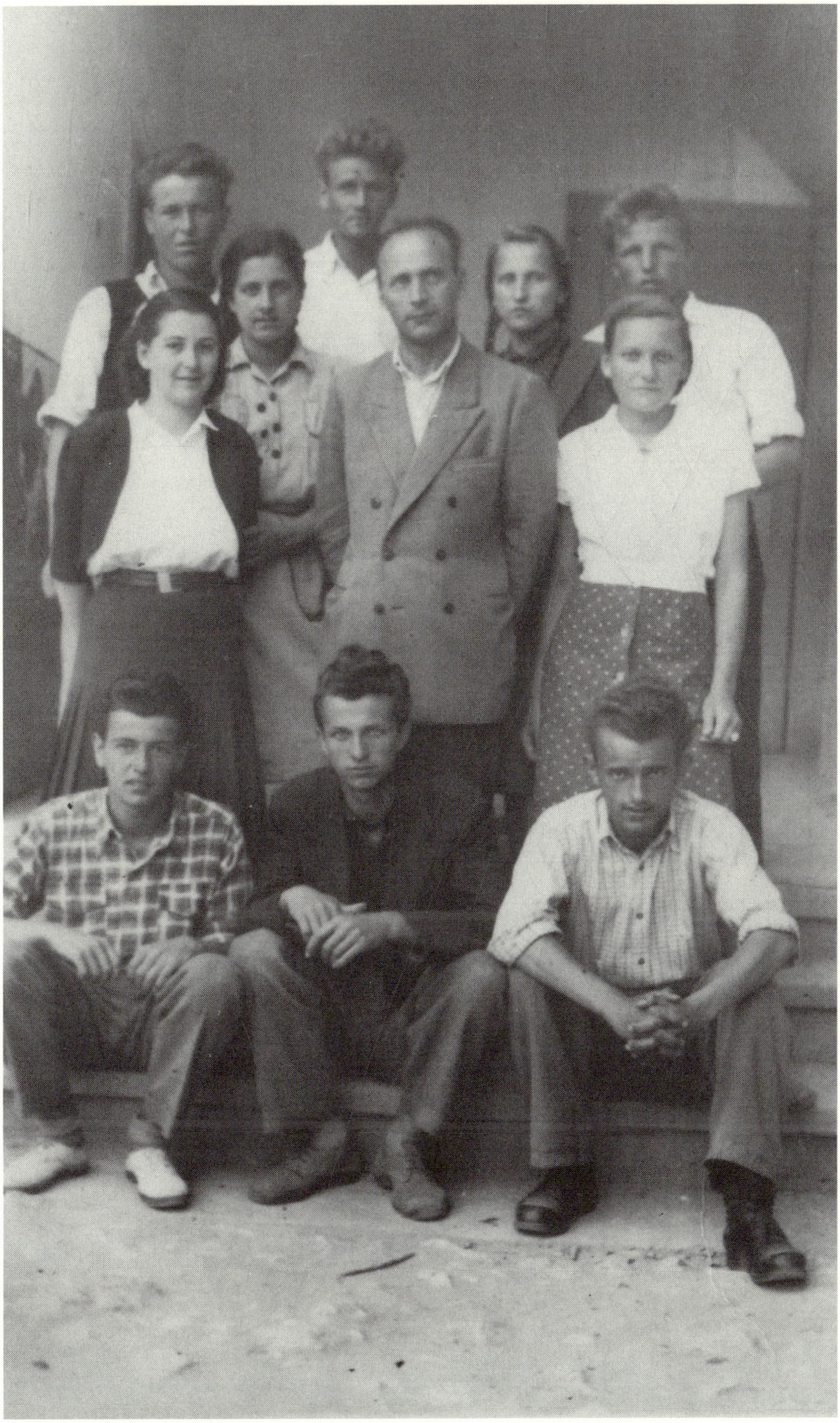

My fifth grade class in the Prijepolje gymnasium in 1950. In the center of the group is the principal, Dobrica Obradović. I stand slightly behind and to the left of him.

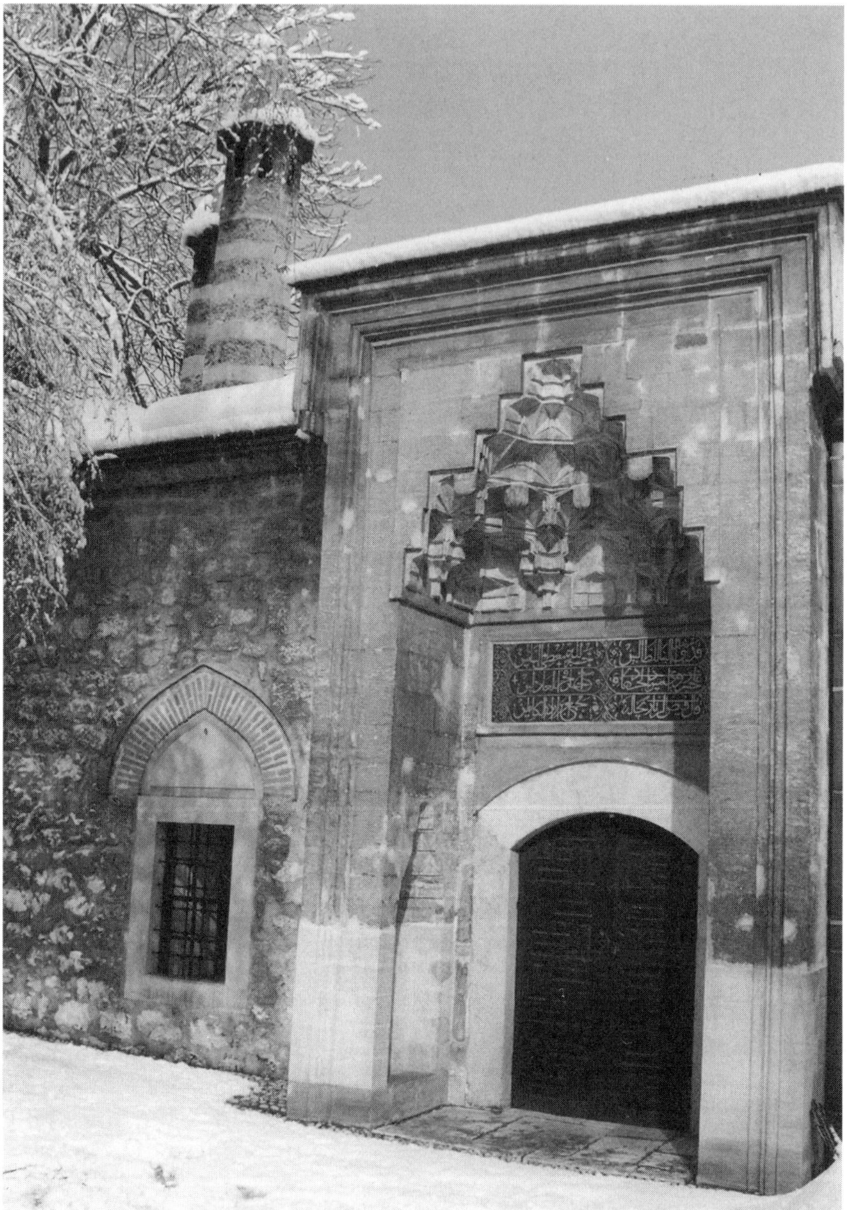

Façade of the Gazi Husrev Beg Medresa–Seldžukija in Sarajevo. It was also known as Kuršumlija because of its lead roof. The *medresa* was built in 1573 by Gazi Husrev Beg, the governor of Bosnia. He named it after his mother, Seldžuka, the sister of Sultan Bayazit II. With only a few interruptions, it has been operating since its foundation until the present. *Courtesy* Gazi Husrev Beg Library, Sarajevo.

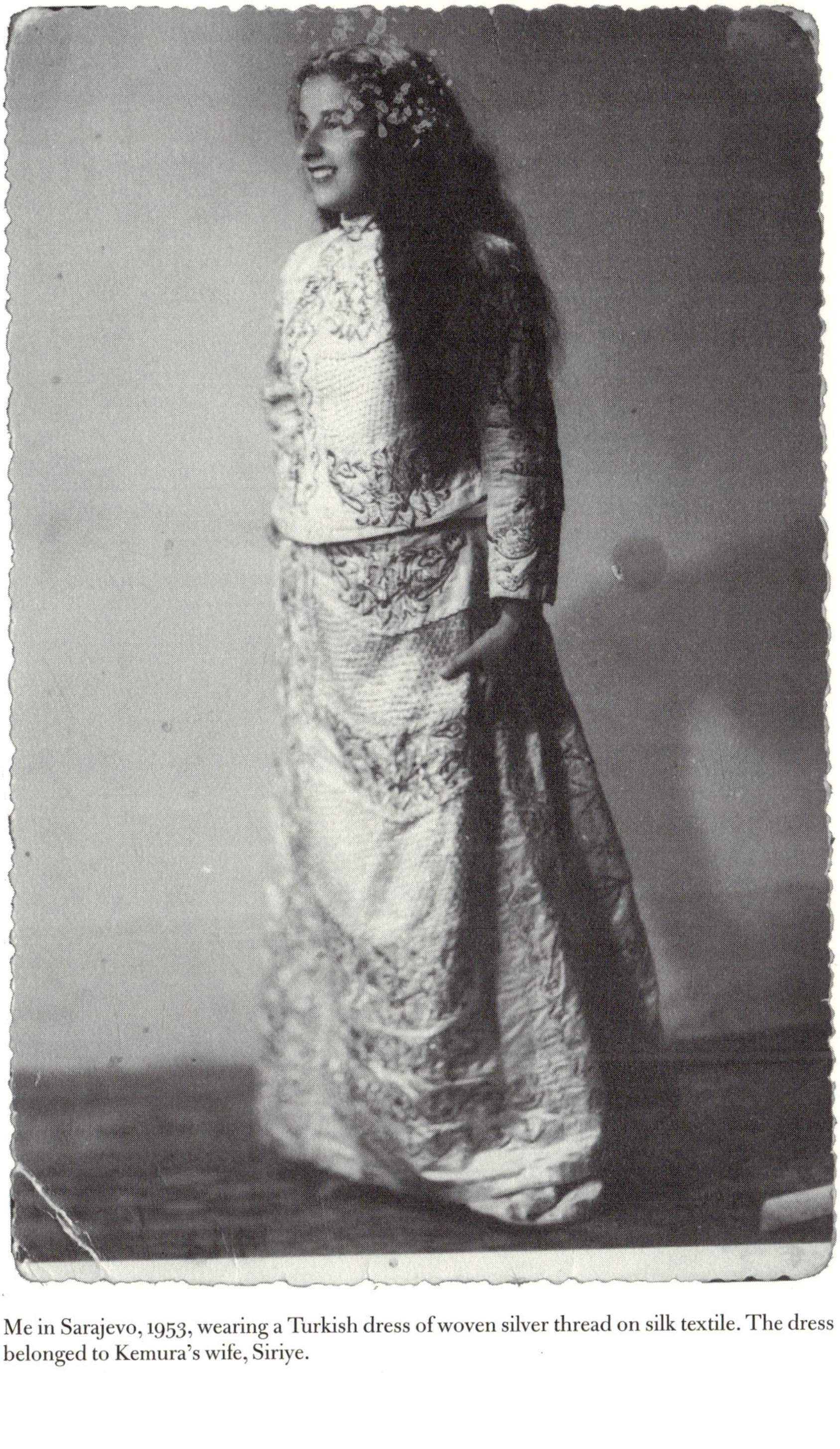

Me in Sarajevo, 1953, wearing a Turkish dress of woven silver thread on silk textile. The dress belonged to Kemura's wife, Siriye.

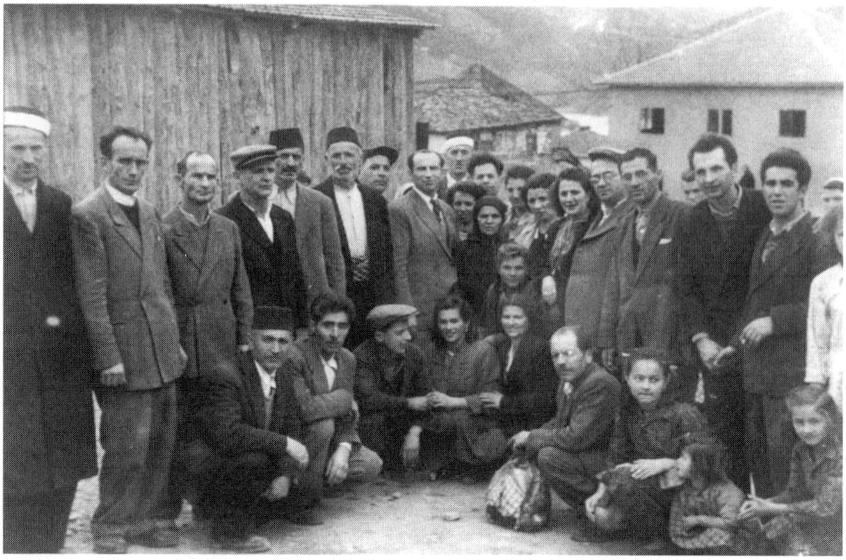

A photo taken at my Uncle Osman's departure to Istanbul in 1953. Relatives and neighbors gathered at the Prijepolje bus station to say goodbye. Standing fourth from the left is Uncle Abid, followed by my father, our relative, Mujaga, and eighth is Uncle Osman. Kneeling first from the left is Nedžibeg, Lady Aziza's husband, and third is my cousin, Avdo, from Polje.

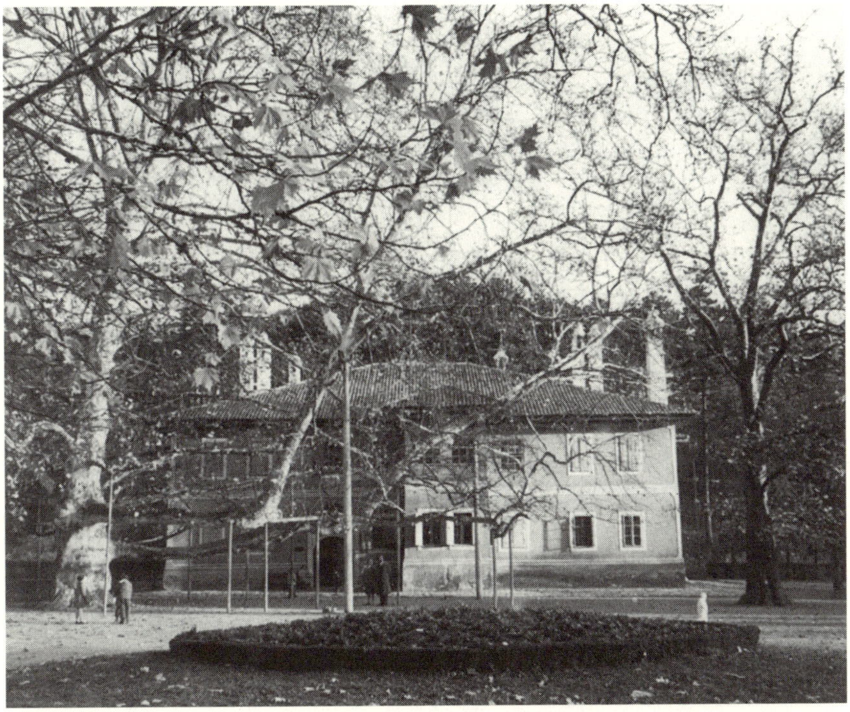

Milošev Konak house in Belgrade's Topčider Park. This house was the residence of Prince Miloš Obrenović. He first became the ruler of autonomous Serbia in 1830. Serbia obtained complete freedom from the Turks in 1878. *Courtesy* Belgrade Museum, Yugoslavia.

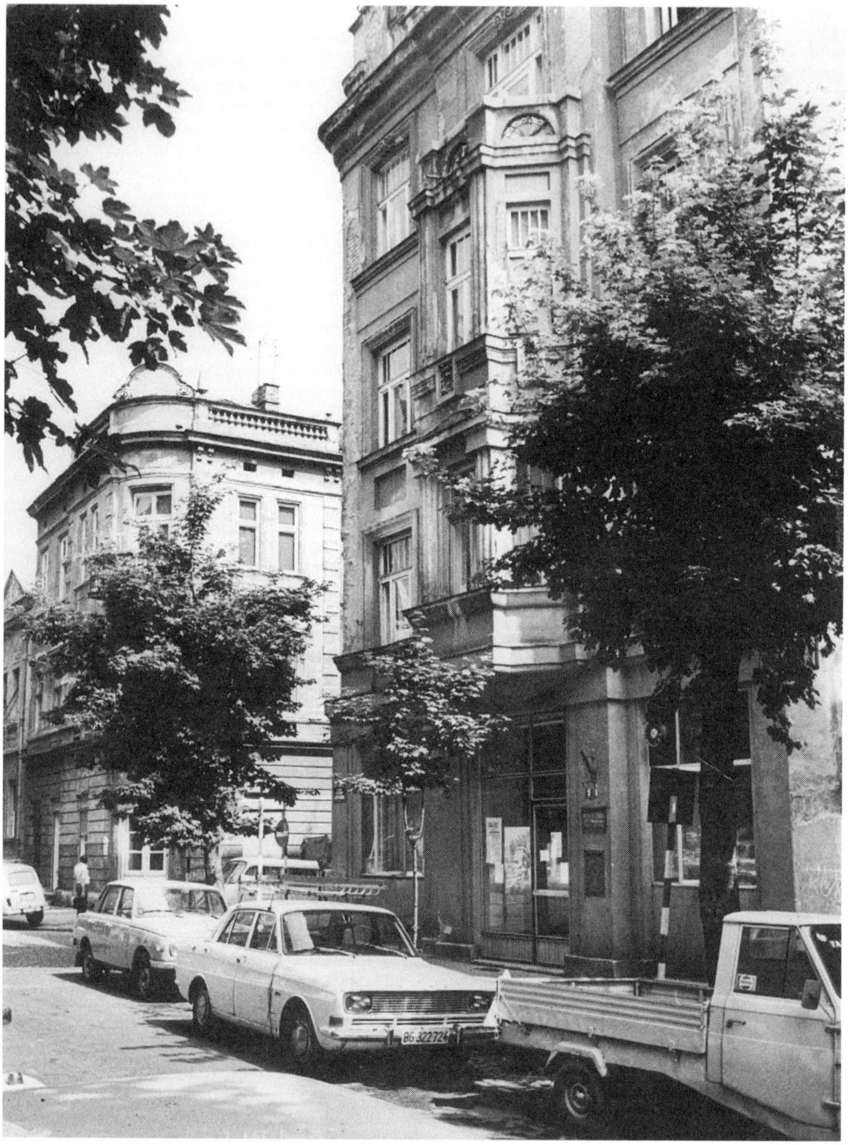

Jevremova Street in Belgrade, an old city quarter near Student's Square.

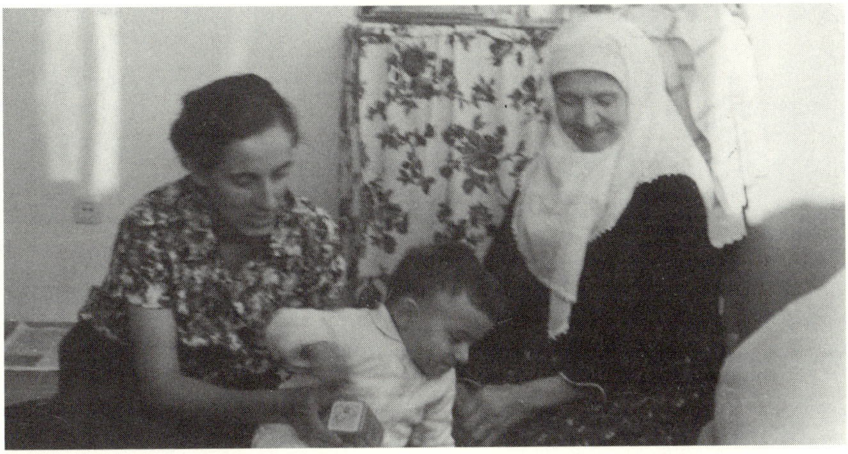

My mother and Kenan with me in Belgrade.

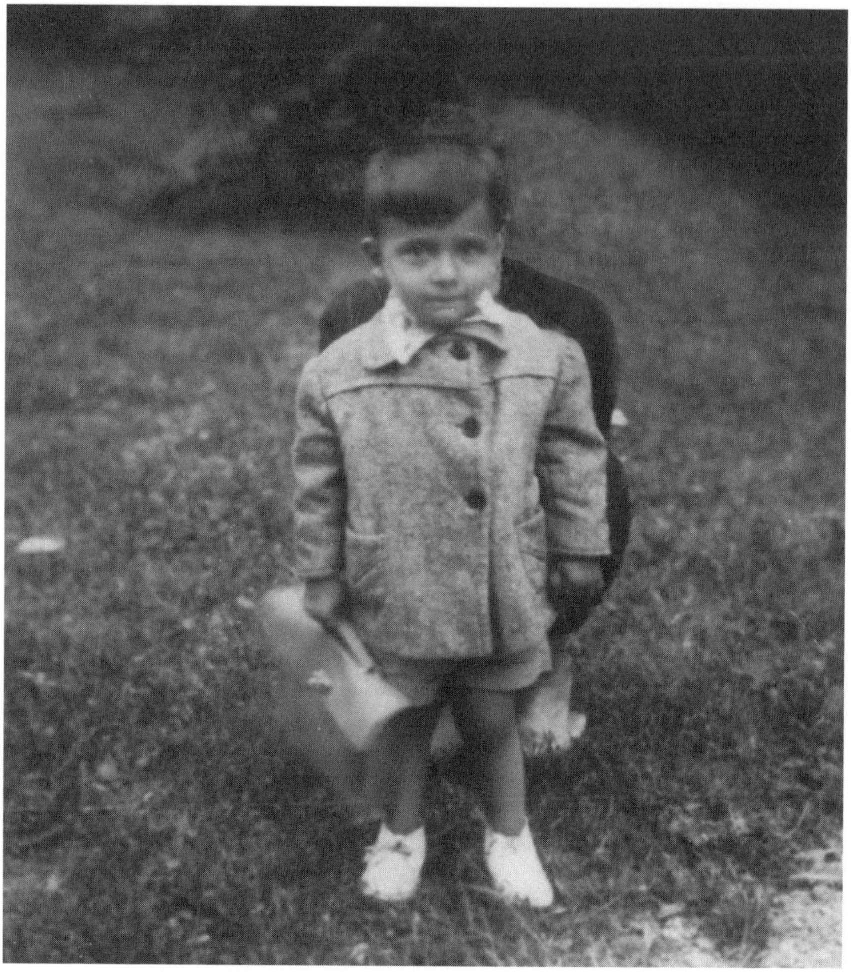

A photo of Kenan going to school, taken in Belgrade Park, 1964.

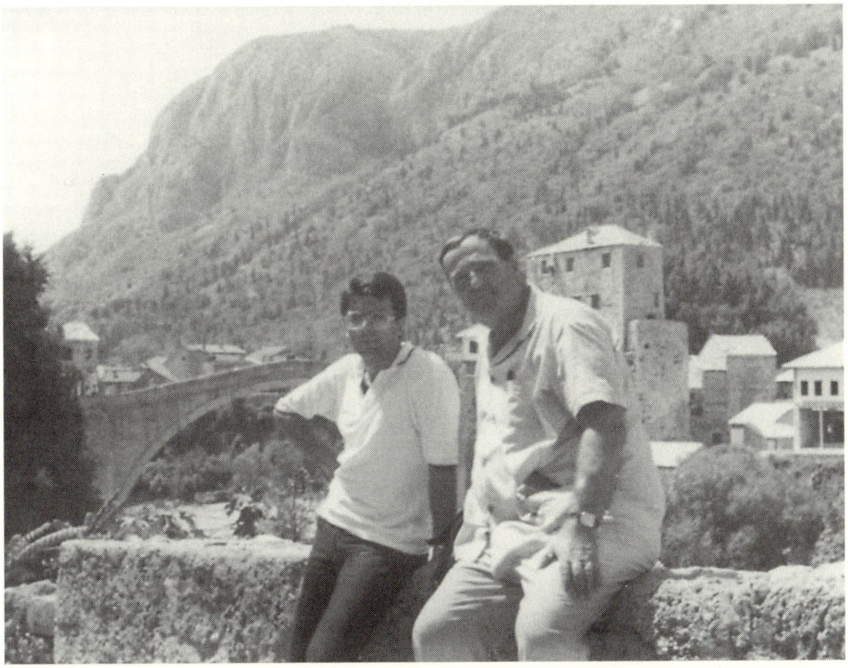

Kenan and his father, Derviš, on the Stone Bridge in the Bosnian town of Mostar in 1985. This bridge was built by the Turks in the fifteenth century and was destroyed in 1993 by Croatian nationalists during the war.

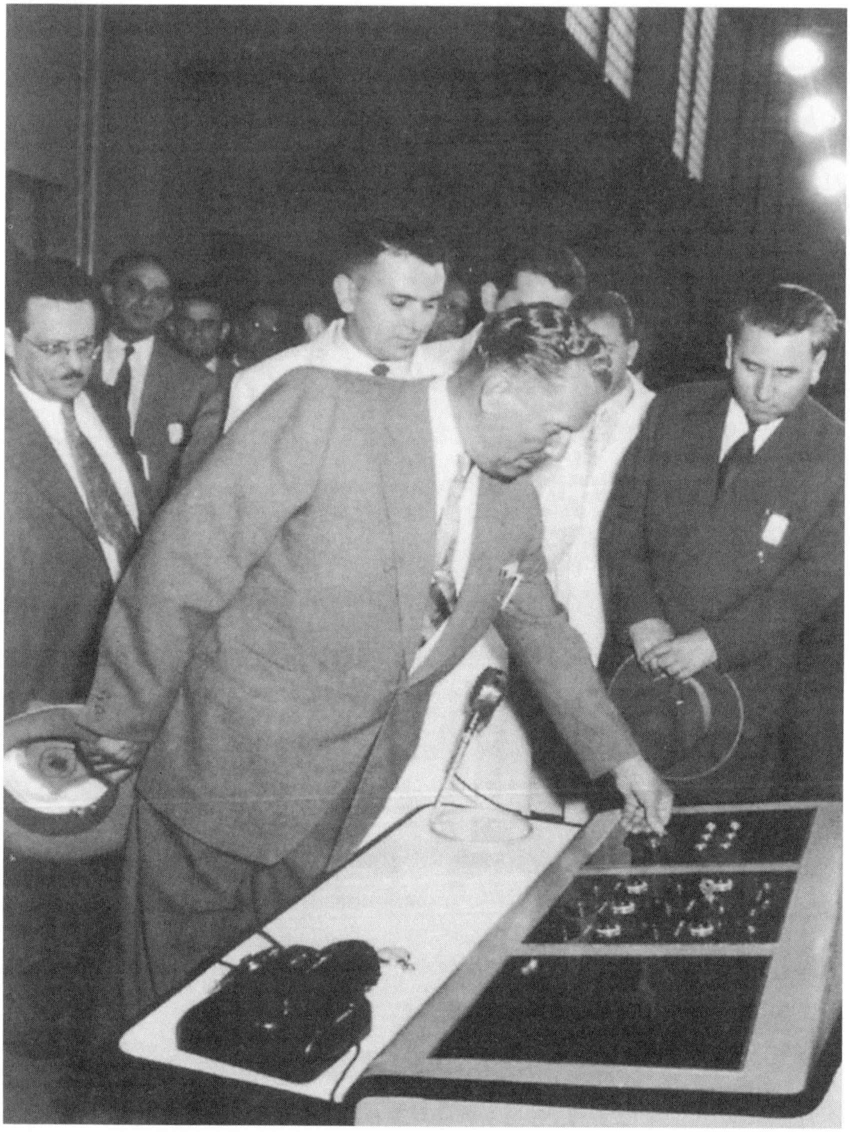

A photo taken at Vinča in 1958. Marshal Tito put a reactor RB of zero power into operation. To the left, behind Tito, is Edvard Kardelj, a Slovenian and a member of the Yugoslav Central Party Committee. To Tito's right is Aleksandar Ranković, vice president of Yugoslavia and president of the Federal Commission for Atomic Energy.

Part III: Tito's Yugoslavia

7

The People and the Regime

Our family returned to Polje in September to live in the lower house, which by then had been repaired. We children were given greater freedom since we had neither school nor other duties requiring our attention. Our elders were so engrossed in adapting to the new order that they did not have the time to control our activities in any way. For us, the important thing was that we were together again and there was no war. We minded our cows and were not prohibited from entering other people's estates, which had become overgrown. We could wander wherever we liked and try to picture what happened when the last army passed through. Two burned-out tanks still stood on our land, having been torched by the Italians when they capitulated. Little by little we reduced them to naked metal skeletons by dismantling and carrying away whatever we could. We liked the little wheels (ball bearings) most of all, using them to make roller skates and carts in which we would roll down the slopes.

Babba reopened his shop in the *čaršija* and life began again. In the fall, however, there were new worries as people prepared to vote on whether Petar II Karađorđević, who lived in London, should be allowed to return. If that happened, the Partisans would leave. We were amazed at that possibility, since they were already here. We sat around the fire once more, discussing the situation. We were all afraid of war and of the Chetniks, who had killed their share of Serbian youths, too—sometimes several from the same family—if they were sympathetic to the Partisans.

It seemed impossible that anyone would vote for a king who had fled the country. However, as we eavesdropped on conversations, we came to understand that free elections would make it possible for the king to return. There were plenty of Serbs who would vote for him and against Tito and the communists. Tito was not "the real Tito," they said, but a Croat impostor whom the Russians had pushed onto the scene after the Germans killed "the real Tito" during the airborne attack on Drvar in 1944. Drvar, a small town in southwestern Bosnia, was where the seventh and last German Balkans offensive occurred. So, in spite of our play and our freedom, we again began to fear war. The elections took place, the Partisans won, and the king would not return. A number of people slyly observed that the elections had not really been free. Voters desiring to cast their vote for the king's return were required to drop a ball into an empty box, which made a clearly audible sound. The result was that few people dared to vote freely.

Many families were divided over the communists—not in a hostile manner, as in some cases—but they *were* divided, as happened with our family. The older generation, including Babba, his brothers, and Mujaga and Arifaga were against the communists, whereas the more modern and younger Ahmo, Arifaga's and Smailbeg's sons and daughters, and their grandsons were either in the Partisans or had worked actively in the underground.

The elders were against communist ideology, especially its atheism. In addition, they said that the communists believed that everything should be communal, that is, that no one should own their own houses or farms, and that even the women were to be shared. "Strange people, indeed—God shelter and save us from such ignorance," our people remarked incredulously.

I listened to the talk and feared the communists. I could not imagine Babba having another wife, or that Zlatulja would not be our cow, or that our fields, the plum trees, and the plants I loved would suddenly become "communal." In that case they could cut them down, sell them, or do what they wanted with them and we could not prevent it. Supposedly, that was the way people in Russia lived.

The first time I heard the word *communist* was when the Germans came and Ahmo began to spend the days in our upper house. It was whispered that he was a communist and we had to hide him. In fact, I recall that when his mother used to come to parties at our house before the war, Ahmo and his wife would appear beneath the window and announce they were "going to Prijepolje," which meant that they were going to a meeting of their communist group. Ljuba Radičević and her husband Branko, who was a professor in the gymnasium and later died in the Partisans, were members of the same cell. Ljuba was with her husband at the time of his death and gave birth to their daughter Nataša while in the Partisans.

Muslim antipathy to the communists was also a result of the fact that the Muslim communists distanced themselves from Islam, so that everything from the past, including customs and our bonds with Turkey, were regarded as backward. On the other hand, it was considered progressive not to believe and to eat pork, as well as for women to go unveiled and to wear dresses instead of *dimije,* and to marry people of other faiths. Muslim communists, at least the first ones and those who joined right after the war, "liberated" themselves from religion as they worked their way through the communist literature, which spelled out everything for them. They justified their changed outlook on the grounds that they were tired of the backwardness of our people, which they attributed to the long Turkish rule and to Islam. Their longing for Muslim equality with the other nationalities in Yugoslavia, as well as for a better life, led them to identify with communist ideas about society. Many Muslims also saw the communists as their protection against Serbian and Croatian nationalists.

An accelerated set of fundamental changes began when the Partisans took over in 1945. Those who had been active Partisans or served in the underground resistance during the war got jobs whether they were literate or not, regardless of their qualifications. Many of the common people got jobs, large stores were opened as well as small-scale enterprises, and peasants relocated from village to town. The result was that towns grew while the villages emptied—although not as much as they did later.

Courses were established to teach women to read and write. Pero Koković ran one such course in Mujaga's little house. Mass work drives were organized to clear away the debris of the war and to reforest the bare hills. A key slogan was "No rest until reconstruction!" People would go to conferences—we learned that word, too—sponsored by local societies, enterprises, and schools. Every new drive had to be explained and every new decision was pounded into people's heads. People already knew who the Communist Party members were even though their meetings were secret and they did not talk about what went on in them. The majority were so-called good political workers and very active when work drives or meetings to support the Party's leaders were needed. They used to come forward as organizers of meetings, bringing up proposals that we discussed, but the end result was already predetermined.

The communists finally seized firm control. The old wartime administration was dissolved and its leaders, who were accused of having "collaborated with the occupier and native traitors," were arrested. I remember the jail up by Dosković Brook, high in the meadow opposite Polje. We used to watch the prisoners from a distance as they were being led out of the barn for a bit of fresh air. We heard that Alefendija Aginčić, who had served as mayor during the Italian occupation, was one of the prisoners, as were Rašidaga Jusufagić's sons. There were also Principal Jovičić of the gymnasium, the lawyer Varagić, and other Serbs. One day there were no more prisoners. We learned from muffled conversations overheard in the house that they had been shot. Some of their families moved away from Prijepolje.

The communists began their disempowerment of the rich with a law on "expropriation and nationalization" in 1946. The law directed that the property of the rich and those who had been "enemies" of the people during the war be confiscated. Free trading was abolished in Prijepolje. The result was that the few remaining prewar shops were not even opened, except for small

were not allowed by their parents to continue school because of the Muslim fear of the new and the tradition that girls should not be educated but should instead prepare for marriage.

Most people were short of everything, including textiles, during the period immediately after the war. However, 1947 was the first time we ever experienced a food shortage. An organized system of food distribution was instituted using coupons. Office workers and laborers received "R" cards. Babba, as a private businessman, got a "G" card, which they said was for "parasites." It contained half as many coupons as the "R" card.

Right after the war we received help from the United Nations Relief Agency (UNRA) in the form of packages of food and clothing sent by Americans. We had no connections, so we received only one or two packages. In one of them I found a beautiful silk dress with floral decorations, long sleeves, and two pleats in front. It fit as though it had been made for me. I wanted to go outside in the dress, but I was ashamed to ask Babba for permission. I found out through Nanna that he would not let me anyway. I continued to go to school in my *dimije* and I did not get to wear the dress until I completed the lower grades of the gymnasium. When not in school, I used to walk barefoot, even to the *čaršija.* This was nothing unusual for smaller children, especially in the summer heat. It was even considered healthy since it was said to prevent flat feet. We wore clogs made of wood at home. Some girls in town already had sneakers they were able to buy with coupons through people who had connections. Indescribable crowds would form in front of stores when the word got out that certain goods had arrived. People would begin lining up at midnight, but because of the connections that had developed you were never sure that you would get a chance to buy anything. A salesperson had more status than a college professor during those times. I did not get my first pair of sneakers until 1950, when they first began to be sold normally.

In September, 1946, I began my second year of gymnasium in the old grade school at the head of the *čaršija.* A new one had replaced the destroyed town hall. We had no textbooks or notebooks and we wrote on any kind of paper we could find, taking down notes from our professors' lectures. Nanna got me a prewar geography text from Naca's library but I, curiously, had no desire to learn. I grazed my cows in Prota Šiljak's garden and at Banka, taking my book along but not opening it. I spent most of my time with Vasvija and Hajrija. They did not go to school anymore. They already dressed well and we began to flirt with boys. Once, I got a note from Hasan, who was an apprentice in the trades. I hid it in the straw in the stable. I did not like his writing and did not answer. Then Vasvija's relative, Fahro, an excellent student and upperclassman, appeared on the scene. His parents, who were agronomists, came to Prijepolje. Fahro and I took an immediate liking to each other. Since Vasvija and Hajrija had already begun to write letters, we now wrote together to Fahro. I wrote my letters on pastel paper with flowers at the top and a line from some popular album. Sometimes, Fahro and I would converse shyly at a party where jam was being cooked en masse. Sadly, Fahro left for Sarajevo for further study and soon became seriously ill. Thus our group flirtations came to an end.

In June, 1947, our class traveled to Rudo for a one-day outing to see the place where Tito formed the 1st Proletarian Brigade. We went by truck from Prijepolje to Uvac on the Bosnian border, where we transferred to a narrow gauge railway known as Ćira. This was my first experience with that train, which I would take many times in the future to schools in Sarajevo and Belgrade. Babba journeyed to Bijeljina, to visit his brother Ibrahim and returned with my cousin Šadija. She was ahead of me in gymnasium and as we walked together through the *čaršija* she and I would compare notes about our schools. I learned from her that they had a Young Muslims chapter in her school—I am not sure whether it was public or secret—and that it had many student sympathizers. The Young Muslims was a secret organization that arose immediately after the war to promote Islamic values. I thought at the time that Bijeljina was larger than Prijepolje and had everything. Some years later, I was to meet some Young Muslims without knowing it.

I finished my second year with a "very good" rating and given a red kerchief at the closing ceremony—even though I had not achieved a grade of "excellent." Other students who had been rated "very good" were also awarded red kerchiefs. The rest received green ones.

The communists formed several auxiliary organizations under their control. Prijepolje had its own Party Committee, whose secretary was the most important person in town next to the mayor. People often did not know who the mayor was, nor could they distinguish between the functions of the two offices.

So-called conscientious comrades filled these positions. Frequently they were members of the same family. We heard the term conscientious comrade daily—it meant a person devoted to the Party's goals. The official form of address was "comrade." Thus, Tito became "Comrade Tito." The People's Front was formed as a citizens' organization that, years later, was replaced by the Socialist Alliance of Working People. It aided the Party in daily life, gathering voluntary contributions for various building projects or obtaining valuable monetary aid from the owners of small service businesses, like Babba. The Union of World War II Veterans was very active and influential.

It had its own newspaper and could overturn many decisions, as well as put its stamp on candidates for various jobs in local government or factory administration. It also played an important role in the selection of children for admission to military school. Later, it became the Party's "iron fist" when it became necessary to remove a high official or deprive him of his benefits, as was the case with Aleksandar Ranković, a vice president of Yugoslavia. Sindikat, the Union (later Federation) of Labor Unions was charged with protecting workers' rights, but they were already overly defended and had plenty of benefits. Thus, there was no talk of labor strikes or rebellion during this early postwar period. Employees became the members of the union automatically and their dues were deducted from their pay in advance. Around 1950, the union was given a magnificent structure, "Union House," which was the reference point for that area. The building was in the center of Belgrade, on Marx and Engels Square, opposite the Central Committee building, where the Party newspaper *Borba* was published. The Antifascistic Women's Front (AFŽ), already existed during the war. It, too, was a powerful organization, as its members fulfilled functions in the Red Cross, in state institutions involved with education and the youth, as well as with women and their protection while on the job. The employment of women on night shifts was prohibited. Women with large families were revered and if a woman had an eleventh child, Tito became its godfather. Such children received scholarships when they went on to higher education. Children under fifteen years of age were enrolled in the Pioneers, while youngsters could join a Youth League called Omladina. Young people wanting to continue with advanced education had to obtain a character reference from the Omladina in order to get a stipend and receive housing. This document contained basic information about the young person's parents—whether they had belonged to an enemy group during the war—as well as how the student had performed as a member of the Omladina. The presidency of the Yugoslav Youth League was considered a good testing ground for future high-ranking Party functionaries, as well as for ambassadors and directors of large economic systems or their representatives abroad.

There were numerous perquisites for employees: free health care, schooling, cheap travel, scholarships, and housing, as well as a whole scale of pensions for invalids and the elderly, the military, and others. Institutions gave their employees low-cost apartments. Although not large, the apartments were comfortable, featuring parquet floors and balconies, and usually having central heating, hot water, and telephone service.

Those who were employed in town sold their land or gave it to their relatives in order to be eligible for the children's supplement, which often exceeded the pay of families with several children. Officials received building lots on land often expropriated from Muslims or from "enemies of the people" whose property had been confiscated. In addition, they were given cheap credit, at interest rates that were not recalculated for years. Natives of the city, who constituted a certain form of opposition to the regime, did more poorly than the *arrivistes* and the poor: they enjoyed fewer benefits, were deprived of their property, and gradually developed into a new class of poor. They usually could not obtain an apartment because they lived in their own houses, for whose repair they were responsible, and their children could not obtain scholarships and housing if their parents had any kind of property or were private employees or tradesmen.

The newly employed became accustomed to living on their pay, leading to a new lifestyle. Before, every family in a town had its own vegetable garden and seldom bought vegetables. Little by little, people stopped growing their produce. Food supply enterprises, called Granapi, sold vegetables imported from Serbia. The new food supply system regulated things in ways that seemed strange. We now bought by the kilogram, where before we had measured things by the basket or sack. Meat buying also employed an exact measure, whereas we used to order by the leg or shoulder. This depersonalized the process somewhat. In the old days, you could say to the butcher: "Cut me off this piece, from here to there," adding, "Only, goodness, give me a little more fat—you know, she wants to cook something."

Bread was not baked at home anymore. Cows, too, gradually faded from the picture. People ceased to raise chickens, and it was against the law to keep cattle and other creatures in town. In the same way, people began to buy milk—which once had been unimaginable. However, when refrigerators were introduced, what was once unimaginable became customary. Women sighed in relief: they did nothing and a bottle of milk appeared at their feet!

People had much enthusiasm in those early postwar years. In Prijepolje, youngsters erected the Seljašnica hydroelectric station, thus electrifying the town as well as some villages. Later, when Prijepolje was included in Yugoslavia's energy grid, all the villages were electrified.

Girls who did not go on with their education were able to get jobs in the new textile factory, including Muslim girls who were receiving their first paycheck. A construction enterprise called "Work" was founded, and several housing projects sprang up, which had an immediate effect on the way of life. The intimacy of living in a single-family home was lost, and people of different faiths and classes found themselves as neighbors. The restriction of private property eliminated the basis for class differences, and the question "who's who?" was no longer important in marriage or in friendship. Slowly, social interaction became freer and looser. We all took part in special work drives: planting seedlings on bare hillsides, clearing fruit trees of caterpillars, and picking medicinal plants that were sent to large centers for processing. By 1947, the country was almost completely renewed. The government then passed a five-year construction plan. The dinar was stable and a national loan was announced. My Babba earned enough that he was able to put money aside and to buy bonds.

Meanwhile, the national agricultural plan had serious repercussions. Peasants were forced to enter *zadruge* (collective farms), contributing their land and their livestock. Farmers knew about the Russian *kolhozes,* which were described as a plague. I remember that right up to 1952, peasants from as far away as Montenegro were driving their sheep through Polje, trying to sell them for whatever they could get before entering a collective farm. For a time after the war, raising mountain goats was prohibited as well. They supposedly nibbled at young tree seedlings, and so were destroying forests that had already been largely devastated during the war. There was a strong popular resistance to the annihilation of the goats, and many people hid them in rural villages.

I personally knew a certain "Mara Jurukuša" in the village of Izbišnje who kept over fifty goats, living with them in her house as though they were her family. She was descended from a rich Serbian family and her brothers had their own estates not far from her house. Mara wore Serbian women's garb made from coarse cloth: a broad-pleated skirt, white blouse, and sleeveless vest. When it grew cold, she wore a short sheepskin jacket. She wore a gray kerchief on her head, and on her feet the traditional peasant leather *opanci* with the turned-up toes, as well as long woolen stockings to protect her feet from snakes. Mara was not quite "all there." Or maybe she was! Her ground-floor house had an earthen floor and a slab in one corner on which she slept. There were goats all around her. She made cheese and did not separate the kids from their mothers because she did not know what to do with all that milk. Mara gave her extra goats to the farmers with the proviso that they not slaughter them, which they promised not to do. She usually would spend the whole day in the forest with her goats, a pruning knife tucked in her belt for cutting branches with which to feed them. When the law was issued banning the keeping of goats, the government had to put Mara in jail in order to remove her animals. They deposited the reimbursement fee for her goats in the bank, but she had no need for money!

A bizarre side of Mara was that she was in love with Petar II Karađorđević, who at the time was in London. Whenever an airplane passed overhead, she would think that it was carrying a letter to her from King Petar, and that it was dropped from the plane into the forest where she could not find it. This fantasy probably originated from the fact that her father and brothers were great Serbian patriots and that she had been raised on tales about the Serbian rulers. Also, nearby, above the Lim and the village of Toci, loomed the ruins of the citadel of the "Cursed Jerina," a French medieval princess who had married a Serbian king. The name was preserved among the Serbian people, who believed the medieval kingdom of Kosovo fell because its rulers married foreigners.

When I would meet her in the forest, where we sometimes used to mind the cows, I would ask her: "Mara, has the king got in touch with you?" She would answer, "Yes," and explain that he had dropped a letter into Toci and that she was waiting for a villager to bring it. In fact, the villagers did bring her letters, but they would only write something that they thought looked like an official royal letter. In exchange, Mara would give them a full bag of her delicious fruit. Sometimes they would bring her a kerchief, supposedly a gift from the king to her. Because she did not cultivate the land and raise grain, her whole estate became overgrown with woods and glades where medicinal herbs grew, as did fruit trees that gradually aged from inattention. Mara had just about the best pears in the region. She was stingy with them, however, and would give them only to us, who were shepherds like her.

The communists gradually came to understand that Russian-style communism did not suit our people, and by 1953 they were already scrapping collective farms and starting to introduce other reforms.

Lack of freedom and the Communist Party's baton were bearable as long as the people had work and were able to live well. But employment benefits gradually exceeded the profit that was being created and, to make matters worse, Yugoslavia found itself in trouble with the rest of the communist bloc—to which it had belonged since the beginning. Although there had been little or no public discussion, the people knew that Yugoslavia was not getting along with the Russians. Almost everyone feared the Russian system, and a constant topic of discussion among friends was: "Will Russia attack us?"

Muslims did not like the Russians because they oppressed the Muslims in central Asia, wiping out Islamic culture there. In addition, the Russian Orthodox Church was alien to our culture. The Russian people were said to be incapable of doing anything on their own. Croatians and Slovenes leaned more toward Europe in their way of life, work habits, and religion. Serbs and Montenegrins were divided—some were for Russia, others against it—but the majority desired close ties with Russia, regarding it as their historical friend and protector. They also wanted to keep the Russian people at a distance, for them to remain where they were.

In the summer of 1948, a breakup finally occurred. I remember how, at the height of a heat wave, loudspeakers around town began to broadcast the speeches of delegates to the Fifth Party Congress. It was held in Belgrade on the occasion of an International Bureau of Communist Parties (Cominform) attack on the Yugoslav administration, claiming that its policies were destroying the unity of the Russian-led socialist countries. Russia and the surrounding socialist states first established the economic blockade secretly and then publicly after 1948.

Our government's policies had our approval because people hoped they would bring us better times and greater freedom. Stories circulated that Russia had been taking our grain and other riches, and that their soldiers had tried to control our airports and other vital points in 1947, interrogating people as to where they were going. It thus happened that, in spite of the deprival of our liberties and the use of the Party's baton, the first breath of freedom blew through our country in 1948. The government was once again with the people, as it had been during the war. Our self-confidence became especially strengthened when Tito announced in 1949 that the country was not going to starve and that we would be purchasing grain from America so that we could feed ourselves. Once more, "that America" was saving the country, just as it had done in 1945 with its packages! Tito's message meant more to the people than the fact that we were going to get wheat, since we had never been in great danger of starvation. "They do not dare to attack us," everyone said aloud.

The breakup between Yugoslavia and Russia released forces for the building of a better life in our land. The majority of the people stood with the state government, but the seeds of idleness and of power and privilege had already been sown.

When the communists came into power in 1945, there was religious freedom, according to the law. Mosques and churches remained open, but they were visited only by noncommunists or people who were not working in government service—including tradesmen, villagers, and independent professionals, such as lawyers, employees in some foreign embassies, and others. It was understood that professors and students could not be believers.

Communists who visited a mosque or church were punished and then ejected from the Party. A government worker, especially a teacher, professor, or judge would lose his job. Nonetheless, people somehow kept their faith. As far as I can remember, there were four old mosques in Prijepolje—one for each quarter of the town. They were two stories high, of square construction, and had tile roofs and white brick minarets. There was only one entrance, and the women's area was on the second floor. It had an open gallery that extended half the depth of the mosque so that women could follow the imam's preaching. Mosques were unheated, had no water, and served only as places of worship. Outside, in the courtyard, was the *šadrvan,* a round water fountain where people who did not live nearby could perform their *abdest.* From the minaret, the *mujezin* recited *ezan,* the call to prayer, five times a day. The first call awoke those who had overslept, and *ezan,* as well as the roosters' singing, dispelled the darkness of unknown content. According to old women's tales, such darkness made its abode in remote places and old houses in which dwelled genies and other invisible, unfriendly creatures. Such houses were called "heavy."

After the war, the number of people who came to the mosque to pray the obligatory *namaz* diminished, but a sufficient number still came to *džuma* at noon on Friday. Women went to the mosque less often than men. After doing household chores, they usually had less time available. Besides, mosques were not always nearby. They used to come to the *teravija,* the special sequence of evening prayers during Ramadan, as well as to the women's Mevlud, a recital in Bosnian about the Messenger's life, performed on Muhamed's birthday. Sometimes men and women attended the Mevlud performances together. Women liked to attend lectures by teachers from Sarajevo and other cities, on topics of interest to women, such as raising children, family relations, and proper dress.

Muslim society supported the imams and *mujezins.* These resources were raised by voluntary donations. Once private property was drastically reduced, Muslims no longer were able to give anything toward their *zekat* (annual contribution), which is given to the needy in an organized Muslim community.

Rarely did one find a mosque in the village. People used to get together in someone's home to do the daily prayers, whereas they would go to town to perform a *džuma* in a mosque. Right after the war, I went with Babba to Zalug, where he performed the *teravija.* We did the *teravija* in Smailbeg's house because, after Arifaga's death, he was the eldest in Polje. We did five *namaz* daily in our house, and had the *sabah* together, before Babba left for his shop and I for my classes. We read from the Qur'an every day, and at noon on Friday Nanna would stop work, pray, and read the *sura* El Kahf (The Cave), which speaks of God's miracle called life. The feeling that *džuma* time is something special remains engraved in my soul.

The *mektebs* were officially closed in 1946, even though they were never really opened after the war. It was the same with other religious schools. Children were required to go to public school through the first eight grades, during which dialectical materialism was the foundation of their education—as was science, which negates the existence of God, according to the communist view of science taught to us.

Muslims continued to give Muslim names to their children. Thus, a person from Yugoslavia could tell who among us was of the Muslim faith. There was very little difference in people's names. For example, Džengiz, Orhan, and Ayhan could be found among the Turks, whereas Albanian Muslims had their own national names, including Afrodita, Fljora, and Veton, in addition to the usual Muslim ones.

All Muslim nationalities had names connected with Turkish sultans, such as Osman, Murat, and Mehmed, which were converted in the Bosnian language to Osmo, Meša, and Meho. Certain names indicated divine features, such as Rahima (Mercy) or His messengers—Adem (Adam), Ibrahim (Abraham) and Ismail. The name Muhamed was given less often because it was seen as obligating the bearer to be a true Muslim, which could be unsustainable during stormy times, especially under communist rule. Common female names were Emina or Ema after the mother of the Messenger, Fatima or Fata after his daughter, or Aiša after his wife. As time went on, those who worked in the cities began to seek more modern names. Mothers wanted their children to have similar names, like Alma for a daughter and Almer for a son, Jasmina and Jasmin, and others that had no real meaning but were merely concocted.

After the war, only the more modern women called their husbands by name. The old custom of including their title lasted for a long time afterward: for example, Mujaga, Alefendija, Orhanbey, Alibeg. Upon getting married, women, especially those in the country, would acquire their husband's first name, plus the added suffixes *in* plus *ica,* with *in* denoting possession and *ica* the feminine particle. For example, Avdaga's wife was called *Avdaginica,* and few people would know her original first name.

Only simple women referred to their husband as "my man." It was not proper to say "husband" in public, but rather *efendija.* In front of strangers, a husband would address his wife as *hanuma* and very rarely say "my wife." In general, husbands would avoid any mention of their wife or sister in anyone else's presence. They would mention their mother more often, especially if she was deceased, in which case they would say "*rahmetli moja majka*" ("my mother, may God grant her mercy and peace"). The term *rahmetli* was used for any deceased person, just as the Serbs would say "*pokoj mu duši*" ("may his/her soul rest in peace").

The *hadž* or pilgrimage to Mecca (for Christians to Jerusalem) was always regarded as something holy. Yugoslav Muslims did not go on the *hadž* immediately after the war because they did not have the money. It seems that the first group travel to Mecca did not take place until around 1952. We had at home a small book titled *A Hadž Journey.* That book, which was popular among the people and read with curiosity, described the route to Mecca before the war.

Postwar connections with the Muslim countries were very poor, and although most people felt this lack, they did not wait for things to improve. Instead, those who continued to consider themselves Muslims and did not take the road of assimilation strengthened their Muslim feeling through mutual contacts. They greeted one another with "Merhaba," or "Es Sellamu Alejkum," which signified that they wished peace for the person so addressed. When visiting someone's house in the evening, they would say, in accord with the old Turkish custom, "Akšam Hajrula" or, in the morning, "Sabah Hajrula," meaning, "What's new? Are you all right?" The person addressed would answer, "Allahraziola" ("may God be happy with us both, I am all right"). When they left, people would say, "Allahimanet" ("may God be with you").

It seems to me that "Merhaba" was more an official form of address, used in the *čaršija,* although surreptitiously immediately after the war. Serbs, especially in the country, would greet one another with "Pomozi Bog" or "God help you!" The other person would answer: "Bog ti pomogao," meaning, "May God help you!" Muslims and Christians would also greet each other with more recent forms of address, like "Dobro jutro," meaning "Good morning," or "Dobar dan" ("Good afternoon") and "Doviđenja" ("Goodbye"). Only young people would say "zdravo" ("hello").

Some Muslims discarded the prefix *hadži* from their last names. In this way, Hadžišehović became Šehović. Some sons, especially those from mixed marriages who inherited the title Spahi, would change it to Spahijević so as to mute any reminder of the Turkish *spahis,* who were landowners.

Muslim communists not only did not believe, they also buried their dead without doing *dženaza.* This was especially unacceptable as far as older people—mothers and fathers—were concerned. Women especially could not reconcile themselves with such a practice. If a husband or brother who held a Party job or was in education, the courts, or the military died, they would secretly go to some male believers and entreat them to do the *dženaza* and offer surreptitious prayers. As far as I know, the Serbs did something similar.

Later, when there was more freedom, people made arrangements with physicians who issued death certificates to wash dead persons quickly and wrap them in their burial shrouds while still in the hospital, before putting them in their coffins for burial. Muslim atheists were not carried to the gravesite in an open coffin, nor did they have a grave marker with a green moon and star, but rather a red star. In Bosnia, especially in Sarajevo, there was even an atheist chapel, and atheist death notices were printed. However, there were still employees and communists who fasted sometimes during Ramadan or had their children circumcised during annual leave. They would go to Turkey or to their relatives in another town to have the procedure performed.

During that period—as almost always during the Second Yugoslavia—believers connected with government service in any capacity were like the first Muslim believers, who had to pray in secret.

Like the seizure of Vakuf property and the limitations placed on religious freedom, Muslim women's attire was eventually attacked. After the war, most women continued to wear the veil and to absent themselves in the presence of strange men. However, around 1950 there was a drive to remove the veils. Working Muslim women and the wives of important directors and officials, as well as the female members of Partisan families, ceased to wear their veils immediately after the war, whereas peasant women, women in the trades, and the wives of men who visited the mosque—including Nanna—continued to wear their veils.

Because the government wanted to carry out this drive "voluntarily," respected women were sought to set an example, as was customary in those days. Nanna, who was a religion teacher and literate, was one of the first they approached. They urged her to remove her veil before the law went into effect. She refused, so they called her to the headquarters of the Udba, the local branch of the interior police. When those discussions also proved unsuccessful, political officers changed their tactics and began sending reputable members of the local government to our house. I still remember a visit paid us by Džemila Hašimbegović, who came with the president of the District Court, an Albanian from Kosovo. Džemila was a late *muftija's* wife and a great activist in the AFŽ. A *muftija* is a Muslim scholar who is eligible to issue Fatwa (Islamic rules). As the mother of two sons in the Partisans, she herself had been jailed during the war and had spent considerable time in various German concentration camps. My parents welcomed Džemila and the judge, offering them special homemade pastries, but their visit was unsuccessful.

Muslim women found it difficult to remove the veil and many felt ashamed to go outside, so they did not. However, from 1950 on, that was the law. The first time Nanna went out without her veil was when she went with Babba to vote. The election was scheduled a few days after the law about veils went into effect.

One other innovation changed the nature of the Muslim family in an essential way: mixed marriages. They began to occur toward the end of the war and increased in number after communist power was solidified. Even though Muslims, Serbs, and Montenegrins had lived together in the Sandžak since ancient times, they had observed a certain boundary in their mutual relations. Mixed marriages simply were not performed. For a Muslim girl to marry a boy of another religion was worse than death. Christians felt the same way.

In the divided prewar society it was relatively easy to prevent such marriages because each group lived according to its own customs and religion, and Muslim women remained at home. We had greater opportunities for association in the new state: in school, at work, and at party functions. The new class that arose from the active part of the population linked to the state and the Communist Party abandoned religious rituals. Since it was prohibited to teach religion in schools, children grew up mainly without religious instruction. The only reminder of their Muslim heritage might be through a grandmother or grandfather whom they watched praying or saying their beads. Thus was the difference between young people of different religious backgrounds diminished.

The first Muslims to marry members of other faiths were those educated in large centers or who went to work in another milieu, or who returned from the Partisans to become directors or distinguished members of one group or another. That process was evident among writers and artists in the First Yugoslavia, although to a lesser degree, and in other Muslim centers in Turkey and the Arab states. Perhaps it was unavoidable, since many Muslim intellectuals had come to accept Western values as a result of their schooling and/or the professions they chose.

When one examines this phenomenon in Yugoslavia after the war, one notes almost a certain rule. A relatively large number of the Muslim women and men who entered into mixed marriages came from wealthier families tied to the previous government either through work, position, or riches. They were the children of imams, *muftijas,* politicians, and large landowners. Sociologists would find such a phenomenon interesting. If such families were studied from the "inside," one could establish that their members did not live like Muslims, even though they adhered to the external features of the religion, such as *bairam, dženaza, džuma,* and the circumcision of children. What did they lack? They prayed irregularly if at all, they did not recite the Qur'an, and they sometimes drank a little. Mothers were especially important in the Muslim religion: the children of those who prayed and recited the Qur'an at home adopted Islamic views of the world. In the prewar period, however, other influences played a role. For example, if someone in the family already belonged to the Communist Party, the rest followed him.

Those in mixed marriages adopted an atheistic way of life. For the sake of equality, no religious holidays were observed. Instead, they celebrated state holidays such as the First of May, the New Year, and the Day of the

Republic. Children were given names from both backgrounds—sometimes Serbian, but more often Croatian—that were closer to western European or even international names. Pork was eaten in the home and alcohol was introduced, which later extended to the whole new class, and even later to ordinary people. A considerable number of these mixed marriages were unstable, which was especially true of marriages entered into right after the war. Divorce was not uncommon in such cases.

The Belgrade Muslim community was quite diverse. First there were the "indigenous" Muslims from the time of the First Yugoslavia. They had settled there from 1920 onward and included Turks, Albanians—also known as Shiptars—Muslims from good families in Bosnia, and people who had come mainly from Bosanska Posavina and Macedonia looking for a better living.

People such as my acquaintances Hajrija and Ilijaz lived for the most part in Zemun and other outlying areas of the city, doing fairly well for themselves—most in their own houses. They were involved in small businesses or worked as craftsmen, while their wives were mostly industrious housewives. They lived in close-knit families and kept in touch with the people in their old regions and with the mosque.

Muslims from Bosnian families of good standing and intellectuals came to Belgrade in a variety of circumstances: on business as representatives of foreign firms or remaining there after completing their studies. Some became renowned professors, as did the Oriental academician Mehmed Begović and caricaturist and travel writer Zulfikar-Zuko Džumhur. Some also worked as officials of the Islamic Association. The chief *muftija,* Zekerijah *efendija* Činara, was of Sandžak origin. I knew Alibeg Kulenović, and by reputation his brother Mustajbeg, both of whom had married "out of the faith." Alibeg was married to Mara, who came from a prominent Serbian family named Todorović in Belgrade, and Mustajbeg to a French woman of Jewish origin who died young, leaving him with a very gifted daughter named Ćamila. Muslims of this type moved in high society and thought of themselves as Yugoslavs. They did not keep to the religious prescriptions, although they maintained contact with believers and would visit them for Bairam and go to *dženazas.* They spoke foreign languages, mainly German and French, even at home. They would organize get-togethers, lunches and dinners; attend Serbian Orthodox, Jewish, and Catholic festivals, and associated with upper class Belgraders. Some people from this class were known to have collaborated with Nedić's regime, so the Partisans executed them after the war. General Milan Nedić was a prime minister of Serbia's quisling regime during the German occupation in World War II.

Other prewar Muslims included Turks, Albanian Muslims, and Gorani Muslims—people of Slavic origin from Skopska Gora in Macedonia who were involved in confectionery, bakery, and other crafts and private businesses, or worked in the Turkish Embassy or the mosque. The best-known confectioners' shops were those of Pehlivan and Medžed. Medžed's pastry shop, located on Knez Mihajlova Street near the American reading room, was a meeting place for young people and was always packed. The authorities did not rest until they got rid of it in the eighties, since it did not suit them to have people meeting in the center of Belgrade in a "Shiptar's sweetshop." Pehlivan's confectionery survived; it had the best ice cream in town. The Albanians and the Turks had the closest-knit communities, with their orderly lives, large families, and well-run businesses. They socialized among themselves, maintained family and business relations with their people in the homelands, and extended their businesses to major cities and sometimes into Europe and Turkey. These people, who were almost immune to all kinds of upsets, survived the war and rapidly found their feet in communist society.

The largest group was the Shiptars: working people who did the toughest jobs as porters, wage laborers in the fields, and selling in the markets—these last were not so poor, although they lived that way. Most of them were single men with temporary accommodation who had left their families at home. Turks, Albanian-Muslims, and Bosniak intellectual believers made up the core around the Bajrakli Mosque. The imams themselves were Bosniaks, sometimes married to Christians who deeply respected both their own and the Muslim faith and rituals, and were even members of the Islamic committees.

The Gypsies, including the Muslim Gypsies, did the lowliest jobs. Most of them were street sweepers who lived in the very poor areas in hovels made of wood and cardboard, alongside the river, on the city outskirts, or in slightly better areas as already long-established indigenous people. One such area, the largest of its kind in Belgrade, was in Zemun's upper town, by the flea market. The people there already had houses, although they were tiny, with light, water outside the house, and small streets. Gypsies were also employed in factories after the Second World War, were allocated apartments, and more and more of their children went to school.

One postwar group of Muslims was composed of communists, former Partisans who had been awarded positions for their services in various institutions and commercial organizations or were from a slightly younger generation and had worked in the local agencies of foreign firms, or as officials and military personnel. They were dependent on the state for the most part, and as a result were almost without exception communists by conviction or need. Those Muslims gave their children modern names or gave them nicknames so they would be closer to the environment in which they lived. On entering a mixed marriage, their children lost almost all of their Muslim identity, and their grandchildren often were christened when nationalism revived and the church became stronger.

In Skopje and Ohrid, as in Macedonia as a whole, people of very different origins had lived in mixed communities, quite peacefully it can be said, for a very long time. However, the Skopje of the past, with its large Turkish community and rich houses nestled in their courtyards and gardens with streams running through them, has disappeared. Mubedžela—who was married to Sulejmanpašić from Sarajevo, an official in the Turkish Embassy in Belgrade—and Dželal, son of the *muftija* Činara, had both grown up in such a house. When the Partisans came into power, most of them had their property and gold expropriated after an investigation. Upon leaving prison they emigrated to Turkey or dispersed around the Sandžak and to Sarajevo and Belgrade.

Albanians moving in from the villages mostly replaced Turks. It was very hot when I arrived in Skopje in June, 1965, and I soon found myself among the Albanians above the *čaršija* Bit Pazar (flea market). The houses in that quarter—located along the *tekke* (a small mausoleum) itself and the Turkish *iptidaija* (primary school), now half in ruins caused by the earthquake in 1963—had had large gardens in which smaller houses with high fences had already been built, so that the narrow streets between them resembled a corridor too narrow for a car. Here and there, ditches full of dirty water flowed out of the courtyards. Snotty-nosed, ruddy children, some of them bare legged, squatted alongside the occasional improvised shops with colored sweets, long since gone stale, in their windows. They distrustfully watched the inquisitive foreigners sightseeing in the area. The foreigners clearly felt uncomfortable as they moved through the neighborhood, differentiated by the languages spoken and the fences behind which the people lived their lives. I used to meet Albanian women on the street, veiled and wearing long coats, and almost always in groups. The poor urban Albanians who lived there as if in a ghetto had no need of foreigners. Nothing could be more unlike the parts of the town across the Vardar and downstream, with their modern high-rise hotels, boulevards, and traffic.

After the earthquake, Skopje made huge strides toward transforming itself into a modern city, suddenly increasing its population to almost half a million, with modern hotels, avenues, commercial centers, a university, and many public institutions. The Bit-Pazar and its surrounding quarters housing a largely Muslim population remained. During the time I spent in

Skopje, those people had not yet had the opportunity to add to their old way of life the new European lifestyle, as the Macedonians already had.

At the beginning of July, 1966, I took my annual vacation at Ohrid Lake with two Turkish families: the Sulejmanis and Umers. It was hot during the day, but the nights were cool and pleasant for sleeping because we were about eight hundred meters above sea level. I particularly enjoyed the clear, sunny skies and the crystal-clear lake.

People saw the Macedonian part of Ohrid from postcards, which gave no clue that numerous other peoples also lived there, including Turks, Albanians, and Gypsies. The slopes above the lake were thickly studded with small, orderly houses with little flower gardens in front. The houses extended up the slope and gradually merged into the old Macedonian town with its Byzantine-style churches and excavated relics from the Middle Ages and earlier. The ruins of Samuil's tenth-century fortress dominated the summit. Tsar Samuil founded the first Slavic state in Macedonia. The fortress itself was destroyed in the third century (209 A.D.) when Christianity came to the region from Byzantium. Debris from the Slavic monastery of Saint Pantelejmon, which was built by Saint Kliment of Ohrid as his memorial church in 893, was found beneath the Imaret mosque. Saints Kliment and Naum were the most famous students of Cyril and Methodis, the brothers from Thessalonica who spread Christianity in the Slavic countries. The Imaret mosque was built by Sinan Čelebi, a member of the Ohrizade family, during the period of Turkish rule.

The Turkish quarter was in the plain, with large houses roofed with half-round tiles nestling in their gardens and life lived privately, away from the street. The upper part of Ohrid had Turkish, Albanian, and Gypsy communities, each in their separate quarters, seldom mingling with each other. The older people could make themselves understood in three languages plus Macedonian. They had access to the upper part of the lake, where women still did their laundry by hand, drying it on the pebbly shore. The linen came out whiter than the finest paper. Women from the Turkish and Albanian communities did not bathe in the lake unless they were doing their laundry in the hinterlands, and even then they waited almost until it was dark. All their houses had spacious bathrooms in which I, too, liked to bathe. A decree was issued forbidding the washing of clothes in the lake, probably to "protect" the people from the sewage that poured into it.

The Turks in the region lived and dressed in the European style, but also maintained their own customs and food. I was surprised by the ancient lineage of the families and the lifestyle of their city, with its many wealthy families and their strong links to Turkey after they, too, emigrated en masse after the war. They spoke Turkish at home and Macedonian with others and the older people kept up their links with the mosque. Ohrid's chief mosque was in the *čaršija,* beside a *ćinar,* a huge oak that spread its ancient, worn branches over the wide square from which rows of shops ran down toward the lake. The mosque's courtyard contained a sizable *turbe* and graves where dervishes performed the *zikr* after *džuma* time on Fridays, with tourists gathering round to watch. The *zikr* is the rhythmic repetition of certain prayers accompanied by specific physical movements, mainly of the head. Most of the dervishes were young, and there were some women dervishes as well. My friend Guzide Sulejmani's mother was one of them. People called her Dervišhane. At home she had a wooden *tasbih,* a Muslim "rosary" that was so large it extended all the way around a small room and weighed several kilograms.

Mehmedalija Sulejmani and his son Džengiz were watchmakers and goldsmiths. After the war, when relations with Turkey improved, the women of the Sulejmani-Umer family went into business. Guzide and her daughter-in-law Senije opened three shops in the *čaršija* that sold wedding dresses brought from Istanbul. The shops remained in the family, expanding through their sons' and daughters' marriages, so that by the 1980s it looked like a small business dynasty. Even so, young people from this milieu went abroad to look for work—mainly to Germany, Switzerland, and Austria—and in the process enriched themselves even more.

Meanwhile, the Turkish minority was under pressure from both the Macedonians and the Albanians. The former had taken up all of the positions in the administration, moving in from the villages and beginning a new urbanization of the town, demolishing the Turkish quarters and bisecting them with new roads, gas stations, and other facilities required by tourists. Ohrid could effectively expand only in that direction. All the same, the town looked like a ploughed field, and everything was in a mess. The town probably would have been urbanized differently if it had been the intention to preserve its Turkish character as well—and only then would it have been of interest to tourists and others. Pressure from the Albanians was chiefly observable in mixed marriages: Turkish women married to Albanians could not speak their own language to their children, nor appear in any way different from Albanian women.

The Turks had no gymnasium, so the wealthier families sent their children to school in Istanbul. Guzide and Mehmedalija's daughter Ayhan went to school there. She came back for the summer and learned that her first two years had been difficult even as regards the Turkish language, since the Turks from Ohrid had no real contact with their motherland and, lacking textbooks, were out of step with modern Turkish. Pressure from the authorities was reflected in the fact that Turkish and Albanian children were expected to attend university in Skopje, where the lectures were given in Macedonian. This was particularly true of children from mixed marriages.

One person whose knowledge and different appearance caused him to stand out in the Turkish milieu was Dželadin, Senije's husband and Guzide's brother. As a young man, despite being from a wealthy family, Dželadin had joined the Partisans at the beginning of the war. He had fought mainly in the region between Macedonia and Albania, close to the wartime borders with Italy and Bulgaria. Since Dželadin knew Turkish, Albanian, and Macedonian, and could get by in Serbo-Croatian, he was involved in getting Partisans, illegals, and goods across the frontier. I found it interesting that the Albanian and Yugoslav communists and Partisans had collaborated so closely and that they had had the same objectives.

Dželadin was demobilized when the war ended. He returned home and married, according to the customs of that time, a young woman from a wealthy neighboring family, the beautiful and capable Senije, who gave him two sons and five daughters. Until taking premature retirement, Dželadin worked as a police inspector, and was a communist by conviction as well as a believer, though not a particularly practicing one, as was his family. He lived a quiet life in retirement, occupying himself with his garden.

The last time I was in Ohrid, in 1987, neither Dželadin nor Dervišhane, his mother, were there: both were dead. The waters of Ohrid Lake became blackish and foamy from the sewage dumped in it, even though the lake is under UNESCO's protection. The well-known song "Biljana Bleaches Linen at the Ohrid Springs" ceased to be topical.

The younger generation had taken on an important role. Its members had built better houses with the money they had earned in Europe and with their business, and had extended into Turkey. Turkish property in the expansive Ohrid plain was gradually taken over by Albanians who had moved into other people's property, although they were not able to transfer the property into their own names legally, but instead took out ninety-nine-year leases on the land and houses. Only Serbia and Macedonia had laws in force that were so discriminatory toward their own citizens. Yet people still managed to get around obstacles and cope. Of course money did its bit, too, helping in various ways.

In 1946, the Sandžak was partitioned between Serbia and Montenegro. It remained a strategically important region with a mixed population, linking Serbia with Montenegro and the Adriatic Sea. In the 1960s, the Belgrade–Bar railroad via the Lim Valley still had not been constructed, although work on it had begun several times since 1904, only to be halted. That was how it was in 1953, too. People said that the Austro-Hungarians had not allowed Turkey to build the railroad. Later, the conflicting interests of European countries and of Russia became embroiled in the matter.

The Sandžak remained economically undeveloped, with only a small amount of crude, low-revenue industry. Freight was transported by truck over poor roads. Schools for business students, which remained poor in general education, were opened for working-class youth. The Sandžak had no faculty, not even a department. Nor did it have a single school of higher education, nor a single laboratory. It had no theater, either.

Two or three textiles factories were erected, one in Prijepolje for making military tents, the other in Novi Pazar for clothing. As for large-scale industry, the Sandžak acquired a FAP automobile factory in Priboj. For want of anything better, dirty industry moved in. Coalmines and lead and zinc flotations were opened in the Pljevlje area, and a cement factory and smaller metal smelting facilities were constructed. The paper factory in Ivangrad poisoned the Lim, and its clear green waters turned black. The rich life of the mountain river, particularly its fish, was at risk. The fry of quality fish was almost destroyed. This drove people away from the banks of the Lim, and bathing places that had once been full of people were closed. As a protest against such negligence, nature-lovers made the film *Rivers Are Dying Downstream.*

Nevertheless, fundamental social and economic changes had taken place. Many people had left villages for towns. At the same time, the national makeup of the towns was altered, to the disadvantage of the Muslims. The majority of those who moved in were Serbs who found employment and occupied the better positions or served in management. Proportionately, they were allocated more apartments and home sites on which to build houses. The Muslim population continued to lose its economic status. The trend begun in the Ottoman period had continued in the First Yugoslavia with the Agrarian Reform movement and the emigration of the people to Turkey, and went on again in the Second Yugoslavia with the expropriation of private property and houses.

In my day, the Sandžak did not have enough educated people. It acquired its first doctors, engineers, and professors from the postwar generation. Some of them, like Safet Čičić, a doctor of geology, became university professors and noted businessmen when they moved to Sarajevo. Of those who remained in the Sandžak, I remember the early-deceased Ejup Mušović as being first in education and capability. He received a doctorate in history at Belgrade University and, because of circumstances, was prevented from studying the history of the Sandžak more deeply. As director of the museum in Novi Pazar, he laid the foundation for that institution's Bosniak Department. In the field of law, one of the heralds of the emancipation of the Muslims of the Sandžak in that period was Sait Bosović from Plevlje. A brilliant student, he received a scholarship from the government of the First Yugoslavia. After the war, Bosović was sent to Czechoslovakia for further study. The break between Yugoslavia and the Soviet Union resulted in his being sent back to Belgrade, where he studied law and ended up as a judge-president in the Sandžak. Another lawyer—who went on to become a judge in Serbia's Supreme Court—was Obrad Cvijović, a Serb who came from a Prijepolje Partisan family that lost several members killed by the Chetniks, including his mother and two sisters.

There were few educated Muslim women. The first we enrolled in 1953 were Berka Bajrović, the granddaughter of a pasha who went from the Pljevlje gymnasium to study chemistry in Sarajevo, and I, a student of physical chemistry in Belgrade.

The population migrations continued. The Serbs, for whom the first step had been to leave their villages for towns, moved into the wealthier regions in central Serbia or to Belgrade and Vojvodina. Many of them left for economic reasons, for better pay or to be closer to centers where they could obtain an education for their children. Meanwhile, Muslims began to move to Bosnia, in particular to Sarajevo, Mostar, and Banja Luka. It was said that people from the Sandžak held half the professorships at the University of Sarajevo.

In the Second Yugoslavia, the first mass migration from the Sandžak was to Turkey—and for much the same reasons as before: because of the poor economic development of the Sandžak, disagreements with the communist authorities, and mistrust of living together with Serbs and Montenegrins. The migration of Muslims to Turkey ceased for a short while during World War II. After the war, it was very difficult to mention Turkey. The communists accused Turkey of collaborating with the Germans and of offering asylum to the communist opposition. Postwar contacts began in 1950. The people most interested in emigrating were peasants and traders from the urban areas whose property had been nationalized. With the abolition of the private sector, they were left without either property or occupation. Intellectual believers emigrated: professors, doctors, and engineers. They could not reconcile themselves to the changes, nor, as believers, could they find jobs. The unresolved national status of the Muslim Bosniaks affected many and gave rise to still greater mistrust of the authorities.

Muslims were particularly affected by the impact of bolshevism on society after the war. They could not hope for better positions and status with such a strong Communist Party and Udba. If, for example, a pupil applied for a scholarship or went to military college or a well-known crafts center such as the one in Kragujevac, he had to have a "characteristic." The characteristic went for further checks if there was anything not quite in order with the family. Questionnaires asked questions about the candidate's parents, what they had done during the war, if they were members of enemy units. They also wanted to know if candidates had any relatives abroad and if so, whether they were in touch with them. Sometimes army officers sought permission to get married during their military service. Some of my girlfriends were required to wait several months before their future husbands obtained the necessary permit. Nevertheless, it was possible to live. Still, the Sandžak Muslims who survived the slaughter and the second or third war since the departure of the Turks from the area were not ready to take many risks.

So, the Muslims began to emigrate. They came covertly to Belgrade and besieged the Turkish Embassy to see if they could prove that they were Turks, since that was what they were called, or that they were at least of Turkish origin, even if they were not. Because there was a treaty between Yugoslavia and Turkey allowing the Turkish minority to emigrate, Sandžak Muslims discovered that it was easier to emigrate from Macedonia, from which many Turks were leaving, and where there were fewer checks. My sister Ferida and her family, Azizehanma with hers, and many others emigrated in that way. In 1965, Hasan *efendija* emigrated with three sons and a daughter, leaving four children in the Sandžak and Sarajevo with their families.

I got my Aunt Veza, as we called Arifaga's second wife, and her son Bahrija out. I first went to the customs office at the station to have her things inspected. Only then could they be packed and handed over to the shippers. The customs officers removed all the copper utensils from her things, but let her off in the case of some plates, since they saw that she did not want to be separated from them. They did not allow her to carry even the butter churn that she had encumbered herself with so as to make our Sandžak butter, which the Turks do not have. Nor could she take her electrical apparatus, which was very expensive in Turkey at that time.

I still can recall the moment when we bought her tickets for Istanbul at the international travel counter. In order to obtain the ticket, I first had to hand over Aunt Veza's canceled identity card, which signified that she had been deregistered as a Yugoslav citizen. There was a huge crowd at the station because we had completed everything on the eve of a national holiday: November 29, 1956. We were finally able, with the help of a customs officer, to push our way through to the train and to settle Aunt Veza and Bahrija in the compartment somehow. I could see my aunt across the crowd of people, waving and crying. I was smiling through my tears: "It will be fine for you there. All our people are there."

Aunt Veza would never again walk across Baskije and drop in for breakfast and coffee in the lower house at Uncle Abid's place. Baskije would be the poorer after the loss of yet another of our families from Polje. All this went through my mind as I forced my way through the dense crowd toward the station's exit.

I also accompanied Aunt Zina to Turkey to visit Osmo. Even with her, there were things to be done. Her documents also had to be regulated at the Turkish Embassy. While this was being done, Milena Dumić and Coca Borisavljević, some old Serbian friends of hers then living in Belgrade, invited her to visit. She promised Milena, who had to boil up all the dishes from which they would eat, since Aunt Zina was afraid of pig fat. Milena did everything that was necessary.

At the station, where I had come to meet her, Aunt Zina got out of the bus carrying a demijohn of water. She wanted to drink her own Priboj water. I pointed out the demijohn to her daughter Kimeta, who simply smiled at me behind her hand. While we were making our way to the taxi Aunt Zina did not want to be parted from the porter who was pushing her things on his cart. "The porter has a number. I've memorized it," Kimeta told her. "What good is a number to me if my presents go missing?" Aunt Zina asked stubbornly, afraid that the porter would run off.

We went to Milena's place; she was living in Slavija. Coca and the Raketić sisters had come to welcome her. Milena went to make coffee, drawing water from the tap. "I won't have that water, it's coming through a hose," said Zina. Milena was surprised. "What hose, Zina?" She had had to remove the rubber hose, which helped to prevent the water from splashing, from the tap, "and it could not even be boiled." We all laughed. "How did we eat before, Zina?" they teased her. "Well, that was Prijepolje," retorted Aunt Zina.

The following day, I took her to the embassy to regulate her documents. When he was finished, the clerk asked her to pay the required fee. "Here you are," she said, turning away from the clerk to take out her money, which was trussed up in a belt around her waist. "Why are you holding on to that money?" I asked. "They might take it from me," she replied. "Who?" I demanded. "I don't know," she said, agitated. "People steal in Belgrade." She finally found her money, counted out enough to cover the fee, and gave it to me. The clerk had been watching all the while and smiling covertly. He had often seen similar things when dealing with people from the Sandžak.

"I've been in your Bijograd, too," Azizehanma told me. "When?" I asked. "Before we came here," she replied. While telling me about her forthcoming move to Turkey, she vividly described one particular situation to me. Just before setting off, she had gone to Belgrade to visit her brother-in-law Juso, who was married to Buba, a woman from Belgrade. Buba's family had some wedding, and had invited Azizehanma, too. They were cooking some food (pork and beef) on a stove in the garden outside their house, and had set a dish aside for Azizehanma with some meat on it, close to other utensils in which the food was bubbling. "Oh, oh," she said. "I saw from the window that there were bubbles coming from their pans that could have splashed into mine." She would gesture to show how the bubbles were seething up and that "some drops could mingle," continuing the description: "They were all rising and could at any moment have splashed here or there. So I went down and moved the dish to one side. Never mind the food, I upset the hostess." Juso brought her cheese, jam, and yogurt. "Oh, that yogurt was wonderful," she said, ending her story. The yogurt was indeed good in Belgrade at that time.

My first visit to Turkey in 1968 had been very exciting. I was on an official visit to the Çekmece Nuclear Center in Istanbul. I looked forward to seeing what Turkey looked like as I traveled by train from Bulgaria. I knew so much about the country.

In Istanbul, I stayed with Hatidžehanma and Hasan *efendija,* but I could just as easily have chosen to stay in the European part of the city, at Taksim, where Uncle Osman had a place. The Veljović's's, now Velioĝlu, had become accustomed to Turkey. They were preparing to build a house at Erenkoy, in the Asian part of Istanbul.

In its extent and its international appearance, Istanbul reminded me of Paris. One could live there easily despite its size, and everything could be bought there, summer and winter. It need not be said that there were luxury hotels, and famous gymnasiums with a long tradition such as Galata Saray, the American and German colleges, and large Greek, Armenian, and Jewish communities with their churches and synagogues. There was also the Ecumenical Patriarchy, dating back to the time of the Byzantine Empire, the Bosporus and Dardanelles Straits sailed by great ships from all the countries of the world. For me, Istanbul was a great story of peoples through history, with the breath of the past to be felt at every step.

I could not easily choose what I liked best. But my heart was attached to the Suleiman Mosque, which from the boat looked as though it had grown organically from the earth; it dominated the quarter, reminding us for ever of Suleiman the Magnificent, the Lawgiver, and his broad legal vision of the order of such a great empire with its different peoples. The Suleiman Mosque also reminded me of the great Vezir, Mehmed Pasha Sokolović, one of our people, whose *turbe* (mausoleum) is hard by the mosque in the wide, shady courtyard. I was also impressed by Sultan Fatih's Mosque, from which mass *dženaze* of the victims of mutual killings set off during the time of unrest in Turkey in 1979. I had the opportunity to see this myself. When the procession set off from the mosque, it looked as though a black sea of people were pouring in waves through the broad streets, carrying on their shoulders the green islands of the victims, who were covered with green drapes, moving toward their final resting place.

When I returned to the Institute at the end of 1978, it was unsafe to be on the streets. We went through crossroads between double rows of armed soldiers standing so close that we could have touched them with our bodies. The military were escorting students to their classes after first separating rightists from leftists.

It happened that, while waiting for the bus to return from work, I unexpectedly found myself in the line of fire between rival groups. That winter we sat in almost cold laboratories at our work in the Çekmece Center. I used to freeze in the library packed with books. I would go out to find a tepid radiator to get warm. There I would talk sometimes with the students doing practices and with young associates, although it was rather dangerous to talk about politics. I used to ask them what they thought about the situation. We in Yugoslavia admired Ataturk both as a person and for what he had done. Here, listening to the young people, I began to doubt that some of his ideas were correct. They obviously had not been so universal as to be accepted by the entire Turkish nation and for the country to experience a renaissance.

I noticed that Ataturk's followers came particularly from among intellectuals, from education, and from among the wealthier classes. For them, the idea of Avrupa, as they called Europe, meant everything. They were not believers; on the contrary, they were atheists who wanted to be "emancipated." Looking at them, I at first could not believe that they were greater atheists than our own communists.

I wanted to see what had become of our people. They could be divided into two groups: those who had emigrated prior to World War II, and those afterward. Members of our family were everywhere, but mostly in Ankara, Istanbul, and Izmir. Few of them had made good, but their children had been educated and had a good social position.

The Turks called our people Bosniaks. Having emigrated during the period when development was at a standstill in the Sandžak, they continued to live as they had before. They were not very literate, the women barely at all, so traditions and stories were transmitted orally. Thus, a gap developed between them and us in Yugoslavia. Many of them pitied us and did not understand us. They had left the First Yugoslavia because they did not want to be under Serb domination, and had heard that in the Second Yugoslavia "everyone mixes, men and women, as in other faiths; they dance together." And, too, that "young people get married without regard to class or origin, sometimes not even to faith." Seeing them, we could see what a social revolution there had been in Yugoslavia during and since the Second World War; how our lives had been shaken to the core and oriented toward modernism.

The second generation that had emigrated after the Second World War was better able to cope. There were plenty of educated people among them who had held good jobs prior to emigrating to Turkey. Almost all of them had immediately bought or built houses and found employment, including many of the young women. The result was that they had rapidly stabilized, and their children had already graduated from university or the military academy. However, they had brought some socialist habits to Turkey with them, pressing for their rights, and were more critical. They did not blindly believe in nor were they simply in love with Turkish society. Moreover, even if some of them had at first lived worse than they had in Yugoslavia, they told me that they felt freer because they were not under pressure. "Everything's the same, except that there is not that pressure," they would repeat, adding, "We breathe more freely." Those from the Sandžak in particular said this.

One day I went with Azizehanma to visit Aya Sophia and Sultan Ahmed's Mosque. I wanted to show them to her and hear her impressions. We visited everything, just like other tourists. Finally, when we emerged onto the spacious square, I asked her whether she liked Aya Sophia. "Not at all; my word, what huge stones," she replied, perhaps to ease her pangs of conscience at entering what had once been a church. Our women did not go into churches. I laughed at her remark. I knew that, raised and living as she did on soft cushions, dressed in silks and velvets, she did not like to see the bare expanses of Aya Sophia, regardless of the fact that each of its pillars, its doors, and its spirit led us back deep into the history of the region and of the eastern Mediterranean, for these pillars were brought from destroyed temples to build Aya Sophia in Constantinople, the capital of Byzantium.

On another occasion, when I had to go to the Esenboĝa Institute for Water Resources Management near Ankara, I took Hatidžehanma to visit my sister Ferida, Lato, and other acquaintances. We were there for some fifteen days in winter—such as it can be on the high plateau deep inland on which Ankara is situated. One Sunday, we visited the mausoleum of Kemal Ataturk. We saw the changing of the guard and recited the *fatiha* for Ataturk and the students buried on the slope beside the mausoleum the authorities had killed during the unrest in Menderes's time. "Peace be on his soul," said

Hatidžehanma as she folded her hands after reciting the *fatiha,* "he made it possible for us to go about this country freely."

We returned on the comfortable Ankara–Istanbul train, which was not at all like ours in Yugoslavia at that time. Just before sunset, we came within reach of Istanbul. At one point in her story about old Hamam, Hatidžehanma noticed the area and the gentle rays of the sun through the window of the train that was now traveling somewhat more slowly. She said as though breathing a sigh of relief, "I thank the Lord when we return home," thinking of Istanbul. Probably this region and its people reminded her of the Sandžak more than did Anatolia. Thus it was that I came to know almost with surprise how much of a sacrifice it had been for them to leave their house, meadows, shop, and a fine lifestyle in small Prijepolje in order to come to Istanbul and start all over again in their old age. I looked at her and said, "We're back." Then I thought, "And where is my home: Belgrade or here?"

The period from 1960 to 1980 was the most prosperous time in Yugoslavia's history. We all would gather in Hasan *efendija*'s house in the summertime—those of our cousins from Turkey as well as those from Prijepolje, Sarajevo, and Belgrade. The house was lit up as if for a celebration and the Turkish neighbors were amazed that so many people came. No one knew how to enjoy themselves like the Yugoslavs. Some would sit at the dinner table talking while others sat in the drawing room watching television, for the news was very topical. Still others would be saying their prayers in Hatidžehanma's room, known as "Anna's room." The young people washed the dishes and talked as they prepared to serve sweetmeats and after-dinner coffee or tea, as people chose.

Those of us in the drawing room talked about everyday events, reminding each other of life in Prijepolje. Hasan *efendija* was glad to be in Istanbul, and said that everything was good in Turkey, even the cowboy films were adapted to the viewers. One heard "Merhaba" openly said, instead of its rough translation, "Good day," as in Yugoslavia. To which Halil, already an engineer from Istanbul's Faculty of Electrical Engineering, added, "Well, Babba, they have to translate it, since half of their people are illiterate." Hasan *efendija* read *Tercuman,* which was regarded as a somewhat right-wing newspaper, and thus formed his views of the situation and commented on events accordingly. One of his sons would suddenly interject, "And do you know, Babba, that the director of your newspaper is not a Muslim, but a *Jehudija* (Jew)?" We would all smile, but Hasan *efendija* was unperturbed. "What do I care? Let him write and do his job well."

In those days, Istanbul was being greatly spruced up. Highways were being laid along the sea, linking the city with expressways while preserving its historical antiquity. The opening of the bridge over the Bosporus to traffic was a major event. It was the first time that Asia and Europe had been linked "over ground." The bridge was overwhelmed by the Bosporus. Instead of disturbing the beauty of the area, it looked like a fine thread swaying in an arc over the water.

Abdullah, Hasan *efendija*'s son, one of the chief designers of traffic projects in Istanbul's city hall, had the opportunity to apply his knowledge, acquired in the Faculty of Traffic and Economics in Belgrade and in practice in Sarajevo, to the ancient city. The projects were expensive, since every inch of Istanbul, particularly in the old quarters, was scattered with antiquities above and below ground as soon as excavations began. Of course, they had to be preserved.

The low cost of travel and the frequency with which we met created the illusion both with them and amongst us in Yugoslavia that things were good for us and that we were close to one another. It remained so until prices began to rise steeply on both sides and there was unease because of the approach of war, the death of the older people, and the coming of age of the young—who regarded Turkey as their only homeland.

School and Party

8

I enrolled in the third year of gymnasium in September, 1947. There were two groups, each with thirty students. Students were not all the same age, since the schools had not been open during the war, except for a short period. My generation, like the previous one, finished the first segment of gymnasium after the third year, taking the so-called *mala matura* or "minor matriculation" as a test of our maturity. The Republic of Serbia was in a hurry to get educated cadres, so the government shortened the traditional period from four years to three for those who wanted to go to work or to vocational school. The majority of boys from Prijepolje went to technical school—especially in Belgrade, where they could expect scholarships and housing—or to the pedagogical school in Novi Pazar. Girls took jobs at institutions in town.

In the spring of 1948, the students in the gymnasium revolted concerning the selection of the president of the youth organization Omladina. I joined them, even though I was not yet a member. We began our strike by skipping school and meeting off campus to discuss the situation. It looked like we were going to win, because some members of the Omladina committee agreed with us. However, those members changed their minds after several meetings, so we went back to school. Our punishment was having our behavior grades "conditionally" reduced from "excellent" (five) to "very good" (four). "Conditionally" meant that our grades would be raised if our behavior improved before final exams that year. Students taking finals were supposed to appear with pencil and writing paper in the classroom where they were to take the exams, the first of which was composition in the Serbian language. In my day, the common theme was the revolution. The process lasted one week. Students were given a hundred questions for each subject in advance, of which we were expected to draw three at the exam. If we did not know the answers, we could change them once, with a special notation being entered to that effect. We had to answer at least two. Students who flunked one or two subjects had to take makeup exams; anyone failing three was required to repeat the grade.

When the commission members entered the room to tell us our overall grades, I was expecting to finish among the "excellent" students, who were absolved from taking the *mala matura* exam. However, because of the four rating I had received in behavior, I was not in that group. This came as a real shock to me, and for the next two hours I stared at the blank sheet of paper in front of me. It was only at the urging of a classmate that I began to write. After handing my composition to the proctor, I barely managed to pull myself together on the way home before I encountered a second punishment—this time from Babba. The principal of the gymnasium had dropped in at the shop and complained about my behavior. Babba ordered me to go to our "small room" where I had studied for my exams day after day, with Nanna bringing me my food. In the end, I passed the *matura* with an "excellent" rating and my behavior grade was then upgraded to five for the year and for the *matura*.

In September, 1949, I joined a group of about a dozen students from various parts of the Sandžak who continued on with the five-year program in the second part of gymnasium. We studied in a new building that had been erected on the place of the old gymnasium beside the bridge over the River Lim. It had sports fields as well. The new building was near the former Italian graveyard above the Catholic church. The mounds were already leveled and bushes and small trees that we had planted covered them. At one point during that winter, Italian women began coming to find the graves of their loved ones. We watched them from our classrooms as they wandered around the churchyard. We were not used to seeing foreigners, especially women, but we did not dare ask any questions. The janitors in the gymnasium told us who the women were. They had been told at the town hall that there was no graveyard here.

A new bridge was being built to replace the old one, which had been damaged several times during the war. On my way to school each day I saw the German woman who was supervising the work as the chief engineer. People said that she spoke our language. She was continually making calculations in a small notebook she held in her hand. The woman lived in a small barracks building and wore overalls and her hair up in a bun whenever she was at the work site. I was intrigued by her vocation. She left town when the bridge was finished in 1950 just as inconspicuously as she had lived among us. A number of German prisoners of war still remained in town, waiting for permission to settle in West Germany because they did not want to return to the torn country's eastern half.

Because there were few of us in the class, we had close contact with our professors and one another. We felt special because, as the oldest students in the school, we were permitted to answer questions in class without standing up and to behave rather freely in the presence of our teachers. I continued to mind cows in Polje and my fellow students would visit so we could study together. We would write, bracing our notebooks against the trunk of a tree or holding them on our knees as we sat on a verge. Even in the house we did not all have tables. I had my special corner in Mother's room where I would write on the wall seat while sitting on a *kilim.*

Professor Žarko Mihailović, who was said to have been exiled to Prijepolje from Serbia proper and to have been disfranchised, taught us math, physics, and geography, as well as botany in some grades. He was a good professor—perhaps the best I had. He was very strict, but he knew how to explain things and to ask questions so that we developed a clear understanding of each subject. I especially liked math and physical geography. We had several other excellent professors, like Dobrica Obradović. He, too, was an outsider from Serbia and served as both principal and our French teacher. Our class was his chief responsibility. We learned how to develop respect by observing his dignified approach to everything.

What Professor Mihajlović was for us, our relative Sadik Hodžić, who taught mathematics in Novi Pazar, was to the students at the gymnasium there. As their professor, he influenced a dozen students to complete their engineering studies at Belgrade Technical University. Most of them returned home afterward to work in their area. As a believer, however, he was forced to abandon his teaching position. He wandered from one school to another until 1957, when he emigrated to Turkey and became a professor at the military academy in Izmir.

It was in just such a school atmosphere that I began my preparations for entering society. After the Fifth Congress of the Communist Party, we became conscious that the Communist Youth League of Yugoslavia (Skoj) no longer existed and that some of our colleagues, especially those who lived in the dormitory, were either members or candidate-members of the Party. Their meetings were no longer secret and students who wished to were allowed to attend them.

I began to read newspapers in 1949, starting with *Borba.* It was full of accounts of trials in the Eastern bloc countries of communists who supposedly confessed that they had worked for Yugoslavia. The bookstore received only a few copies of *Borba,* so I submitted a request for one of my own. A little earlier, in history class, we were assigned *The Communist Manifesto* and after that *The History of the Soviet Communist Party.* One book we read in groups, each waiting for a turn. It all seemed like a great discovery to us: the struggle for justice and truth. I remember that we also shared *Wuthering Heights.* We were terribly disillusioned, however, when in responding to our professor's "What did you read this week," we were told that *Wuthering Heights* was not great literature for a gymnasium student to be reading. Great literature or not, we read Maksim Gorki's *Mother,* and Makarenko's *Pedagogical Poema,* as well as Fadeev's *Young Guard.* I read Sholokhov's *Virgin Soil Upturned.* His descriptions of village life even now remind me of Zalug. His village was redolent of barns full of wheat and of Zalug's cattle pens! At the same time, a world masterpiece like *A Thousand and One Nights* was unknown to us.

We knew nothing about Muslims in our day. In grade school and gymnasium it was as if they did not exist and there prevailed a general confusion about Muslims, as though the prewar doctrine that they were really Serbs was being continued. Muslims were even listed as Serbs or Montenegrins in postwar censuses. We were not even asked what our religion was, as happened to me. My personal documents all reflected that my nationality was Serbian, even though I was not listed as such in my birth records.

We also learned that classic Muslim ballads like "Hasanaginica" and "Omer and Merima," both translated into various European languages during the nineteenth century, were Serbian. This appropriation of Muslim cultural icons was so daring that Europe, without any perplexity, accepted Muslim cultural achievements as Serbian, whereas in Bosnia they were claimed to be Croatian. In other words, lies became truths.

We accepted these facts, but we disparaged the communists for their inconsistency, and we also knew that it would be no different in the Sandžak. We hoped and were almost convinced that by studying and joining society we would strengthen our ability to make our own way, however painfully and slowly. Somehow we also understood that it was better to create, even when others took it from us, rather than have nothing. In taking something of ours, *they* would have to become part of *us.* For example, one could never envision "Hasanaginica" as a portrayal of a Christian family.

Nevertheless, Muslims *were* on the Yugoslav scene. As early as August, 1949, in Prijepolje, I had seen in the newspaper *Politika* the pictures of four Young Muslims—students sentenced to death and executed in Sarajevo—as well as long articles about their activities being hostile to the state. All we could do was feel sorry for them, knowing that the charges were not true. There was no chance in those days of anyone doing anything against the state. We knew what happened to the communists who supported the Informbureau, including young people who were full of élan for building postwar Yugoslavia. Informbirovci, as our people called them, disappeared—and when they reappeared much later, they were completely changed and looked like they had aged considerably. I knew some of them personally later on, when they were having great difficulty finding a job.

During these years I used to visit my sister Ferida in Nova Varoš. While visiting her in the summer 1949, I made friends with Hata, the younger sister of Ferida's sister-in-law Halima. I would spend days in their house in a peaceful corner of town. There was a garden below the house through which a swift little stream ran. A new barn had been built at the head of the garden, with outside steps leading to the second floor, where the hay was stored. Its doors were always closed—in contrast to our barn, the doors of which were always left open and whose ladder we often climbed and then hid in the straw. I corresponded with Hata and was amazed at her fine letters and perplexed that she did not continue her schooling. Our friendship continued until Serbian Christmas on January 7, 1950. It was a Saturday, if I remember correctly, and so cold that even the Lim froze over. The *čaršija* was bare because of the cold, and Babba came home early. Nanna had cooked potato with lamb and brought it hot to the *sofra,* then waited for us to sit down. It had not yet turned dusk, but we had covered the windows with blankets in order to keep out the cold.

After praying the *akšam,* Babba told us that he had heard in the shop that the family of Ibrahim, Ferida's brother-in-law, had all been arrested in Nova Varoš and taken to the regional jail in Titovo Užice. The police had come from Serbia during the night and surrounded Nova Varoš. After tightening their ring, the police reached the barn. There they found Halima's relative, a professor of literature from Rogatica in Bosnia who belonged to the Young Muslims. He had been hiding there for more than half a year. I suddenly realized who had been writing me those letters, and I realized that I had written one to Hata not long before. I did not dare say anything, nor could I eat. I kept looking out the window at home and at school for the next two or three days, fully expecting the police to burst in and arrest me, just as they had done to Hata.

In September, 1950, at the beginning of my sixth year of gymnasium, my classmate Savo Kržavac invited me to the dormitory to chat about the Party. He told me that the communists at school and in town thought I would make a good Party member because I was "a good student and interested in social activity." Besides, they could see from examining my compositions that I had "the correct ideological-political views." First, however, I had to become a candidate. After two conversations I agreed to write a petition to the membership committee requesting that I be made a member of the Party. Still not quite seventeen, I was accepted at a Party meeting in the gymnasium and I remained a member for the next thirty-five years. It was not easy for me to become a Party member—just as it was not easy for me to leave the organization.

I told no one at home that I had joined the Party, thus beginning my separation from home and from the old way of life.

There were several reasons for me to join an organization that clashed with my Muslim upbringing and religion. First, I knew that the Partisans had saved us from the Chetniks and the injustice of the First Yugoslavia and that we owed the present government for the freedom and equality we had attained. In addition, our prewar way of life was spent. My parents began to adapt after a few years of communist rule, yet still lived and worked without any direct contact with the government. I received greater freedom at home, stopped wearing *dimije,* and was allowed to attend school programs after classes.

Upon finishing my sixth year of gymnasium, my parents gave me permission to work for the summer on the construction of the Doboj–Banja Luka railroad in Bosnia. This was almost the end of the era of the great construction drives, like the building of the Brčko–Banovići railroad in Bosnia, the Belgrade–Zagreb highway, the building of the New Belgrade, and the draining of the Pančevo Marsh to create arable land. Older people were forcibly recruited to work alongside the youthful volunteers for many of these campaigns. People in Prijepolje were afraid that their daughters would be mobilized, as had girls in Montenegro. This in fact happened if there were several girls in the same family.

Students from our gymnasium formed the Prijepolje Work Brigade. Its commander was Medo Hašimbegović, our physical education instructor. We spent a month working at Grapska station a kilometer or two from Doboj. We had a well-disciplined brigade and lived in a camp near the school, beside what today is a rail line. Farther on, at the construction site, there was a large international camp with young people who had come from all over the world to take part.

We got up at about 6 A.M. After inspection and roll call we cleaned up our area, then reported for work in formation after eating breakfast. We emptied railroad cars carrying earth for the embankments at a rate of one every four minutes. Each of us received a piece of bread and marmalade for a snack and we took breaks in the meadows along the Bosna River. At noon we marched back to camp in formation behind our flag bearer. We were allowed a short rest after eating and then returned to the railroad line. Because Muslim boys and girls did not eat pork, we had a tough time. They did not have separate cooking facilities for us, but we did not protest—it was normal for us.

We had an unexpected visitor at camp one day: Babba came to visit. He had some business in Sarajevo and decided to stop by en route. Medo brought me back from the work site so I could be with him. I had time to wash and change clothes before he saw me, but Babba still criticized the food situation. Medo had evidently explained to him that there was nothing to be done, that it was simply the way things were. Babba left us some money, but in vain: there was no store there and the town was too far away.

I experienced my first love before going off on this campaign. A classmate and I began to develop a special relationship in the close school atmosphere. He had shown interest in me earlier, sometimes accompanying me to the suspension bridge below Banka. That companionship gradually transformed itself into a mutual love of which we both became painfully aware, especially since I was a Muslim girl and he was of another faith. Both of our parents noticed this and I felt my parents' concern. Even though they said nothing, my conscience bothered me.

We stood up all night on the return trip home, looking out the train window while most of the others slept. Sometimes Commandant Medo would join us. He pretended that he did not notice anything, but it seemed to me he had been watching me vigilantly ever since Babba's visit. We parted for the rest of vacation when we got back to Prijepolje. I went to Sarajevo in the fall while he continued his education in Titovo Užice. We corresponded throughout the semester and met in Prijepolje during the winter holidays, but we both felt that something had changed. Summer came and we got together again. After a couple of dates in Polje it became evident that our individual desires did not match: he sought a freer relationship, although he never expressed it, whereas I wanted a platonic love and companionship that no longer seemed attainable after we left our old school.

I received a letter from him breaking up our relationship after we returned to school. He said we had no future together because he respected his mother, who strongly opposed mixed marriages. Yet after gymnasium, at university, and even later in life, the bond we had developed grew into a kind of friendship.

My small class did not return to gymnasium in the fall. The Prijepolje town council instead decided to give us a one-year hiatus so that the much larger group of students in the grade behind us could catch up. This meant that those of us who wanted to continue our education during the coming year would have to go elsewhere. Babba sent me to Sarajevo, to the home of Pašahanma Mašović in Bistrik. Pašahanma was the daughter of Nanna's Aunt Đula and the sister of Ibrahim *aga* Veljović, whose garden with the Vuk fountain was located above Polje.

I enrolled in the seventh grade of the Second Girls' Gymnasium, which stood on the banks of the Miljacka River in the vicinity of Princip's Bridge, near the place where Austria's Archduke Ferdinand was assassinated in

1914. Pašahanma's sons and daughters were Muslim intellectuals. Her oldest son, Suleiman, was a sociology professor at Zagreb University. His wife, Fatima, was a doctor and the daughter of the Karabeg of Mostar, the translator of the Qur'an. Fatima's brothers and sisters had been imprisoned as Young Muslims. After gaining their release, they emigrated to Austria and Switzerland.

Pašahanma's son Omer, a solicitor and later a lawyer, had recently been released after serving eight months in prison for being a Young Muslim. He was the first to help me adapt to my new environment, giving me books from his personal library—including some in French, which was for me quite a novelty. I got his Latin grammar text from the Sarajevo Classical Gymnasium he had attended, which had been discontinued following the war after being deemed unnecessary. Their daughter Igbala was also a lawyer, as well as the mother of two small sons. The youngest, Džemal, a university student and yet another future lawyer, used to bring me news from the university when he came home in the evening. That was my first contact with university life.

The school itself represented a great change for me, as relations between students were not as direct as I had been used to in Prijepolje. We addressed our teachers as "Madame" or "Sir" instead of "Comrade," as was the case in the Prijepolje gymnasium, and greeted them with "I kiss your hands" instead of "Good morning" or "Good day." Most of the teachers were women, including one Muslim, Belkisa Fazlagić, who taught philosophy and was married to a Christian.

Our building, in which the First Girls' Gymnasium was also located, dated back to Austro-Hungarian times. Similar buildings located on the other side of the bridge housed the First and Second Boys' Gymnasiums, the Economics School (formerly known as the Commercial School), as well as the School of Applied Art. The latter was soon closed after being deemed unnecessary. In spite of the system of staggered recesses used by both schools to keep the male and female students from creating large crowds and from associating with one another during school hours, news of happenings in the different schools quickly became common knowledge. The *raya* (slang for boys and girls) could be seen walking together during *corso* in the early evening on Tito's Street, or more freely along the Wilson Boardwalk by the Miljacka River. However, going from the gymnasium to the *corso* or the boardwalk was like passing from the patriarchal way of life into Western European culture.

Our class had about an equal number of Muslim, Orthodox, and Catholic students. We prepared our written assignments for our professor of Serbo-Croatian, Olga Hadžistević, alternately in Latin and Cyrillic. She singled me out by frequently asking me short questions with the expectation of quick, brief answers. Perhaps she did this to "bring me along" as a newcomer, or perhaps it was from sentimentality since my dialect was *ekavian* (*mleko* not *mlijeko*)—the Serbo-Croatian variant used in Belgrade, where she had earned her degree in literature.

The mother of Nenad Kecmanović taught us history. Before the Bosnian war broke out in 1992, he held an important position on the Serbian side in Bosnia and Yugoslavia. Kristina Kostić, who was responsible for the class during its full eight-year cycle, was maternally strict, causing fear and trembling in all the girl students—especially those she spotted outside after nine o'clock at night. The lame figure of our chemistry teacher, Miss Latal, a true Croat, still lingers in my memory. She used to call me *kiseonik* and *vodonik* because I used those two *ekavian* terms for the main elements of water, while in the Croatian variant they were called *kisik* and *vodik.*

Almost all our books and textbooks were written in Latin letters in *ijekavian* and the Western variant Serbo-Croatian used in Zagreb. In the beginning I would gloss the words in my own dialect, but later I was able to read with more ease, while at the same time managing to retain my own *ekavian* dialect. The girls' uniform consisted of a light blue pinafore with a white collar and a cap with our grade number on it. We were not allowed to put on lipstick, wear nylons, or be seen out on the street late at night.

The communist influence was less visible in this school than in Prijepolje. It seems to me that with the exception of Professors Fazlagić and Danica, the principal, there were no communists among the teachers. Perhaps it is because the Sarajevo professors were older than those in Prijepolje. Serbs were the directors of the gymnasiums, both in Prijepolje and Sarajevo.

Omladina was not very active in our school, its activities being rather limited in both number and variety. Nor did we have a Party organization. Omladina was more apolitical: it had art and literary sections in which students tested their aptitude in one or the other area. There was a lot less enthusiasm than we were accustomed to back in Prijepolje. The girls seldom went on construction drives in the summer and they were unwilling to work for free to help weaker pupils. In fact, one could say that they were mainly individualists. National allegiance was not neglected, however, as students normally observed their religious holidays, going either to their mosques or their churches. Saint Basil's Day was celebrated separately in his church at Bistrik near the Catholic seminary, while Easter and Christmas ceremonies were held in the churches and cathedral not far from the school.

Muslim girls who went to the mosque were not to be seen after school on the street and during the *corso,* nor were they members of the Omladina organization. My friend Nezahat was an excellent student who earned her teachers' respect with her serious comportment and because she knew everything. We spent some time together on an excursion to the steel mill at Zenica, during which she told me that she was going to study medicine in Sarajevo. She lived in her house near the *baš čaršija* (main bazaar) and studied alone.

I had introduced the practice of studying with and helping students who had problems with math and science and who were even afraid of geography because of the strictness of "Kostićka," as we called our class's faculty supervisor. Only Dragica Kalember managed to get a five in geography from her during the fall term. Only two others managed to get a five by the end of the year. Kostićka seldom called on Dragica, but when she did, the girl's answers were exact. The two of us sat at the same desk. Dragica later got her doctorate in law in France and moved to Belgrade, where, as a Serb, she felt more comfortable than she would have at the law school in Sarajevo.

Even if Kostićka was not disposed toward me at first, she was always fair. I eventually became her most trusted pupil. My knowledge of physical geography, instilled in me by Prof. Žarko Mihajlović at Prijepolje, soon became apparent. I gradually gained her favor, beginning with humiliating threes, and reaching fives with my responses to her requests to go to the board and, by using mathematical calculations as well as maps, show how trade winds were formed, monsoons, sea currents, and so forth. I had made up my mind to be better in something than the students from the big city and the well-known gymnasiums. I came out best in the sciences, but the Sarajevo girls were superior in languages, which probably reflects the major difference between the Prijepolje and Sarajevo gymnasiums.

That summer, I went with the Sarajevo Omladina Brigade to work on the hydroelectric dam at Jablanica in Herzegovina. In the ravines of the Rama River we traced out a new road above the future lake. Because of the extreme heat, we often worked at night instead of during the day. We slept on bunk beds with straw mattresses in stone barracks. The heat and the explosions used to dislodge the hard stone for the base of the dam are my clearest memories of that work.

After my return, I received an invitation from the Party's City Committee to become a candidate for membership. I accepted the candidacy and soon after was a member.

The City Committee was located in the center of Sarajevo, opposite the Alipaša Mosque. I had heard of it—and its secretary, Hamdija Pozderac—right after my arrival. It was the locus of political life and planning for the development of Sarajevo. It was an honor for me to become a member and a challenge to be in the company of its leader. Along with that, I felt more at home in Sarajevo, where a significantly higher number of Muslims were in government positions. I went regularly to committee sessions, which usually were held after work. All sorts of things were discussed, including reports from factories and important institutions. Political life in the city was included in the daily order of business, as well as various events in the country in general, and Bosnia and Herzegovina in particular. I remember shabby reports about love affairs in upper class Sarajevo society, with fatal consequences for some, like the mother of my classmate, a Party member, who hanged herself.

Constant topics were the city's lagging development and helping newcomers to make their suburban housing developments more civilized. During that period, the city limits were around Marindvor and the Wilson Boardwalk along the Miljacka. The building of a new railroad station and of New Sarajevo had begun, as well as of the suburb of Grbavica, where hitherto there had been only rows of barracks and little houses in which workers lived. The village of Pale and the Romanija Mountain, through which I used to pass when I took the Ćira train home to Prijepolje, were associated with the Chetniks, of whom people would say: "It happened, may it never return!" Hrasnica Plain was still a farm area with fields of wheat and they were digging the foundations for the Famos complex, a motor manufacturing facility. The suburb of Ilidža (the Turkish name for spa), with its beautiful natural surroundings and its famous row of plantain trees extending from the front of the hotel to the raging Bosna River, was almost unpopulated, except for its hotel.

Hamdija Pozderac expressed himself rationally and without jargon, and did not mispronounce words like *konferencija* (conference), as happened in Prijepolje among the majority of barely literate bureaucrats. He reduced problems to work assignments, thus abbreviating our meetings. If I were to typify my attitude toward him at the time, it would be one of respect, perhaps even admiration. Was it because he, a Muslim, was in such a high position? I am not sure, but I think it was because he was first of all an intellectual, of a stamp that was altogether new. He was more intelligent and educated than any of the rest of us had met until then. As a communist, he had no interest in personal riches, a quality I valued highly. He was a Muslim who was not in conflict with the state—he was creating it. In addition, he came from a large extended family like mine, from the undeveloped Bosnian Krajina. Muslims there were in the majority, just as they were in the Sandžak.

Not long after I joined the committee, I also became head of my school's Omladina chapter. I was elected by secret ballot and had only one other competitor: Nevenka, a Serbian girl. An excellent student, she later studied chemical engineering at Belgrade University. She missed winning by only a few votes.

It was customary for members of the Party Committee to attend the more important meetings of institutions and factories. I was told that Hamdija would be responsible for my school as well as the First Boys Gymnasium, where Željko Ostojić was president of the Omladina chapter. Željko was an excellent student who was preparing for electrical engineering studies in Belgrade, after which he planned to emigrate to the United States. The two of us were responsible for the special secondary schools, including the school of apprentices, whose students were a problem—especially those who lived in the dormitory or were from the homes for neglected children. They wandered the city at night, attacking passersby in back streets. The government sent the more serious offenders to reform schools. Such problems began to mount with the influx of people from the rural population into the settlements around Sarajevo.

At one of our meetings, I received material about the Youth Vacation League (YVL), which had existed in the First Yugoslavia and attracted students preparing for outings and travels. At the beginning of October, 1952, as a delegate from Bosnia and Herzegovina, I went to the YVL's main organizational assembly in Belgrade. It was my second visit to Belgrade in a short period of time, since I had just returned from a tour of Yugoslavia as a traditional part of our graduation program called "Know Your Homeland!" I received per diem for this second trip to Belgrade and stayed at the Hotel Balkan in the center of town. The assembly was held in the auditorium of the City Committee of the Party, at Students' Square. I did not know it at the time, but that square was destined to encompass much of my life, both personal and professional.

The YVL was projected as the first independent organization, and for that reason there was discussion at the assembly as to whether it would develop into an opposition party. That never happened, though. The organization was strangled during the process of formation because the state did not return its prewar properties—buildings in various towns and vacation places on the sea and in the mountains—as it had promised. Possession of those properties would have made the YVL truly independent.

After returning to Sarajevo, Željko and I received invitations to a special concert at the National Theater, in honor of the Day of the Republic, November 29. I wore my school pinafore with its white collar and we sat in the second row with Hamdija.

One of the frequent topics at City Committee meetings was the Muslim youth and the influence on them by the Gazi Husrev Beg *medresa* and mosque. Gazi Husrev Beg, the second real founder of Sarajevo, was governor of Bosnia from 1521–1541. When I came to Sarajevo, no one spoke publicly of the Young Muslims. People suspected of being in contact with them—like Omer Mašović and Muhamed Kemura, in whose house I stayed during the last school year—could not find work. Mašović worked as a bookkeeper and Kemura as a temporary clerk in the State Museum, a job he got through friends. The Gazi Husrev Beg *medresa* was also under attack after communists executed four students.

At a committee meeting, three of us were assigned to go to the *medresa,* which was in close proximity to my school, and prepare to organize an Omladina chapter there—a plan that had been dropped a year or two earlier. This was the first time I entered Sarajevo's *medresa* and its classrooms, which the professors showed us while acquainting us with their work. The rooms were full of squalid furniture and old desks, and the floors were covered with worn out, partly torn linoleum. The pupils' books were neatly arranged on their desks. Everything transpired softly, with little talk, and with self-effacement and even discomfort. We gave them materials about forming an Omladina unit and left. I did not go there again. I related my experiences at the *medresa* to Kemura. He had nothing to say. In the glass-paneled bookcase in his workroom was a library full of books about Bosnia, many of which had been collected by his father, Sejfullah, who was himself a writer and collector of inscriptions from Muslim monuments. One day not long afterward, Kemura advised me to read these books. "When you work late, you can sleep here," he suggested, thus making his room available to me, with its comfortable sofa in the corner and a big desk with plenty of drawers and writing materials in them.

A second topic at the meetings of the Party's City Committee was the gathering of the Muslim youth for the Ramadan evenings in the courtyard of the "Begova džamija," the Gazi Husrev Beg's mosque. This was especially massive during the summer of 1953 and had the appearance of a protest. The area around the mosque, as well as the little streets that house the private shops in the *baš čaršija,* was teeming with young boys and girls. The girls, wearing *dimije* and white prayer shawls, strolled along the illuminated streets.

All this unfolded some one hundred meters from the customary *corso* on Tito's Street. It was as though two different worlds existed—which the state itself had created through its prejudicial attitude toward religion and religious people. The young people belonged to all social classes, but the majority of them came from the trades and former commercial families. Besides those gatherings, home parties came gradually into style. During school vacations, young intellectuals, university students, and the descendants of former "enemies of the regime" or of rich families would meet at these get-togethers. With what was left of family wealth, or through other means, they were studying mostly outside of Sarajevo—either in Zagreb, not infrequently in Austria, or in the Arab lands.

Living with Mašović and Kemura, I was in the same circle of young people. Except for students, I was not interested in gatherings of the descendants of once-rich families, even though I did go to some with Raif, Kemura's only son, who was a student in the electrical engineering department at Ljubljana University. Raif frequented such parties because he knew how to play the accordion and had an almost heavenly voice. As Kemura's heir, he was a desirable marriage prospect in this society, but I seemed to have inherited my mother's aversion to getting rich through marriage.

The City Committee did not take action to block the evening *corso* around the Beg's mosque or in the *baš čaršija.* The majority of members believed that with the continued weakening of religion, the gatherings would eventually cease. Perhaps the administration was afraid to touch such a massive expression of protest within the framework of Ramadan, which the communists could not easily channel in a peaceful manner.

During the holidays, I would go home on the Ćira train via Pale and Priboj. At Priboj, I would try to find a place in the mail truck to Prijepolje, which was not easy.

Returning from a weekend at home on the November 29 national holiday, in an almost completely empty train coach with wooden seats, I peered through the window into the darkness, barely able to wait until we arrived. Sometimes a person would walk by and catch my eye. Once, I saw a tall young man with a red scarf walking through the car. He strolled past me and then turned back and sat down opposite me. It was Derviš Hasanagić, a former student of the Prijepolje gymnasium who had gone on to the well-known Petar Drapšin Engineering School in Belgrade to continue his education. Sitting there on the bench in the coach, he tried to start a conversation, joking and interjecting remarks like: "How's it going, Prijepolje girl?" I did not like that kind of talk, regarding it as provincial. I barely answered him and pretended I was sleeping. We finally reached Bistrik Station, and as I prepared to get off, he helped me with my things and commented that he was a teacher in the technical center for the school district, which was not far from my gymnasium.

After winter vacation that year, Aunt Zina gave me a small package to carry to Derviš. I was taken by surprise but agreed to do it. I went to the technical center where Derviš worked to give him the package, but we immediately got into an argument and I left the center angry. During Ramadan, just before the end of classes, Derviš and I met again and agreed to go on a date. We got together after class on the bridge by my gymnasium, and walked along the banks of the Miljacka. We went through the Bembaša area and when we reached the "Goat's Bridge" we climbed to a valley above the roadway and sat down. Derviš proposed to me, asking me to go with him to Priboj where he had been given a position in the FAP automobile factory, which had just gone into production that year. While trying to tell me why he wanted to marry me, he talked about young people's drinking parties, about some relative who was pregnant and how that might cause a problem for him. He said he had singled me out as the ideal girl "from the other side," that is, from the old-fashioned, patriarchal milieu. I did not understand what he was talking about, except that his life seemed alien to me, and I wanted to continue my studies. I told him no.

While we were talking, Derviš pulled me onto the grass and began to embrace me. I resisted, trying to get up, but when I could not I stopped defending myself for a moment and turned my head away. That gesture seemed to get to him. He sat up and moved away, covering his face with his hands. I stood up and put my hand on his shoulder, as a signal that I wanted to talk with him, but I became afraid when I felt his shoulder tremble. Suddenly, I was conscious of the darkness, which had set in shortly before. I could barely make out his face. I wanted to get home as fast as I could. I got up silently and we walked down through the meadow, parting at Bembaša, near the Emperor's Bridge. I went home and began to wash in order to remove his touch from my face and to revive myself. I felt badly that it was Ramadan, and I asked myself what I was doing.

About ten days later, I encountered Derviš on my way to school, this time in a nearby park. He was with a girl in a beautiful white dress with pleats, which was then the fashion. She wore her black hair in a bun and her face was pale white. He got up from the bench and introduced me to his fiancée. I wished them good luck and continued on to school. I recalled his vague talk in the meadow about modern life, but that no longer interested me.

The final or eighth year of gymnasium ended at the beginning of June, so that students could take the *velika matura,* the major comprehensive examinations. Those who had scored "excellent" overall up to that point, had to take only a written exam in Serbo-Croatian, plus one foreign language—either Russian or French. At that time, English was not studied in our gymnasiums. My composition in the native language was best and was sent to the archives of the student section of the National Library. At the graduation ceremony, the commission declared our class to be the best, with eight students in the "excellent" category and no one having to repeat the grade. For our excellent grades and participation in work drives outside of school, Nevenka and I received Vladimir Dedijer's *Biography of Marshal Tito.* Dedijer later became a Yugoslav dissident.

I said goodbye to Sarajevo, which I had just begun to get used to, and left for Prijepolje to prepare for my university entrance examinations.

During the summer of 1953, our brook flooded Polje, altering it forever with great deposits of sand and stones. The lower house, at the bottom of Polje, suffered the least damage, but it took us some time before we were able to move back into it. In August, Uncle Osman arrived from Istanbul with his family for the circumcision of his son Bilen at the family homestead. We got over the flood and prepared a great celebration. The fences were decked with lights, and guests came from everywhere, including Kemura from Sarajevo and Uncle Ibrahim from the town of Bijeljina in Bosnia. For the first time since 1933, all of Babba's brothers and sisters were together, giving us the opportunity to see them all.

After the circumcision ceremony had been celebrated, the Udba called Babba to their office. They informed him that Osman was an undesirable person and that he had to leave the country—supposedly for having said something against the government. He was given two days advance warning, out of respect for Babba's reputation.

Osman had taken the train from Sarajevo to Priboj during his trip to our home and from there rode the crowded bus to Prijepolje. When he got off the train, he told the conductor, "It's hard to tell who's buying and who's drinking here!" Our elders were at a loss to come up with any other cause for his abrupt deportation, except for that quip. They doubted that it was because of the big celebration for the circumcision. Osman's family left helter-skelter, accompanied to the station by many relatives and friends, including those of Osman's wife, Aziza, who was a Prijepolje native from the family of Pašanović. We took everyone's photograph, as was the custom when people traveled a long distance and would not be back soon.

Babba, who had been thinking about my education, thought of sending me to Zagreb University, where I could stay with some friends of his. We were unsuccessful in that, so I went to Belgrade and signed up for physical chemistry without having to take an entrance exam, as it had been eliminated that year. After enrolling, I went to the window labeled "Students' Questions" to see about housing. I learned that certain groups had the right to state housing and that the children of workers and office employees who did not pay taxes had first priority. Since the majority of applicants were in that category, I was turned down. I returned home to Prijepolje.

Not long after Osman's departure, Babba fell ill. His doctor, Simo Simotas suspected he had liver cancer and told me first. He suggested that Babba go to the mountains to rest. We called Aunt Zina in Priboj and asked her to come and help us. We took him to the village of Kosatica, in the foothills of

Mount Zlatar, right below Merica Cliff. Babba rented a house from the Šantić family. As the disease progressed it became difficult for him to sleep, so we took turns sitting with him. Aunt Zina cooked his favorite dishes, but alas, he could not eat them.

Early one evening, Babba pointed out some barely visible houses in the forest on the other side of the Mileševka River Canyon. He asked me if I dared to go there—to the homes of his customers, Serbs Mihajlo and Radoš. He wanted me to ask them to send horses to take him back to Polje. Even though I was fearful, I told him I would do it. He explained how I should go, what to watch out for in order to avoid meeting men in the forest, and the shortcut to their houses. By the time I reached the fenced-in pasture around the houses it was pitch dark and the cattle had already been fed. Through the spare patches of field I could make out the owners inside their house and I yelled our traditional, drawn-out cry: "Ooooo . . . master of the house!" so that their dogs would not attack me. I also signaled who I was and shouted my father's name and why I had come.

They let me into their compound, giving me a piece of bread with *kajmak* to gulp down while I waited for one of their sons to get ready to go with me into the mountain meadows for some horses. Another son had earlier led the horses there to graze after a hard day's work. We climbed up the mountain with only the light of the moon. Fortunately, the meadows were in the direction of our ultimate destination, Kosatica. After saddling the horses, we continued on, reaching Kosatica about midnight. We helped Babba onto one of them and put our things on the other. Aunt Zina stayed behind to straighten up the house. Again we crossed the Mileševka Canyon, passed by the monastery of Mileševa and went right through the town of Prijepolje, reaching home at dawn. Babba was soon taken to the Koševo hospital in Sarajevo, where he died on Friday, October 23. Omer Mašović and Kemura were with him. Muslims believe that people who die on Friday were good in this life and will enjoy God's mercy in the next. For that reason, they say "Allah's mercy on his soul."

I left Prijepolje for Belgrade two days before he died, because classes had begun. There I learned that the expenses of private lodging were twice what they were for a dormitory room. With Babba at death's door, I knew that there simply was no money for my living expenses, so I went back to Polje. The next morning the telegram came with the information that Babba had died. I was in Mujaga's courtyard at the time and even though people tried to keep the news from me, I felt his death anyway. The men started getting ready to go to Sarajevo for the funeral, while others dropped in to visit. I went down to the Baskije, our fenced area by the River Lim and sat on the verge. I took in my Polje. Everything that had been part of my life was gone, and now Babba had left me.

Zlatulja had been the first to die that summer—it seemed to me that she herself announced this impending end. She could not eat and lost weight. Babba tried to get help from a veterinarian, but he said there was no hope—she had swallowed a piece of metal. They took her to the butcher shop so she would not suffer any longer. Her meat was distributed to the poor, while I was left with memories.

When the men came back from Babba's funeral, Uncle Abid dropped Babba's identification card on the large table in the room where Babba had often cut cloth and wailed: "Ćamil is dead!" His son Muhamed, who was in his third year in the navy, could not attend the funeral because of the Trieste crisis. When he did return, he could only say: "Adžo is gone." It was a big blow to everyone that Babba died so unexpectedly in his fifty-seventh year. In December, Uncle Ibrahim, who still bore the effects of the Chetnik slaughter in East Bosnia in 1942, also died.

We had spent a lot for Babba's medicine and hospitalization. As a private businessman, he did not have any health insurance. We closed his shop but we needed money to pay the various taxes he owed, even for the farmlands that the storm had laid waste. I stayed in Prijepolje for two months, taking care of business. Some people suggested I get a job, but Nanna and I were against that. We sold some sheep from the village, Babba's sewing machine, some land, and gave other things away. But we realized that we had to reorganize our house for a new life.

I would not let Nanna and the rest of my family sell what was left in order to support my university studies. I decided to go to Belgrade and seek help from the *Maršalat,* Marshal Tito's cabinet, to which people turned in moments of extreme need. When I reached the Maršalat, I was led to the office of Jože Vilfan, a Slovene who headed Tito's Cabinet. I asked for a scholarship and housing on the grounds that I was an excellent student and member of Omladina, as well as of the Party, with no right to student lodging because I was the daughter of an independent businessman. I was convinced that I was right: this was *our* country, which we had all worked to build, and therefore we had the right to certain benefits when the need arose. Perhaps my performance and my youth won Dr. Vilfan's sympathy. He listened kindly to my petition and advised me to return home and wait for their answer.

After a week or so, a courier called me to the mayor's office in Prijepolje. "You're sick of us, eh?" the mayor joked, getting up from behind his desk. "No," I answered flippantly. "I'm just looking for aid to go to school." I saw on his desk a communiqué with the word *Maršalat* printed in big letters. I had already been to city hall a month before, when they called me in to inquire about Uncle Osman and what he had done in Turkey. They had begun with the usual, "Tell us everything—we know everything anyway!" At the time, this thinly disguised threat made me think, "If you already know everything, why did you call me in?"

During those years, this was the common way of beginning an interrogation of students, and probably of others as well. When I was a university student, Udba watched how we students socialized. Was it just Muslims with Muslims and Serbs with Serbs, or did we mix? Students joked about the Udba surveillance.

The mayor handed me the communiqué from Belgrade. It said that I had been granted a place in the Student City. It also recommended that the town council grant me a scholarship of five thousand dinars a month from the town's education fund. The customary stipend was three thousand dinars, so this much larger sum would surely cover all of my expenses.

After obtaining my scholarship, I packed my personal effects in a canvas bag and set off for Belgrade at the end of January, 1954, to begin my studies at the Faculty of Natural Sciences and Mathematics (PMF). I had the number of my room in Student City written on a scrap of paper, together with the name of the liaison person. After completing the registration and getting my bed linen I went into the four-bed room in block two, where the women students lived. There I found three fellow students: Zora and Danica, mathematics students from Šumadija in central Serbia, and a Macedonian named Vera, a geology student. At that time, the *brucoši* (freshmen) lived in four-bed rooms on the ground floor of the hostel blocks. Our furniture consisted of a plywood cupboard and a small table and chairs. Each room also had water and a coal-fired stove. It was our job to keep the room clean and to bring in the coal. Life in Student City was only just beginning. There were about five thousand students living in the hostel, including nearly two thousand "illegals," students who did not have the right to student accommodations. For all that, they were living there with the tacit agreement of the administration and remained "invisible" to those making sporadic nighttime checks on the occupants. They slept in the beds of students who were absent, and it seems that there were resales, too.

Student City was composed of five parallel five-story blocks with F-shaped wings, standing in a fairly large area that had just been planted with trees. The buildings were new, with parquet floors in the rooms and the corridors; the rooms led onto balconies with a view of the parks, with handsome avenues between the buildings. At the rear of the hostel, right alongside the fence, was the old Zemun airport, and the road beside the hostel led to Bežanija suburb and the nearby Zagreb–Belgrade "Highway of Brotherhood and Unity."

Student City itself was erected on marshy ground as part of the planned construction of New Belgrade, which had just begun in those days. The deserted, uninhabited area some eight kilometers from Belgrade was dumped day and night with sand from the Sava and the Danube, which was carried by water through large pipes. A little farther along toward the Danube channel, there gaped the concrete buildings of the Federal Executive Council and the Hotel Yugoslavia, begun and then halted by the blockade imposed by the Eastern Bloc. The Federal Executive Council building, which was later completed, was designed in the form of a roman numeral one in memory of the 1st Roman Regiment, which had been located on this site in the former settlement of Singidunum, the precursor of Belgrade—or so people believe—two thousand years ago.

We still had no bathrooms in the dormitories, so we went to the Belgrade baths in Mišarska and on Dušanova Street, where one could stay under the shower for about ten minutes for the ten dinars price of one entry ticket. The cubicles were more expensive, and we did not like them anyway.

To begin with, our canteen was a rather long way away in a hut on the site of the present-day Belgrade department store. Later, a modern, circular canteen was built between the blocks. The food served to us was very poor. Those who had money could buy things at the nearby markets. Most of us preferred to spend our money on the cinema, where the movies were mostly American, and we even sold meal coupons to buy tickets for the movies. The prices were exactly the same, forty dinars, perhaps. We rarely drank coffee, juice, Coca Cola, or similar soft drinks in those days, and we ate a lot of fresh and dried fruit. It could be said that we paid little attention to food. The students had no weight problem. We were served a free breakfast in the faculties, thanks to American aid: a slice of yellow cheese that was rather bitter for our taste, or "Truman's eggs," a little similar to scrambled eggs, with a slice of bread and a glass of powdered milk.

Students associated very little with Belgrade families. Sometimes they would visit people from their region or they would make contact with some family or other. My first acquaintances were of the same type. When our people began to emigrate to Turkey, I became acquainted with a Turkish Bosnian family: Hadija Spahi, who worked in the Turkish Embassy, his wife Nura, and their four sons. Through them I got to know two Albanian Bosnian families. Imer and Rabija lived in a tall prewar building in Students' Square. Farther down the hill, on Jevremova Street, Emin and Veda had their apartment. Nearby was Belgrade's sole mosque: the Bajrakli Mosque. It was at the Spahis's house that, somewhere around 1955, I saw the first

Palestinian refugees who came through Belgrade en route to Algeria and Morocco. Once I saw a young woman with three children to whom Nura served lunch in her yard. We in Yugoslavia knew little about the tragedy of the Palestinian people, although we knew that Israel had been formed in 1948. We often read in *Politika* about the Jewish farmers' great achievements in cultivating desert land, and we used to buy Jaffa oranges in our marketplace.

For the first two years it was very difficult for us to get to the faculty. During those exceptionally cold winters we waited in long lines for the only number thirty-six bus to appear from Bežanija to take us to Belgrade. Both students and other passengers liked to travel as stowaways and thus avoid having to pay the conductor for their tickets. The most popular personality at that time was "Ridgway," as the students called the ticket inspectors. They named him after the commanding officer of the American army during the Korean War. Being able to spot Ridgways and avoid having them check your ticket was a real art. People who did not like to tempt fate paid a flat monthly student fare of about four hundred dinars that allowed them to go anywhere on the municipal bus line.

We rarely studied in our rooms. There was always a lot of coming and going as we got together to talk about the day's events. On Sundays, the football match would be broadcast over the Student City public address system. Male students occupied four of the dormitory blocks and women students lived in the fifth one. Women students could go into the men's blocks during "visiting hours," twice a week from four to eight in the evening, and the men could visit ours in the same way. Drinks and playing cards were banned in the hostel.

Students who had practical classes (ones that involved experiments or use of the library) would spend their days in town, learning and doing the practicals in the faculties themselves or in the university library. They would then go out "into the wide world": to the cinema, to dances, or to the famous restaurants and cafés, such as Stambol Kapija (Stambol Gate). It was not expensive. We used to go to the theater, too, with prepaid tickets or a discount on entry. The best-known theaters were the Yugoslav Drama Theater, which I liked, and the National Theater on Republic Square, where operas were also performed. There was also the Comedy Theater in Terazije, and an experimental stage with avant-garde plays.

The hostel became fuller and fuller at the end of the academic year as students completed their practicals and spent more time in their rooms. Many of our fellow students would let their beards grow until they passed their exams. Their only recreation was brief outings to the canteen and the football world premiers that were broadcast over the public address system. Student

City was lit up like a torch during the June examinations, with students studying until late at night. They would go out onto the balconies for a breather and sometimes break the silence, or rather the subdued murmur, with some loud exclamation or by calling to fellow students living in the other blocks. It was usually only a brief interruption, and then the atmosphere of hard work would return. Few students remained in the City during the summer. Most of them were in a hurry to return home, but there were always hostels "on duty" for those who were doing postgraduate studies, continuing their studies, or had other reasons to stay in Belgrade.

There were only a few Muslims in my faculty. Among them was the Albanian Derviš Rožaja, who later became rector of Priština University, in biology. The older Sandžak generation, held back by the war, was already in Belgrade at the Faculties of Medicine, Economics, and Philosophy (the humanities). There was a largish group of students from my generation, mostly from Novi Pazar, studying at the technical faculties, particularly the Faculty of Civil Engineering. Among them was my friend Smajo Saračević, later known as Victor Sedlar when he emigrated to the United States. The Omerbegović girls came a little later: Mevluda to the Faculty of Medicine and Ulvija to study pharmacy.

In 1954, foreign students from Africa, Asia, the United States, and Canada were already coming to Student City. There was a large group of students originally from our country that had been taken to the Soviet military academy as children. After the break with the Soviet Union, Yugoslavia withdrew them. The students were accommodated in two-bed rooms on the principle of one foreign student with one of ours. They all brought with them their diverse cultures and behavior. The Chinese, for example, exercised in the mornings and afternoons around the compound, regardless of the weather. Our people were amused by all this zeal to begin with, but later they too began to exercise. It became a commonplace, everyday picture. There was talk of the policy of "a thousand flowers," that is, about democratization in China and rapprochement between our two countries. The Chinese disappeared from Student City soon afterward, however, called home when political relations between Yugoslavia and China worsened.

The Russians, as we called them, were not happy, although they had everything: scholarships, hostels, and the right to attend our schools. They were homesick for the Soviet Union. It seemed to us that the Russians had no idea how to be economical. They would run torrents of hot water and not turn off the lights or the cooking ring after use. If we had behaved like this, the administration would have penalized us severely. The Russians also went off somewhere after a while. The Africans had already been educated in the French and English system and for the most part came for specialist studies, particularly in the fields of economics and political studies. Later, we had doctoral students from Canada and the United States, some on study visits, most of them examining self-management.

A large group of students came from India to study specialist subjects and to write their doctoral theses. Among them were Singhal, a doctoral student of geology, and Mishra, who had been in Europe for a long time and was interested in the socialist system and the political program of social democratic parties. All of them except the first two went back home, unable to get used to the food, the cold, and the other conditions. At first there were no foreign women students. They did not come until later, and most of those who did came for specialist studies. Some of them married our students.

Foreign students would visit their City colleagues in Serbia and Vojvodina during the Serbian household saints' days and wedding ceremonies. We used to invite them to our gatherings and shows on the occasion of our holidays, and when foreign arts ensembles were guests in the hostel. It was in this way that I got to know Singhal and Mishra, and in a way to make friends with them. I had already read Nehru's *The Discovery of India,* and his letters to Indira, written to her as a young girl when he was in jail. I knew about the conflict between the Muslims and the Hindus at the time of Partition and the creation of Pakistan.

The PMF was located in its old building in Students' Square. Later, a new building was erected in the neighborhood, just below Students' Park. Next to my faculty were the Faculty of Philosophy and the Rectorate of Belgrade University, in the Kapetan Mišina edifice, together with Kolarčev University, where popular lectures and concerts were held. The Serbian Academy of Sciences and Arts was nearby. A little farther along Knez Mihajlova Street one came to the National Library and Kalemegdan Park, from where there was an extensive view of the confluence of the Sava with the Danube, New Belgrade, and Zemun in the distance. The faculty had about fifteen hundred students in eleven departments or groups, from the departments of mathematics and physics to the departments of biology, geography, and mechanics. It prepared students to be gymnasium teachers, and some who had ambitions to be scientists. Physical chemistry was the fourth group, very new and at that time popular because it was the beginning of the nuclear era. Engineers in reactor physics were educated in the technical faculties.

All the professors, not merely those at the PMF, were tacitly divided into communists and those who were not Party members. Department heads and deans did not have to be communists, and sometimes a noncommunist was allowed to become rector of the university, although this was rare. There was a third group of professors who were mildly or strongly against the regime. This group was strongest in the faculties of social sciences, and had not always been mildly "deviant."

I remember what happened with Vladimir Dedijer, a professor of modern Yugoslav history at the Faculty of Philosophy. I was living in a room with his students when he was finally forced to give up lecturing. It was, I believe, in 1955. He did not openly come out against Milovan Đilas, a well-known Yugoslav dissident, when Đilas published a series of articles in which he called for the democratization of society, and attacked those communists who had acquired a range of benefits for themselves. The faculty's political management persuaded Dedijer's students to boycott his lectures. Students would not go into the classroom. They would watch from other classrooms as the professor entered, disposed his notes on the podium, waited about ten minutes in the empty room, and then departed. For years after that, the students had no lecturer for the subject of modern Yugoslav history.

In our departments of physics, physical chemistry, astronomy, and mechanics, physics was one of the most important subjects. We all listened to the lectures in the famous National Heroes Hall, where other important gatherings for the city were sometimes held. The hall, shaped in the form of a garland beneath the roof beams, was decorated with the busts of almost all of Yugoslavia's national heroes killed during the 1940–45 War of National Liberation.

Professor Dragi Jovanović, head of the Physics Department, lectured on general physics. He was educated in France in the "Aid for Serbia" program for Serbia's services on the Allied side during World War I, and was an associate of the famous Radium Institute in Paris. Professor Jovanović was regarded as a good experimenter. He was also famous for the various comments he made when introducing his lectures. We thus learned from him that the concept of the ideal is wrongly equated with the best. In fact, he said that it is the simplest model for explaining physical phenomena and states. He would jokingly add that "the ideal woman is not the most interesting, either," and everyone in the amphitheater, which was almost always packed with students, would laugh. He used to get irritated when students came in, sat in the upper gallery, and whispered as he was beginning a lecture. Although most of us heard nothing, he would abruptly interject, "Whispering is for Kalemegdan." The physics lectures began at ten and finished at twelve, with a brief break. It was the same every day for two years. It seemed to us that he always wore the same grayish suit with a barely visible stripe, although he went coatless and wore a white short-sleeved shirt in the summer. He had long white hair. He would emerge from the Physics Laboratory through the door at the far end of the amphitheater, dragging his left leg a little. Prior to this, his assistants took the same route to the chalkboard, to ensure that everything was in order.

Until they appeared, one of the students could be counted on to stand at the board and imitate the professor: writing, gesticulating, and turning around and raising his glasses to scrutinize us before giving his explanations. The student would hurriedly take his place and then a silence fell over the lecture hall as the professor came up to the chalkboard, settled his notes on the podium, and began his lecture. He never wrote anything on the large double chalkboard except his own symbols. We did not dare to use the symbols in our textbooks during examinations, since the professor lectured on and asked about more than was in them. Some said he was an anticommunist. He believed that politics had nothing to do with science, and that the situation in the university was not good for the students—or at least we gathered as much from his comments. He was consistent in his lectures, and he expected us to know our subject well and to give clear answers to the questions in his examinations.

Unlike Professor Jovanović, the head of my department, Academician Pavle Savić was occupied with the foundation of the Institute of Nuclear Sciences in Vinča, with his work on the Federal Commission for Atomic Energy, and with visits abroad. He had also been an associate of some European laboratories in which the fission process in heavy elements—still unexplained at that time, around 1939—was being studied. Such studies led, a few years later, to the development of the atomic bomb. Quite often he did not give the lectures on our most important subject: physical chemistry. Nevertheless, he personally conducted the examinations and signed the examination analysis. The physical chemistry program entailed four years of study and was not easy to pass. A committee heard the exams, which were composed of several sections.

Independent experiments, called practicals, were the basis of our physical chemistry and chemistry studies. We would hand in our notebooks with the results at the counter or to the assistant lecturers. If the results were good, after completing a certain number of experiments in a given field we would move on to colloquiums in another field and thus get ahead. If not, we would repeat the practicals until we obtained the true values for each parameter.

The examination analyses were carried out in an almost festive atmosphere. On the day they were administered, the demonstrators handed us all the necessary materials and instruments and we were granted priority use of the laboratory. The demonstrators would help us a little with complex chemical analyses, but the responsibility for entering the correct value in our notebooks was ours. In the early evening we would hand our analyses in to the professors, and wait anxiously to see whether we got a "plus" beside the results or the phrase "incorrect." The latter meant going back over the entire procedure again, sometimes with additional analyses as a penalty.

Old Prof. Milivoje Lozanić lectured on inorganic chemistry in the amphitheater of the Kapetan Mišina edifice. He was the son of Simo Lozanić, the founder of the Department of Chemistry, who had donated his large library of scientific works and journals to the university. The amphitheater, where we attended the lessons, was reminiscent of a classroom from the old days: steep and rather dark, with portraits of famous chemists from earlier centuries and chemical symbols adorning the walls. The professor always wore a well-pressed suit with a handkerchief in the breast pocket and was accompanied by his assistant, Rajko. As soon as the professor said "Rajkoo . . . o" during his lecture, the assistant, knowing what experiment was to be conducted, would light the Bunsen burner and hand the professor a test tube that he would hold in his trembling hand while carrying out the experiment for us. Other than that, Rajko was a semiskilled worker who dispensed to us the chemicals we used for our experiments. Professor Lozanić held no lectures over Christmas and Easter. He, too, had been a French student.

There was one more scholar who belonged to the older generation: Prof. Vukić Mićović. The head of the Department of Organic Chemistry and later rector of the university, he lectured on Organic Chemistry. He was not a communist either. We had three years of this subject. I liked the professor's style of lecturing and conducting examinations. Each student was given a list of questions that had been compiled based upon his success in experiments and colloquia. Four students were given their lists simultaneously as they sat on the front bench, so that they could think about them and wait their turn to sit for the exam. They thus had almost three hours each to prepare their answers, which they were required to give to the professor in writing—either on a sheet of paper or on the chalkboard. Sometimes, however, it seemed as though the exam ended before it began. If the first student did not know the answer to an important question, the professor would unexpectedly ask it of all those who had come to sit for the exam. If no one gave the correct response, the exam would be put off until the next time. Students who were not due to sit for the exams were also allowed to attend; it was the finest way of learning and becoming accustomed to the professor's style of examination.

During the exams, Professor Mićović would sit with his assistant, who succeeded him as lecturer. Other young assistants would write long formulas on the chalkboard before the professor's lectures to save him time during the lecture. If a student did not answer a question in the grammatically proper way, the professor would correct him. He once criticized me when I went to see him about the results of an examination analysis because I had written it in Latin letters (script). He could tell from my surname and accent that I was from the Sandžak, where an "indigenous people" who wrote in Cyrillic lived. He probably thought that the Muslims of the Sandžak were Islamicized Orthodox Christians. The professor himself was of Montenegrin origin. What a coincidence! I have continued to write mainly in Cyrillic to this day, although only a few of my colleagues do so.

Professor Slobodan Ristić, who studied in Germany, also had a crucial influence on my education. He lectured on physical chemistry measurements. "It is well known that there is no science without measurements," he would say, adding, "This is not history," where events are described. Instead, he explained, "Science reckons on the basis of what is measured in the experiment." We thus became accustomed to a logical order of work, which saved us both time and material. "Experiments also call for psychological concentration," he instructed us. Accordingly, he observed, "you need to enter the laboratory with a clear plan for your experiment," properly dressed "to protect yourself from possible accidents at work."

I returned to Belgrade in September, 1954, and enrolled for my second year of studies after spending summer vacation in Prijepolje. I was now living in a three-bed room on the second floor. There were bathrooms in the basement, and central heating had been installed.

I had been in the faculty and had not know that a demonstration had already broken out in Student City on the eve of Republic Day, November 29. When I got to the hostel at about nine, I found the square full of students. The administration had decided to increase the cost of accommodations and canteen meals. The students attending the meeting called for the decision to be revoked. The response to their insistent demands was an announcement over the public address system stating that the University Students' Committee agreed with the decision. Shouts of "let's go to the university" were heard, and the crowd began to pour onto the street and march in line toward Belgrade. Since the Zemun airport road passed alongside the hostel, the students took the opportunity to attack some cars, including those driven by foreigners. Soon the grounds around the hostel were empty. Those who did not join the march, including myself, had all gone inside.

At about midnight, students were seen running into the blocks to take cover. Mounted police from Belgrade had come to confront them, and had dispersed those who arrived from the surrounding roads. The students thought the police would not be able to enter Student City because of the autonomy of educational institutions, but when they saw them in the gaps between the buildings, they began to throw stones and chairs at them from the dark and from the windows. When things finally calmed down a little, an announcement was made over the public address system calling for all communists to attend a meeting. The demonstrators told us that the police had halted the march at the underpass near the Federal Executive Council in New Belgrade and that some students had been arrested. We agreed that a message calling for the urgent revocation of price increases and for the release of the arrested students should be sent to the police.

In the morning, however, they called us again. This time there was a letter from the University Party Committee regarding the events of the previous night. According to that body, the demonstrations had been organized by "hostile foreign elements" insinuated among the students to subvert the regime and to work against the country. Our impression that the demonstrations had started spontaneously began to fade, and our enthusiasm for them to dwindle. The communist authorities ordered us immediately to organize meetings of the students and to "explain" the situation as it was described in the letter. The students came en masse, to take part for the first time in meetings where someone was protesting. The unrest began to spread to the faculties in Belgrade. The City Party Committee then appeared directly on the scene. That body could not permit the unrest to spread to the young workers at the surrounding factories or to gymnasium pupils.

A general meeting of all communists was convened in the Cultural Center Hall in New Belgrade. The secretary of the Belgrade City Committee—Milojko Drulović, a former Partisan from a village in Mount Zlatibor in Serbia—came to the meeting. The hostel's communists were called upon, almost individually, to say what they thought about the demonstrations and where they had been on the evening of November 29. Listening to different versions of the events for a whole morning reinforced my earlier impression that the demonstrations were basically spontaneous, provoked by the rise in prices. When my turn came, I said as much. Drulović, after hearing several others make similar remarks, launched into a diatribe against the demonstrators and their supporters.

Following that meeting, the settling of scores with "suspects" continued and the circle of those who came under the lens of the investigating authorities widened. Slowly but surely, I found myself under that lens.

I returned to Prijepolje during the blizzard of January, 1955, for winter vacation. Mishra, a student from India I had invited to visit, came after me. I put Mishra up in Hamam with my cousin Muhamed Kurtović. Mishra lectured in our language at the gymnasium to a hall packed with teachers and pupils. Then the idea emerged that he should give public lectures and visit our factories. People were delighted to hear something about India, since it was a country that had become quite popular, and many mothers gave their daughters the name Indira. A few days later, however, I was called to appear before the Udba authorities. They warned me that Mishra was a spy and banned him from giving any more lectures. Mishra stayed a few more days and then returned to Belgrade. I do not know if he sensed anything about what I had learned of his "espionage activities."

As soon as I returned from my vacation, the Student City's communist secretary, who I barely knew, called me. He was a former member of the armed forces and an outstanding student, very near to completing his electro-technical engineering studies. He gave me further details about Mishra, saying that he worked for or had some kind of connection with Milovan Đilas and the British Embassy. He then said that "some comrades" wanted to talk to me at the Hotel Belgrade. When I asked who they were, the secretary replied, "Do not be afraid, they are our people." When I asked how I would recognize them, he said that they would call me. I realized from this reticence that I should not ask too many questions.

I went to the meeting at the agreed-upon time. As I entered the hotel lobby, a young man got up from a table by the front window and came to greet me, while another man remained seated at the table. We sat down, and after exchanging pleasantries, the conversation turned to Mishra: Where had he been in Prijepolje? Who had he talked to and what about? I briefly told them all I knew. When I finished, they asked me to summarize what I had said in writing and sign the statement. I refused, saying that I had told them everything and that I did not have the time to write it all down.

I continued to receive invitations to meet with the "comrades." They began to come looking for me in the hostel and at the faculty. What really surprised me was when I discovered that the faculty secretary was collaborating with these people, who were probably from Internal Security. The questions they asked revolved around Mishra and Student City. They suggested that I "establish contact" with some Shiptars, too. When I asked what they wanted with Albanians, I found out that there was unrest in Kosovo. There was no way one could tell that from the newspapers. Until then, I had been unaware of any discord between the Serbs and the Albanians. I got out of it by saying that the Albanian community was very enclosed, that they did not mix with others, and that they spoke their own language. When they proposed that I establish closer contact with Mishra and go out with him in the evening, I said that I did not have the money for the kind of clothing that would require. They then offered me money, but I again declined, saying I needed to study in preparation for my exams. Up to that time I had thought that Party assignments had to be carried out, and that the Party would not use underhanded methods to persuade communists and young people to do bad things in their own country.

The calls became more frequent, but they resulted only in making me feel more and more unsettled. I did not agree to anything. One day, I found out from one of my colleagues that two sisters from a town in Serbia, women we in the hostel knew were no good and did not like the regime, were working for the "Interior." He told me that the police were paying them. As soon as it became clear that money was involved, I stopped short. I could not take money at any price. That much we had learned at home. I knew that I could no longer behave indecisively, so I told him I would not accept money.

Two things helped me to resist, one was money and the other was that I would have had to work against the Albanians. Our people had fled to safety among them during the war to escape from the Chetniks. I also recalled the Albanian Partisans who were the first to cross the Oborce. Many of their soldiers had typhus and died while their comrades continued on to the front to help liberate Yugoslavia.

Following a long period of silence, I was called to a meeting of the inner Party management in the hostel. One of those present at the meeting was Ibrahim Hadžić, a Bosnian Muslim who was an economics student and secretary of the Party's University Committee. I was told that staff problems were on the agenda. When I reached the small hall on the first floor of the women's block where the meeting was being held, the atmosphere seemed extraordinarily tense and the faces of the people present looked like masks. When the meeting finally began, the chairman brought up the "issue of Comrade Munevera" on the agenda and called upon Ibrahim to speak. I was surprised to learn I was on the agenda, but I had the feeling it had something to do with my "indiscipline," for I knew in my heart that it was inevitable that anyone who opposed the Party would be penalized.

Ibrahim brought up the accusations made by the University Communist Committee, with which I had never had any dealings, that I was careless with foreigners and that I was collaborating with them and giving them information. When I tried to deny this, Ibrahim cut me short and said that I probably knew the exchange rate of the American dollar. This particularly hurt and astonished me. It was the first time I had even heard the words *exchange rate.* I do not think I had even seen a dollar before then. I asked of what charge, specifically, I was guilty. Ibrahim quoted some of my sentences from conversations with foreigners, such as "that's not done in the same way here." It was true; I *had* said that when commenting to colleagues about Singhal's remarks about life here. Ibrahim then read another statement I had made—"we do not have good roads"—while describing for Mishra the effects of the war on Yugoslavia and explaining that it was being rebuilt, beginning with the roads. My accusers gave a different meaning to every sentence. It was clear I had not only been speaking to my colleagues: there were spies among the women students in our dorm rooms. I learned later that these were often girls from the faculties and groups that were at that time of lesser importance. They were not good students and had probably agreed to spy on us in the hope that after graduation they would find jobs in Belgrade. But there were high-class spies, too: the roommates of foreigners who could speak foreign languages. Singhal had one such roommate. They later obtained high-ranking positions in the state institutions in Belgrade.

I was dismissed from my duties as secretary of the hostel communists of my faculty in short proceedings. No one came to protest, and a proposal calling for my expulsion from the Party was sent to my faculty Party organization. I thus found myself on the agenda there, too. The meetings were held in the amphitheater where we had chemistry lectures. There were many members present, probably because of the interesting agenda. The secretary was Vladeta Borojević, an older colleague of ours who had been a soldier. Ibrahim Hadžić also came to the meeting. He presented the conclusions of the management of the hostel communists and the University Committee. When asked to elucidate the charges, Hadžić kept to his assertion that the details could not be provided for reasons of the interests of the state, saying that it was "the conclusion of the Committee, which gives it the force of an obligation." The meeting lasted for nearly four hours. No one accused me, but neither could they openly reject the charges. A way to salvage the situation was found in the request for further details. When the Committee did not provide the desired information, the organization found a compromise solution: I was reprimanded, and the conclusion was passed on to the University Committee.

I saw this penalty as cruelty on the part of the Party and as a great injustice in which the powerful came down on someone in order to diminish them and befuddle their brains. It was hard for me to defend myself against the accusation that I was keeping company with foreigners and giving them information, and that they were perhaps seducing me. I was ashamed to speak about my problems to anyone. To this day I do not know who knew about my punishment, or the allegations that led to it. Yet I have carried its stigma with me throughout my life.

The students from our department set off on a professional excursion to visit our colleagues from Sarajevo University in April, 1956. I visited my Babba's grave and went to the City Party Committee, of which I had once been a member. Hamdija was not there; I was told he was in Ilidža, preparing a lecture for a conference. Since we too wanted to go to Ilidža, I left a message to give him my greetings in case I did not see him there. I had seen Hamdija twice since leaving Sarajevo. He was in Belgrade in 1954, and he dropped in briefly to see me and express his condolences after Babba died. The second time was in March, 1955, when he came to a Party meeting and dropped in on the "basement" of the faculty, where I was doing some experiments. He said he was working quite hard and joked that Sarajevo was "still in the same place."

My colleagues and I went to Ilidža. On returning from Vrelo Bosne, the source of the River Bosna, through the Avenue of Plane Trees, I saw Hamdija on a bicycle coming to meet us. He drew up to us with a smile and said, "Good day, Belgraders!" He then came over to me and dropped a hand on each of my shoulders and gave me a friendly hug. We talked about our impressions of the source of the Bosna, which most of my colleagues were seeing for the first time. Hamdija then took his leave of the group, asking them to leave me with him and saying he would bring me back to Sarajevo.

The two of us went into a small roadside café for some hot tea. We then went off toward the Hotel Bosna, which was empty, like the other hotels in the area. There was nobody, I think, except some cleaners who we saw in passing. We went into Hamdija's apartment, a modern room of the kind I liked, with books and papers scattered everywhere on the table and the armchairs. I sat on the edge of the bed near the foot and he at the head, leaning back on the pillow. "I'm so glad that you came and that you have not forgotten us," said Hamdija, for the first time a little more outgoing toward me. "There were those who were in love with the little girl in her school apron, always smiling," he continued, jokingly. "But commitments, differences—everything got in the way, my little one," he said, addressing me in this way for the first time. He asked if I still lived in Students' City, how I got to the faculty because of the crowds in the buses, and how long it would be before I was done with my experiments and "that stifling basement."

I said a few inconsequential things out of old habit, lacking the courage to speak to him about my problems with the Party and the fact that I was behind in the faculty. Then suddenly some barrier in me gave way and all of my strength and will to speak and to resist vanished. In fact, I did not know what to say. Certainly nothing personal, and any other kind of explanation would be lengthy and impossible. Tears sprang unbidden to my eyes; I do not remember having ever before cried in front of anyone. I sensed an awkward silence and discomfort, and it seemed to me that a shadow flitted across his face when I looked at him at one point.

He drew closer and hugged me. I leaned my head on his shoulder and the tears began to drench his shirt. He did not ask me anything, probably because he thought I did not want to speak, that I still felt set apart from people by a huge invisible distance. He drew me protectively close and said simply, "Don't cry." I slowly melted into a kind of darkness and peace. The calming proximity of his personality, which did not challenge but soothed, filled my soul. The pleasant feelings of that closeness still remain with me. Although everything was quiet, and it was somewhat somber outside, with the still bare branches blocking the view, in my surrender and search for protection it seemed to me that I could find it. Then my mind turned back to my faculty and to Belgrade: It's the same thing again, I thought. A feeling of even greater loneliness washed over me. I felt incapable of overcoming that internal barrier and telling him what the problem was. Hamdija said that he was preparing to come to Belgrade to enroll in pure philosophy. He took me back to Sarajevo, where I joined my colleagues, or rather went to my room to lie down and reflect.

The following day he came to the station, where we were already in the compartments and at the windows. He brought us a big bar of chocolate and whispered to me, "I'm coming to Belgrade." He kissed me on the forehead, which was later his way of greeting me, and hugged me warmly. Then off he went, tall, stooping a little, always well dressed in his own style, as I followed him with my gaze and a smile.

The penalty had its effect on my faculty. I failed physics and went on with the experiments—but only for a while, then stopped that, too, and began to avoid the faculty. I found at least some peace in the National Library near Kalemegdan learning physics from the beginning and extensively, which took me still further from the curriculum. I passed some colloquia and part exams with experiments, and finished my third year in June, 1956, but unsuccessfully, without the main examination. When Prijepolje withdrew my scholarship, I went home to see what I could do. I did not want to go cap in hand around town asking the reasons. They claimed in the municipality that they needed the money to support medical students, and perhaps that was so. Nanna changed several ducats secretly, which gave us a breathing space.

I returned to Belgrade in mid-August, but again avoided the faculty. One day I asked myself why I was in Belgrade. "To graduate," I said to myself, a reminder of my major wish. "But graduation does not happen by itself," came my own unwelcome response. It was clear to me that I had to face up to the curriculum, however difficult it might be for me to deal with colleagues who had left me behind, when once we had been the same. I went to the library at the Physics Institute, took out several Russian physics textbooks, drew up a program to meet the demands of Professor Jovanović, and began to study and to do the experiments. As soon as I had begun I felt a sense of relief. I passed both physics exams, not brilliantly, but with a seven out of a possible ten.

My scholarship was restored in September, including the arrears. I was surprised. I found out that Savo Kržavac, my classmate from gymnasium, then a student of literature and editor of the newspaper *The Communist,* had put my case to a meeting of Sandžak students. Velibor Ljujić, our national deputy, had attended the meeting and intervened on my behalf, telling the Prijepolje councilors that it was important as many people as possible from the Sandžak get an education and that it was less important where they did so.

A little later, Nanna applied for a pension on the grounds that she had worked as a teacher for more than twenty years in old Serbia and the First Yugoslavia. Shortly thereafter, I received a call from Selmo Hašimbegović, secretary of the Serbian Assembly, to visit him. Selmo, like Ljujić, was a Sandžak Partisan who had fought from the beginning of World War II, and a lawyer of Prijepolje origin. He had also been a pupil of Nanna's there. I went one morning and was taken to Selmo, who I met that day for the first time. He welcomed me kindly and explained that Nanna's pension would be sorted out as soon as some formalities had been completed because of certain problems arising from the fact that she had not worked since the war.

After asking me about the life and work of students from the Sandžak, Selmo stressed that it was important that we complete our studies on time and take our place in society. He said it was particularly important for me, as I was still the only Muslim girl student from Prijepolje. His secretary later took me to an office where a gift from the student aid fund awaited me. I went inside, signed my name, and the secretary handed me an envelope containing five thousand dinars. I now understood that his getting up from the table to greet me and the friendly smile with which he saw me off were a message telling me what I should do: graduate and get a university diploma. Nanna soon got her own pension.

In September, 1956, I enrolled for my fourth year, although I still had exams to complete from previous years and had not finished all of the experiments. Hamdija came to the Faculty of Philosophy. He stayed with his own people on Dositejeva Street at first. We used to go out in the evenings. I spent the days studying and completing my experiments. We usually went out so Hamdija could have dinner in a restaurant around Republic Square. Then we would go to the cinema or the theater, to Kalemegdan, or sometimes to visit friends. I did not eat with him in the restaurant, nor did we go to cafés. Hamdija was opposed to alcohol and liked sports and skating, which he had come to like back in Moscow, where he had graduated from the Party's Lenin High School after the war. I usually ate dinner in the students' canteen near the faculty at about six in the evening after finishing my work in the laboratory, and met him later.

Sometimes we would meet up with his colleagues working as Party or state officials in Belgrade. I thus began to get an insight into the lifestyle of the new class at firsthand, although I had had some opportunities to do so even before then. We had understood the basis of the new society and the proclaimed equality very simply, not knowing what this equality was or where it lay. But here there were servants, cooks, salons, elegant furniture, exclusive but inexpensive summer resorts, and expensive gifts. It was like the life of the wealthy in any society, the kind of thing communists claimed to be against. At first I thought they must be doing important work, and that it was for this reason they were so richly rewarded. In the course of our conversations I saw that it was indeed true of most of them, but their households spoke more about position and money, about how "so-and-so has fallen on his feet" and "such-and-such is up to his neck." They had less to say about their own jobs. Position had begun to become an obsession with those people. Is that really how a communist state is run? I wondered.

At one time it was fashionable for officials' wives to learn literacy by attending "Partisan schools," as the people called them. These schools had short curricula, and the officials' wives would obtain jobs in places that were reserved for them. A special external gymnasium opened in Zagreb for this purpose, and candidates sometimes came for assignments that they had to do for their examinations. Children of officials who had difficulty completing their education also attended this school. In some cases they would come to me for help, and sometimes I went to them. I recall vividly how Persian carpets of exquisite design and fine knotting caught my attention. On the other hand, I was in our stifling basement every day doing my experiments and listening to my colleagues' anxieties about finding work and above all apartments. Our high level of expertise, which was up to the world's standards, was no guarantee that we would find space for the kind of life we wanted. When our professors could not get good apartments but were happy to be allocated a one-bedroom apartment, how could we expect to do so? We constantly asked ourselves this question and harped on it in our thoughts.

Hamdija, as least as far as I could see, had not lived such a life, and as an intellectual and politician was occupied with programs and visions for the future of Bosnia and with books. Yet he too planned to buy elegant furniture as a wedding gift for his cousin. Who were the people who bought such gifts? Where did they get the money?

We had yet diverged on one topic. Hamdija was an atheist by conviction and belonged to the circle of Bosnian intellectuals who wanted Bosniaks to have equal rights with others in the country, but who did not keep to the customs of Islam. They regarded Muslims as an indigenous people who had based their culture on the values of Bosnia itself right back to the Bogomils, who in the Middle Ages were the believers of the Bosnian church. However, it seems impossible that, given such an upbringing, Hamdija had not been able to foresee that times would change. It was inevitable that the basis of an Islamic identity would be one of the major factors shaping Yugoslavia's Muslims.

We had not become much closer as a result of seeing each other, each of us going our own way. He was moving ever closer to his class and to officials from Bosnia. I had the feeling that he perhaps knew something about my problems in the Party. He could already have heard about it from the faculty, but I still did not want to say anything. Moreover, he who could have created the opportunity for such a discussion did not do so, which was for me yet another reason to turn away from him. We began to drift apart spontaneously in early 1957, but he continued to have a great influence on me. I think that as someone older and more experienced he realized that I respected him and that that was one of the reasons for our distance.

I completed my experiments at the beginning of 1958 and finally had some free time to prepare myself for the remaining examinations. I remained in the hostel studying with colleagues in an effort to speed up this process. We would spread blankets in the corner of the corridor by the windows and radiators. I studied all day, every day except Sundays, with a short break for lunch. In this way, I was able to successfully complete the chemistry examinations. I continued studying for the other exams, this time in rather better conditions in the flat of a female student, a former Partisan. We would stop studying at eight in the evening. I used to go to the cinema, the theater, and sometimes to parties with people from Novi Pazar at Stambol Gate or the Dalmatian Cellar. As the students of Novi Pazar would jokingly say, the cafés where there was singing and the high-class restaurants were their "second home." I remember singers getting good tips when people asked them to sing "Even Bairams Are Not What They Used to Be" or the "Drina March." Both were banned in the cafés: "Bairam" as a reminder of the "rotten Turks," and the "March" of Serbian nationalism from the time of the First World War. For all that, the singers would agree to sing them late at night when the atmosphere in the cafés turned into one of general abandonment.

In April, 1959, I passed the last examination and took the finals. I completed my experiments at the end of September and continued to work up the results and to write my dissertation, finally handing it in to the committee at the end of November. I had to wait until February the following year to defend it, since dissertations were defended in groups.

Finally, on February 16, 1960, I passed my finals. I came out of the old faculty building into Students' Park to take a breather. So, I had graduated—very soon after the crisis and with a high degree and the right to work as an intellectual, perhaps even a scientist.

I decided to stay in Belgrade after graduation and began looking for a job. My goal was to work at the Vinča Institute, but I was afraid that I would not be able to obtain employment there since I had neither graduated on time nor been sanctioned by the Party. In order to be employed at Vinča I needed to reside in Belgrade. There was a tremendous housing shortage in the city at that time, but I was able to find a room with Spahi's family friend, Ljubica, who had a large, centrally located, prewar apartment at 16 Gračanica Street. Immediately after registering the apartment as my living place, I applied for work and, despite my fear, was hired to work in the Physics Laboratory, one of the best in Vinča. My employment began on April 20, 1960. It was a truly happy day for me. I felt much as I had when I completed the first grade of gymnasium in 1946.

From the beginning, I worked well—becoming involved in testing the work of one of Vinča's reactors after an accident in which a group of associates were exposed to radiation. Most of their lives were saved with bone-marrow transplants—the first experiments with that procedure in the world—at the Curie Hospital in Paris from October, 1958, through the first half of 1959.

However, my scientific debut was mingled with personal misfortune. Less than a month after I began work, Nanna became ill and had a minor stroke. After she had improved a little, I went to Prijepolje to bring her to the Military Medical Academy in Belgrade for a checkup.

Hamdija graduated from university a few months earlier and obtained a job in the ideological section of the Central Communists Committee in Marx and Engels Square. In May he invited me to see him and to say good-bye. We met in a restaurant on Vasina Street, ordered bread rolls and yogurt, and talked. Hamdija told me he intended to return to Sarajevo because it was "not possible to make oneself felt in Belgrade." Besides, he felt that Bosnia "needed him more." He joked that now that I was a nuclear scientist, nobody could do anything with us scientists any more. Thus, we finally parted. I went off toward Students' Square, to catch the Vinča bus. It seemed to me that I was slowly detaching myself from the Party and that the two of us were taking different paths. My leanings were toward Islam and the unattractive and uncertain calling of researcher, whereas he was off to build Bosnia—about which I had no doubt. I was a little sorry for all that: Could I not have contributed to that, with his help perhaps? Yet I also liked Belgrade, that extensive city, and Vinča, and my colleagues—of whom there were many in the laboratories. I sensed that this was the environment for me, that the laboratories were my finest and best home.

I had no further personal contact with Hamdija. Nor I did not regret the past. I continued to follow his public life, curious to see how Bosnia was progressing—until his tragic death just before the war in Bosnia began in 1992.

Meeting Derviš Again and Kenan's Birth

9

In the mid-1960s, university students from Prijepolje living in Belgrade had the idea of organizing Sandžak games in which young people would compete in sports and cultural activities. The games, which lasted about ten days, were hosted in various towns, and in August, 1957, Prijepolje was the site of the event. During this time, Prijepolje had the look of a metropolis with a festive atmosphere. The streets were clean and brightly lit, full of the townsfolk and guests, and the shops stayed open until late at night. Many people opened their houses to guests, since Prijepolje had only one hotel, the Polimlje.

One afternoon I saw the games in Vakuf with Subha Sadović, Prijepolje's first actress, who was also a guest. We were thirsty, so we made our way to the fountain and sat on the stone wall that surrounded it, awaiting our turn to get a drink. There was an incredible crowd all around. All of a sudden, a motorcyclist wearing a helmet and smiling broadly detached himself from the crowd and came toward me. It was Derviš. He came up to us delightedly and offered the usual Sandžak greeting: "What are you doing these days?" There was a degree of emotion in his voice, for Subha had been our classmate in gymnasium back in 1947. We extracted ourselves from the crowd and sat down on a stone slab near the Mileševka River. Subha left us.

I had seen Derviš several times since our parting in Sarajevo. He would pretend not to have seen me, or would laugh from afar. Sometime in May, 1955, I met Derviš with his eldest brother, near my faculty; on this occasion we asked after each other's health, Derviš was interested to know where I was and soon came to the basement in the faculty where I did my analyses. We went to Kalemegdan to talk, and he boasted about going to the FAP branch in Vienna for a two-year specialist course. As for his personal life, he said he had made a "mistake," and that he had a daughter. When he suggested some kind of relationship between us, I refused and the conversation came to an end. I accompanied him in the direction of the train station and we parted on good terms.

To meet again in Prijepolje by chance among such a huge crowd of people introduced a sense of destiny to our feelings, which finally broke to the surface on that relaxed, pleasant summer day.

Derviš had returned from Vienna. He said it had been hard for him to get used to these confined surroundings and that he was unhappy with his wife. He wanted to divorce her and resume his university studies. He added that he realized I had been right to opt for more education. He proposed to me again, as he had in Sarajevo in 1953. This time, however, he said he was willing to begin his university education in Belgrade. For this reason, his question, "Will you marry me so we can make a start together?" was also the expression of my wishes. "Yes," I barely managed to say in my agitation, finally breaking down the barrier toward him I felt within me. We were finally caught up in the illusion that we were really so close and not impossibly opposite. It seemed to me as though our modernism, acquired in a new world, was a magical conjunction with our culture and customs. Yet, in the quest for a conjunction of the old with the new lurked a conundrum: what did all this mean for us? Were we not both returning from a world that was to us somewhat alien, momentarily finding in the promise of marriage a psychological way out of our difficulties: I from my wanderings about the faculty, the Party, with Hamdija; he with his knowledge of life in Vienna and the discrepancy in his family between the aspirations and ambitions of two spouses?

We parted after a day or two with some fairly firm plans about what each of us should do: that I should graduate and that he would get divorced.

I soon went to Belgrade to sit for my exams. I continued working well and was already on my best form. Derviš often passed through Belgrade on his way to Vienna on business as his duties at the FAP factory involved the import and export of goods. I went to Prijepolje for the November 29 observance. It was snowing heavily and he turned up unexpectedly. We spent a few moments together between the bus departures for Priboj. I felt within myself some uncertainty, I do not know why, even though our relationship seemed much stronger than I could have expected. While he was in Belgrade on business we would go to restaurants where we could talk in peace. We both smoked—I had been a smoker for two years—on one occasion, by chance, the same cigarettes, the red Herzegovina. Derviš wrote to me from everywhere he went, and I wrote back. In his letters he described some of his family and business problems, saying that he had grown tired of the obligations of the large family he loved and helped. He represented everything he did in these circumstances as quite natural, and he probably believed it to be so. I accepted this and I did not look for much for myself, nor would any kind of argument between us have been possible, it would have seemed shameful to me.

After two years of this I felt as though I had gotten nowhere. Our circumstances had changed, and so had Derviš's position at work. After some reorganization of FAP's leadership structure, new managers surfaced. Among them was Derviš, who had obtained an important position in the foreign trade division. The number of major company branch offices increased in Belgrade. Derviš, fully committed to his new position, finally found himself: at work and in the family.

In June, 1960, Derviš came twice, briefly, after a long absence, friendly letters, and congratulations on my graduation. I recall a conversation about our future. For the first time he asked whether he should divorce his wife or not, even though we were together. During our conversation he mentioned that he had visited his mother and that she had "made him swear" not to divorce his wife. "All that is strange to me," he continued, "in fact, mother and my cousins do not understand it." Derviš came back to the old topic of the war as yet another obstacle to our relationship, one that his mother "could not get over." This was the story of the Partisans who had "done wrong" to his family. He linked our cousin, Ahmo Šehović, and Jasika, the prominent head of the Udba with this. Arifaga's daughter Nadira, herself a Partisan, had just married Jasika, a Serb. I countered this, saying that during the war we had just been children and had suffered enough. Besides, the Hasanagić family, like many others, had been split. Many of them served in the 3d Sandžak Brigade with Ahmo and had already performed important state functions in Belgrade by 1945.

My Babba had mourned Derviš's brothers: Emin, who as a Muslim militia member had been shot by Partisans on entering Priboj, and Ćamil, commanding officer who was among the missing in the Muslim units that had retreated with the Germans toward Austria in 1945. Those rifts in my unconscious doubts about Derviš manifested themselves. As I slowly crossed Students' Park after parting from him with icy feelings of emptiness, it seemed to me that Derviš had forgotten everything.

In July, I felt some discomfort and changes in myself. We were working hard and I attributed it to tensions at work and getting settled. The staff at Vinča went on collective annual vacation, during which I went to Prijepolje. Before leaving, I gave a urine sample for a pregnancy test at the First of May pharmacy on Tito Street but then did not go back for the results. I spent August in Prijepolje in a strange state of mind with nightmarish dreams. I sensed beyond doubt that I was pregnant, but I also felt that something was not right with the child and me. Derviš did not call after June, nor did I look for him at work.

I went on working when I returned from vacation, thinking one day that the pregnancy had not happened and the next that it had. Finally, on October 22, I summoned the courage to go in for a checkup. The doctor told me I was in the fifth month of pregnancy. I left the clinic on a very pleasant, warm evening of the kind that is common in Belgrade in autumn. I set off slowly along Višnjićeva Street toward Nura's house. I felt that something had conclusively changed in me and that something entirely new was beginning. I was overcome with loneliness. It was as though my entire being had come together in a single skein in which connections with the outside world had ceased. I went to Nura's place and said nothing. There was still a small hope that Derviš would understand and that he could do something to help.

Besides that hope, I began to develop awareness that my "great love" was no good, and that great difficulties lay ahead of me in facing up to that fact. Pain and misery arose within me, and I knew beyond a doubt that I would always have to live with that pain. Thus, at the age of twenty-seven, my personal life seemed to have come to an end.

Derviš came a few days later and we went to Kalemegdan. We sat on a bench by the path near the tram route. He told me that his wife was pregnant and that he had obtained a transfer to Belgrade. He would come there to live. He said that he and his wife had visited his mother in the summer to tell her the news. A little later he added, "My mother again made me swear not to get a divorce." I could not see his face, partly because it was rather dark and partly because I was staring straight ahead. I finally plucked up the courage to say, "I am pregnant, too." A silence fell over us, which he tried to break with a smile. He tried to persuade me to have an abortion, saying that a child would bring me nothing but trouble. He said he would have felt better if I had told him I was beginning my doctoral studies. He expressed the wish to draw closer to me. At one point he said, "Resolve it, and we'll celebrate the New Year together." I thought fleetingly, "It would be the first," and then freed myself from his touch. The feeling that our relationship was on the "road to death" began to work within me. His proximity did not touch my heart, but instead settled somewhere in the nausea I felt.

We remained in this conviction until morning. I was now painfully trying to explain to him that the child was part of my feelings for him, that our relationship encompassed everything, and that I had not lived with a married man solely for the sake of sex. However, I did not mention our agreement that was also part of my story and his. We rose from the bench shortly before dawn and walked around Kalemegdan, then set off via Knez Mihajlova Street and Terazije, and soon found ourselves in Marx and Engels Square. Dawn had broken by then. Yellow leaves were scattered about the Square's red paving slabs, and we saw a few early passersby moving down Moša Pijade Street. We leaned there together, on the edge of Fontana. I looked at him properly for the first time and saw dark circles under his eyes that he had not had before. His tired, white, sweaty face, was powerfully altered. I sensed that he would never face up to his problems, and suddenly felt sorry for him.

"Why I am troubling him?" I wondered. "I have to get away. If I don't, I shall continue headlong." I saw that I was not the only one suffering: he was, too, and he was clearly afraid. I think our fear was the same: shame at our relationship and its hopelessness in our eyes. For the first time I understood the simple truth: he had been living a normal life with his wife. I wanted to escape, to go somewhere far away from him. His presence hurt my eyes as if stilettos were piercing them and lancing me. My eyes hurt so much! I closed them and turned away from the force that drew me toward it. I realized my child would have no father—and not only in the formal sense. "Let's go," I said. We walked silently until we reached the door of the building on Jevremova Street where I was staying with my friends Veda and Emin. We parted "normally" with just a brief good-bye.

After two or three days we again found ourselves having the same conversation. I said that it was too late for an abortion, but he retorted that it was not, that he knew someone who did such things. I finally agreed and went to a doctor, a professor, who confirmed that it was too late and advised me to have the child. The committee in the gynecological hospital on National Front Street also confirmed that it was too late.

I had to tell Nanna, so I went to Prijepolje for the November 29 observance. I cleaned up the whole house for the last time and then told her with great difficulty all that had happened. She did not reprove me in any way. Instead, she demonstrated greater understanding than I had expected and seemed truly sad for me. When I returned, I first told Nura and Rabija, and then my chief at Vinča, Prof. Đorđe Bek-Uzarov. We were working on a project that had to be completed on time, so I was constantly busy. Derviš and I had stopped seeing each other altogether.

On Monday, January 29, we sent a report on the project to the International Atomic Energy Agency in Vienna and breathed a sigh of relief. I returned from work to Nura's place to help Rabija's son Labdoš with some school homework. Before the lesson was over I suddenly began bleeding. We were alone, Labdoš and I. I told young Labdoš to call Džafer, Nura's neighbor. Džafer was an Albanian medical student. He came and called an ambulance. Then Nura came back from having coffee at Rabija's place. They took me to the hospital on National Front Street. At about midnight, the director of the hospital came to visit me. The Vinča doctors had called him. The hospital's doctors had determined that I was giving birth prematurely and that both my child and I faced complications and risks. They put me in the maternity ward and held me for observation.

On evening of February 1, a Wednesday, Kenan was born. I looked at him as the doctor lifted him up and then nodded in satisfaction. The effect of the narcotics overwhelmed me and I fell asleep. I awoke around midnight after an intervention. The following afternoon, a nurse brought Kenan so I could see him. He was so tiny, having been born prematurely. A few days later the house doctor, Dr. Ivan Radovanović, told me that the child was losing weight while he adjusted to his surroundings. The uncertainty lasted until the end of February. Kenan weighed 950 grams at that point and soon began to make real progress.

One Saturday at the end of March, the duty doctor told me that Kenan had developed an impacted hernia but that he was too small to undergo surgery. When I asked if there was anything I could do, she shrugged her shoulders. I got up and asked for permission to telephone Dr. Radovanović at home. I begged him to try to save my child. He came to the hospital and called me into the doctor's room. He gave me a cigarette, and said that Kenan must be transferred to the children's hospital on Tiršova Street for an emergency operation. He hoped that all would be well, since he had showed signs of improving. "If you agree," he added, "sign here." I signed the consent he held out to me and then he and a nurse took Kenan to the children's hospital.

Milena, a nurse who was an acquaintance of Nura's, also came to see me. She asked me about Derviš and what, if anything, I had thought about doing. I asked her to go to him and tell him what had happened. She returned a few days later and said that Derviš had received her in his office without sitting down. Upon hearing that he had a son, he had said nothing. She then resolved to leave, since there was nothing more to be done. Kenan was successfully operated on and recovered fully. They finally released me from the hospital at the end of April. Since Kenan was still in hospital, I returned to work. Everybody at Vinča was very kind to me. It was a great relief, like balm on a sore wound.

I finally invited Derviš to come and meet with me. I told him all that had happened and asked if he wanted to acknowledge the child. He raised his eyebrows archly and glowered at me. "No," he snapped. I looked at him and saw that his face was an impenetrable mask and in it I could discern a readiness to blame me. This stung me like a whiplash, and deepened my wound still further. "All right," I said. "I had to ask you, because of the child, who has that right when he has come into this world. It is odious for me to have to beg for your mercy." He softened a little and said that he would like him to be called Kenan. "Fine," I replied coldly. We parted.

I went to Savski Venac municipality and registered the boy with the name of Kenan, my surname, and left blank the space where the father's name was supposed to be entered. So this was what our "great love" had come to: a child of shame. The idea had begun to haunt me and there remained only the hope that perhaps one day, Kenan would understand.

The first problem arose when it came time to register his nationality. "Let him be Yugoslav," I suggested to the official. "He can't be," she replied. "But I have no other nationality," I responded. The official went out several times to consult with someone and finally returned, saying, "In that case, this space is to remain empty." I agreed. Although Kenan had been given the name his father wanted him to have, he remained fatherless and without a country. It was all so strange: They taught us that we were Yugoslavs, but then said we were not, that we were born in love and thus had no father. These were complicated and dangerous times in which we were living. A woman and mother were left to bear everything. Because she cannot say that it is not her child, many people are ready to blame her alone, without any further reflection.

Just before the First of May celebration, I met Derviš in company with some other people one noon on the Terazije. They were cheerfully walking along, laughing. He spotted me moving toward him and left the others. We sat in the Mornar Café on Moše Pijade Street. I said that I had named the child Kenan just as Derviš had asked and explained that he was still in the hospital receiving treatment. "I have to go to Priboj, but I have no money for the journey, we still haven't been paid," he said as if joking. I knew that he did not need money, but that was just his way of breaking the awkwardness of seeing me. I took out some cash and handed it to him. He had to take it now, there was no way out. We talked for a while, not so coldly this time, but about inconsequential things, avoiding touching on the "topic," and then parted for the next twenty or so years.

He did not tell me that he was expecting or had just had a son, nor that he had obtained an apartment in Belgrade and would soon be moving there from Priboj with the rest of his family. It was a mark of great privilege in those days when an enterprise or state institution transferred one of its people to Belgrade, where an apartment and important work awaited him.

My first concern when I got out of the hospital was to rent a room for Kenan and me. In addition, I had to find and pay somebody to take care of him while I was at work. That is why I was delighted when Veda suggested that Kenan, Nanna, and I stay with her for a while. It was also important that Nanna feel comfortable in Belgrade and that she spend time with Kenan. As Veda was from Prijepolje, I was optimistic. My cousin Muhamed brought Nanna from Prijepolje at the end of June, and Kenan was released from the hospital at about the same time. Thus our life as a threesome began.

Hatidžehanma and my Aunt Arifa sent presents for Kenan, but the rest of them did not want to have anything to do with me, since what I had done was a severe blow to the whole family and a major surprise to them all. I did not even get angry; I simply did not have time for that, what with having to manage with a small child, a sick mother, no apartment, not enough money, and a *very* demanding job.

At the time, renting an apartment in Belgrade on my pay was impossible—except in the suburban housing estates filling up with people from rural areas. My colleagues were aware of this and were trying to help me. While I was in the hospital, Prof. Fedor Borelli, the head of the physics laboratory, had asked Vinča's housing committee to find me any kind of accommodation, even if all it could come up with was a room in one of the Vinča apartments. The process was slow, however, and some of the women on the commission saw little need to give mothers with children born out of wedlock help and encouragement, although all of them had very good "political credentials" and lived in comfortable three-room flats with one child or none. For all that, they allocated me a little room of some eight square meters on the top floor of a house on Uralska Street in the Karaburma district of Belgrade, with shared use of the kitchen and a bathroom. A bachelor technician was allocated the official occupancy rights to the house and the large room on the first floor. Gleda, who had a job with Vinča and whose husband had a job in another company, got the room on the second floor. Her unmarried sister, a clerk, both of them from Lika, a Serbian Partisan area of Croatia had already been allocated a nice apartment in the Vinča building in the town center.

Once we finished moving into that little room, Rabija and her husband Imer found Bulka for me to look after Kenan for a rather large sum of money. After meeting all my expenses, I was left with very little on which to live, even though Nanna gave me her pension. Unfortunately, there simply was no other source of income.

I remember one Saturday when I was left without a single dinar. I said nothing to anyone, but instead went to a Turkish working-class family in a part of town close to the Danube, where they lived in a single small room, and borrowed some money from them.

Not a day went by without some problem. I lost weight, but I could not afford to be ill. I *had* to keep well. At the same time, I got more and more behind on my work. I hardly had time to read the newspapers, and we had neither radio nor television, which really was not a bad thing. Nanna and Kenan got along well together, and Bulka, although she could be crotchety, had become like a member of the family. I went to buy some household items. I bought spoons, some enameled metal plates, and a clothes rack that is still in use today. I took out a loan and bought a top-quality heater. It was expensive, but it also had a fan. We got through the winter with it, turning it on only from time to time so as to save on electricity. I bought a gas ring and put it in a corner of the kitchen. Gleda made her kitchen in another corner. We set up a little electric ring on a stone tile in our room and used it to make coffee and heat Kenan's food. He slept in a secondhand cot and Nanna and I slept on mattresses on the floor. Autumn came, and with it a pay advance for November 29. I used the extra money to settle our debts, buy some food for the holiday, pay Bulka for babysitting Kenan, and wound up spending everything before the month had even begun.

My only leisure was to go out with Kenan in his little pushchair in the early evening to the self-service store to buy supplies. It was my relaxation. I knew that I needed about ninety dinars a day, but that was more than I could afford. I also used to enjoy putting Kenan to sleep at about eight in the evening and then taking the bus to Students' Square, to Rabija's place, so we could have coffee and chat together. And so my life went by, hour by hour. Early in the morning, before going to work, I would buy bread and milk in the dark and then set off to work from Karaburma at 6:30 in the Vinča bus. I would get back at about four in the afternoon, after Bulka had already left. In early 1962, I went on my first official visit to France. I stayed for a month, missing Kenan's first birthday. Upon my return, I found Kenan running a fever after receiving a vaccination. He recognized me when he saw me, but he sat on the corner of his cot for a long time before he finally smiled at me. I had a few French francs left over, so I changed them at the bank. The extra money helped me to pay off some debts and start running into debt all over again. I was perpetually short of money for two years, but there was nothing else I could do. I made some acquaintances in Karaburma, too. Hasan, a man from the Sandžak, lived nearby with his family. I had known Hasan's brother, Arif, an older medical student, since our student days, and even in Prijepolje had noted that he was interested in me before he knew me personally in Student City and found out that I was a "Party activist." Before graduating he got a job in Bosnia and married a nice, hardworking woman with a trade whom I met in Hasan's house. After a while, Arif came back to Belgrade to finish his university studies.

One day he called me at work and asked if I would meet him, that he needed my help. He said he was free in the evening. Since Kenan would already be asleep by then, it suited me, too—although I really did not want to go out. We met at the entrance to the playing fields in Karaburma below the Zvezdara Observatory. We crossed the playing fields and sat down on a bench. The night was still warm, the moon shone on the bushes, and it was very quiet.

I asked him what kind of intervention he needed. Sometimes people wanted information about the levels of radiation treatment after Vinča had supplied radioisotopes to the hospitals. I had thought of that first, but had asked him nothing on the telephone out of discretion. It turned out, however, that he had called me for something else entirely. He suggested that we should "see" each other since he would be in Belgrade for at least six months, explaining that it would be better for us to "see" each other than for me to go out with "others," meaning non-Muslims, and for him to do the same.

I was upset by this unfair remark and felt even more estranged from my people. However, knowing what Sandžaklijas thought about "independent" women, I was not that surprised. I had to endure all kinds of things now, and this was just another knife wound, reviving a sadness that was almost tangible. The painful feeling that evokes others, when the person you long for is not there, flooded into the emptiness within me, and the wound again began to throb mutely: "There's nothing, nothing . . . there never will be, the dead can't come to life." A love forced to die had made me indifferent. "Thanks for the offer," I replied calmly. "But if I were to fancy anyone I wouldn't worry about who he was. For now I can't go out with anyone." A painful silence followed and I suggested that we go home. We quickly set off, dispelling the embarrassment by talking about other things until we parted. I did not blame Arif. He was essentially a decent man and I understood that men, too, after the war, needed time to get used to and understand emancipated women.

Arif's brother Hasan met me some months later on the city bus. "Why don't we see you these days?" he asked in a friendly fashion. "Come and visit us on Wednesday," he suggested as he left the bus. I promised I would, and I did so, after first putting Kenan to sleep. He opened the door, and when I entered I saw that there was no one in the apartment. "Where's Zineta?" I asked, going into the dining room. Hasan answered in an offhand manner that she had gone to visit her parents. I realized that he had invited me knowing that his wife, Zineta, would not be there. I tried to keep the conversation going, because I respected him, too. We finally settled on the topic of some of our old acquaintances. When I felt that I could leave without being impolite, I stood up in the middle of our conversation and paused by the fireplace. He also stood up, lightly barring my way by standing in front of me.

This subtle effrontery of his made me stop putting on an act. After a few moments of silence I finally began to speak, avoiding looking directly at him so that he would not cajole me into something I should not do. I went out into the corridor, still trying to be amiable, bringing the conversation back to commonplaces. He paused briefly and then accompanied me, unruffled, with the remark that we were "living beings." As soon as I was outside I finally began to breathe more easily, walking along the street quite beside myself, not knowing what I was doing. I returned to our little room and found Nanna reading the Qur'an, which was how she relaxed. You're lucky, I thought, you know what peace is.

We spent a year in that little room in Karaburma. Then, in October, 1962, we were allocated a room in a twelfth-floor apartment shared with another Institute employee, Rada. Rada was the occupancy rights holder because her husband Simo was employed as a lawyer in the Belgrade municipal offices. The high-rise was on the Boulevard of the Revolution, a little way up from the Zvezdara. We spread rugs on the floor of the room. Kenan slept on a cot and Nanna on a nice modern couch. We cooked on a gas ring in the room and also did our washing there, boiling it in a big pan. I stayed behind once a month to tidy the apartment and shake out the carpets before Rada came back from work. We bought an Obodin refrigerator on credit. It has worked ever since without giving any trouble.

The apartment was new and comfortable, but difficulties soon arose—unlike at Karaburma, where we had all got on well together. We could not use the kitchen because they accused us of being dirty and untidy. We, on the other hand, were disturbed by the television, which Rada had installed in the dining room right by our door. Their guests also disturbed us. They would often stay late, particularly on vacation days—especially Sima's friends, mostly clerks from the city municipal authorities and a few office-holders. This was the period of liberalization in Serbia. They would gather around the table, laughing and commenting on the latest events, telling jokes at the expense of the Yugoslav leadership, and eat and drink a little, as if we did not even exist. And yet they made it difficult for anyone to visit us. From the very start it seemed that they did not want to live with Muslims. They interpreted everything back to front and always unfairly. For example, it annoyed them when Nanna took *abdest* in the bathroom, although the corridor separated our room from the rest of the apartment. They even went so far as to complain about us to the Vinča management.

We might have understood their criticism of our way of life, perhaps, if Rada and Sima had not also made use of perfidious methods, accusing us of immorality and practicing religion. We certainly did have visitors from time to time: Nura came, then Hadija, and also Prijepolje Muhamed Čelebić, who was preparing a collection of local handcrafts for the opening of the national museum. He used the opportunity of coming to Belgrade to ask Nanna's advice about recording the origins of *mahramas,* towels made of a fine white fabric embroidered with gold or silver thread, and *čevras,* kerchiefs embroidered with gold thread at the corners. Nanna herself had her own embroidery collection, including silk *mahramas* more than a hundred years old that her Aunt Paša had woven when she made her own silk. We did not even know that silkworms had once been raised in Prijepolje.

My colleagues who knew what was happening in the administrative offices told me about Rada's letters to the administration saying that a mosque was being made in the house and that suspicious people were visiting us. They advised me to take steps to defend myself and to try to get another apartment.

I went to the Institute director for assistance. He did not say so, but from the conversation I concluded that he too knew about the letters. He advised me to turn to someone outside the Institute such as the editorial writer for the newspaper *The Communist.* I did so, writing a letter complaining of the attacks being made against my moral integrity and my mother's freedom of religion, explaining who she was. Rada's letters themselves must have given away the identity of their author when the *The Communist* found it appropriate to intervene, letting it be known to Vinča's administrative offices the Institute had gone too far in supporting Rada and the people behind her. To obtain an apartment I had to go through a rather long process. First, I obtained confirmation of Nanna's condition as an invalid, and wrote that I was living in a single room with my mother and a small child. Although he was small, Kenan understood something of what was going on and was afraid of Rada. He began to refuse to go into the apartment. We often slept at Bulka's place or in the neighborhood with a Muslim family from Bosnia.

Finally, after three and a half years of hell, in 1965 I was formally allocated a new, comfortable apartment measuring forty-five square meters on John Kennedy Street in New Belgrade. We moved in at the beginning of July. Although the apartment had only one large room, it was spacious, with a sunny balcony and loggia running the length of the room so that Nana could make a little flower garden. The corridor had deep, floor-to-ceiling cupboards, and the kitchen also had a door opening onto the balcony. The building itself was modern, with a broad, well-lit staircase and lifts, which we did not use since we were on the second floor. The occupants of the building were almost all selected from federal and military institutions and hospitals. I loved that apartment; we stayed there for twenty years. We quickly got used to it and bought some furniture, a radio and a television, a Tobi stove made in Slovenia, and began at last to live a normal life. The area where the apartment was located was close to Student City. I liked New Belgrade, known as "the dormitory of Belgrade." Many people did not like coming there across the Sava, thinking of and alluding to the fact that during the war the region had become part of the Independent State of Croatia, the infamous NDH. Everyone was scrambling to get an apartment in a "better" location because there was fear "the Croats might come again." For me, New Belgrade was handsome, with its broad, tree-lined boulevards and international street names. My street, Kennedy Street, was lined with mature lime trees whose fragrance filled the apartments. Limes grew right beneath our window, and a little farther on was a large sports ground for children and young people. On the corner was a foreign language school that operated in a famous "Shack." Then came the main post office and the large, modern health center for children and adults. Above the house was the maternity and children's hospital, the gift of an American foundation to Belgrade, and across the park the Zemun Hospital, with its great and long tradition.

There were several schools in the neighborhood, too, including Kenan's Marko Orešković School. A little farther along in the direction of Student City was the Ninth Belgrade Gymnasium, which Kenan also attended, and on Paris Commune Street one could catch the bus to the Belgrade airport. A number of bus routes crisscrossed our quarters without entering there, including the famous Number Sixteen bus that linked New Belgrade via Lenin Boulevard and the bridge at Brankova with the Zeleni Venac Market and continuing through the town from Republic Square along November Twenty-ninth Street toward Karaburma. A little farther down Kennedy Street one came to the banks of the Danube and the kilometer-long promenade toward Zemun. On the other side, below the Federal Executive Council (SIV), toward the confluence of the Sava and the Danube, was the Yugoslavia Hotel, a modern facility where my colleagues and I would sometimes go in the mornings for "coffee and cornbread with clotted cream" in the Danube Room. In the immediate neighborhood there was a sports center with swimming pools, where one could go with an annual pass that cost very little.

Later, I crisscrossed the more distant regions toward Zemun Polje in connection with my work. This gave me the opportunity to get to know the way of life of the people outside of Serbia proper, their rich agriculture, and the quality of their water and living environment. Upper Zemun had been home to a large German community that was resettled in 1945. Their properties, with spacious single-story houses, were nationalized and divided mainly among people who had fought as Partisans in World War II. There I found our people from Divci village and Ivanje.

The rich Zemun market, located close to our place, was composed of two large sections: the meat market and the fruit and vegetable market. They were always packed with goods and people from all over the place, especially Macedonia and Kosovo. There we found produce of all kinds: the famous sour cream of the region, meat, game for tasty soups, and river and sea fish. The prices of fruits and vegetables were a mere bagatelle in the autumn, when everyone could afford to buy them to make winter preserves for the cold days when the Košava wind blew from the east and there were fewer people and less traffic on the streets because it was pleasanter to stay indoors in our warm apartments, most of which had central heating.

New Belgrade also had a lot of waste spaces overgrown with sparse, stunted grass. These reminded me of Polje and appealed to my sense of freedom in natural surroundings where everything is closer to one and where I could walk with Kenan so that he could play and learn to recognize individual plants, trees, birds, and beetles. Kenan also had plenty of space to play around the house.

In the building itself, we quickly got to know the family of Alija Mustafović, a retired JNA officer from the Turkish community of Skopje, his wife Mica-Milica, a Serbian lady from Titovo Užice, and their three children. We used to leave a key with them, and would drop in before going back to our own apartment. In one of the flats reached through the other entrance to our building there lived Adil from Rogatica, a precision mechanic at Vinča, and his Serbian wife Cana, from Titovo Užice, a telephone operator on our main switchboard, and their daughter Fadila, who was a little younger than Kenan. In the apartment right next to ours was a family of military doctors with whom we got on well as neighbors right from the start.

The buildings had apartments for their caretakers, who were responsible for their upkeep. The city housing authority paid for repairs and for the cleaners from the rent paid by the residents. Besides the caretaker, the larger apartment buildings, like ours, had their house councils, which the apartment dwellers elected for two- or four-year terms. Their presidents often were former Partisans or retired military personnel. They tried to maintain order in their buildings and organized social activities, such as contributions of money in the case of accidents, as well as the establishment of burial funds. In every building, a list was posted in a prominent place inside the door, giving the names of the residents. Regulations relating to order were also posted. The president's role had its political side to it. To a certain extent, the presidents were the link between the residents and the governmental and police organs. For example, in New Belgrade, through which passed the roads to both the civil and military airports, the presidents of the house councils checked—in an unobtrusive manner—what was going on in their buildings, what mail was coming in (especially from abroad), and the movements of subleasers, especially the ever-increasing numbers of foreigners. It happened that students were prohibited from going anywhere for one or two days if an important guest was coming on a state visit.

In 1963, we took our annual vacation in July. My cousin Mehmed came from Skopje to procure some goods for the public utility company at which he was then working. So, Kenan and I decided to go to Skopje and spend a short vacation with them. We prepared some food for the journey, Kenan's plush bunny was given a bath, and Kenan, who did not sleep all day because of the excitement of going on vacation, fell asleep early that evening. Our train was scheduled to depart at about ten in the evening. I really did not want to wake him, and when I noticed that I had failed to get our medical care cards certified I suggested to Mehmed that we set off the following morning instead. He agreed.

We rose early and had coffee. Having no radio, we did not listen to the news. I went to Vinča and got my medical care card certified. The Institute was almost empty everywhere, since most people had already left on their vacations. I went outside to wait for the bus and encountered Veljko, the head of the Institute, who drove me back to Belgrade in his car. "Where did you say you were going yesterday?" he asked. "To Skopje, our train leaves at eleven," I replied. "What do you mean, Skopje? There's been an earthquake there." We turned on the radio. Everything was already abuzz with news of the earthquake, which had occurred that same morning, July 27, at 5:15.

The railway station was destroyed just as the train on which we had first planned to travel was arriving. A second train that left a little later had been halted outside Skopje. We packed a little food, and I went with Kenan to accompany Mehmed to the station. Only people with Skopje identity cards were being allowed onto the train. Mehmed checked his ticket and came with me to the Putnik, a travel center opposite the station, so I could return my ticket. We stood there on the corner saying good-bye.

When I turned toward Karađorđeva Street, I saw Derviš in an empty space outside the travel center, a meter or two from us. He did not look my way, although we were right there beside him. I was holding Kenan's hand; he was wearing a little blue suit that I had bought for him in France. That was the first time Kenan saw his father. He was two and a half years old. I went on talking to Mehmed and, shortly after we said good-bye, set off with Kenan along Balkanska Street. My intent was to visit a pastry shop run by some Albanians I knew to purchase an Italian cake. The question had again come up of what to say to Kenan about where his father was. I could tell from the fact that Derviš had moved on that he had not changed his mind, which hurt me once again.

I had yet another encounter with Derviš while taking Nanna for a checkup at the Military Medical Academy. We were sitting on a bench above the old academy building on the Deligradska Street side, waiting for the desks to open to the public at four and for the crowd around the entrance to disperse. I was smoking and the air was chilly; it was perhaps May, 1964. All at once a group of well-dressed, bejeweled women appeared and surrounded Derviš, who looked extremely dapper in a good-quality suit with a shirt and tie to match. They were standing close by, pretending not to know us. His niece—whom Nanna also knew, and who had married in Prijepolje—was there, too. They were talking among themselves, standing in a circle. Derviš, apparently casually, chose a position opposite us and began to stare openly at me—but more so at Nanna, whom he was seeing for the first time. I pretended not to notice anything as I sat there on the bench with my legs crossed, smoking a cigarette. I was looking in their direction, but through a gap in their ranks, gazing icily "all the way to Kosovo," as our people say when things become too much for us.

Yet my thoughts were wandering, deep inside me, without finding expression on my face, wondering what Kenan's fate would be and whether this injustice had any deeper meaning. Was this a sign that Kenan and I must endure endless suffering? It seemed to me that perhaps by bestowing suffering on someone it makes that person somehow elect, bound to look for the strength to forgive and transcend human misfortunes. I also felt certain that Derviš shared a part of that suffering. What else could this contrariness mean? To be as close as we had been, and now so far apart? It seemed to me like going from Heaven to Hell.

It was time for us to go. We stood up slowly and went to the other door, where Dr. Kičić waited. After checking all the test results, he announced that Nanna was perfectly well. He could not believe that at her age she had been able to regain strength in her right arm and the power of speech. "Mother, teach me the secret of maintaining your vitality," he said in an attempt to cheer her up. Nanna smiled, took out a box of fresh biscuits that she had brought as a gift, and handed them to him. "Thank you, Doctor, work in good health for many years to come." My Nanna had been beautiful and had kept her tall, slender figure. She also had a paler complexion than mine. Her doctor once exclaimed to me, "Please don't be angry, but your mother was more beautiful than you, and now see how young she looks for her age!"

Nanna rarely washed her face with soap, and when she did, she used only soap over which she had read "Sura Yusuf" from the Qur'an, telling me that half the beauty of the entire world had belonged to the Prophet Joseph and that the other half was shared out among all the other people "who have ever been and who ever will be." She then would pour the water she had used for washing onto the ground for the flowers to drink, so they, too, could take their share of the other half of the beauty.

It suddenly got warm in the spring of 1968, and everything began to burgeon. On Saturday, March 24, I went to Zagreb on business, taking Kenan with me. I left Nanna well, getting ready to clear up the terrace and prepare the flowerpots. On Sunday we went to the zoo in Maksimir and I spent Monday in the Ruđer Bošković Institute. I dealt with my work and we returned to Belgrade that same day on the night train, reaching home in the morning. We found Nanna sitting by the front door. She looked different, but I acted cheerful, saying, "What are you doing there by the door, Nanna?" She complained of feeling poorly and said she had seen us through the window and got up to open the door. I went to fetch the doctor, who came quickly and prescribed some medicine for her blood pressure. I saw him to the door. "I don't know why she's upset," he said as he turned to leave, "we'll soon see."

I asked her if she could eat anything. "I could manage a little spinach pie," she said with great difficulty and went to lie down. I made some for her. We slept a little that afternoon, and in the early evening she perked up. We watched a program about nature parks with babbling streams running through them, cascading down in waterfalls. This delighted her, reminding her of how she had always loved water, especially running water, liking to be beside it, enjoying its freshness and listening to its music. She said that she would no longer work around the house as hard as she had the past two days, adding, "One has to know one's limits." Those were her last words. Soon after that we all fell asleep, Kenan and Nanna and myself after them.

It seemed as though I had only just fallen asleep when I was awakened by a crash. It took me a few moments before I remembered where I was, and then I saw a light in the kitchen and jumped up to look for Nanna. I looked in the kitchen first. She was lying on the floor. I ran up to her, calling her name, thinking she had fallen. There was only dead silence. Hearing no sound from her made me realize what had happened. She showed no sign of life. On the table opposite where she had been sitting I saw an open Qur'an and a half-eaten pear. It was 3:35 A.M. I dashed to the telephone and called for emergency services, then called Cana and Adil to come and take care of Kenan. After returning the handset to the cradle I ran to our room, took a pillow to put under her head, and returned for Kenan. He was standing there in the dark.

I took his clothes, which I always kept in the same place, and took him into the hall. He wanted to turn around so he could see Nanna. Then Cana and Adil arrived. Cana took Kenan while Adil went out into the street to wait for the ambulance. I went back into the kitchen and found Nanna in the same place. After a moment she gave a few gasps, and then everything was quiet again. When the paramedics arrived on the scene they examined her briefly and established that she had been dead for several minutes. The whole episode had lasted just six minutes. I thanked God for taking her soul; she would have hated being incapacitated and a burden on anyone.

After the paramedics left, we went back inside. Adil stayed there and at about four o'clock I set off for Ljilja's apartment. She was my closest colleague at Vinča. As soon as I rang the bell, Ljilja came down to open the street door. The moment I saw her, I began to cry. We went in. Lale, Ljilja's husband, was getting ready to take Nura and Hadija from Belgrade and to phone Muhamed in Prijepolje. At about seven, I went to the Health Institute for the death certificate. The same medical team that had answered my emergency call came and examined her at home. They found a bruise on the left side of her back where the blood had collected.

Ljilja and I then set off to find a burial site. We chose a place we liked in the Old Bežanija cemetery in the Muslim section. Nura and another woman had already come and washed the body. In the early evening Nanna's nephew, Muhamed, arrived from Prijepolje; I had not even called my own people. Muhamed went out to buy *ulčitahte:* thick wooden planks placed above and below the deceased's body. Every Muslim used to keep *ulčitahte* ready in those days. Nanna's were made of solid beech wood, but they had been too heavy to bring with her from Prijepolje. He also bought a *ćefine,* the white linen shroud used to wrap the body after washing, and arranged with the imam for the *dženaza.* When all was finished, they put her in an inexpensive coffin that I had bought in accordance with her desire that nothing should be extravagant.

In the bundle of things she had kept ready for her burial, I found some *kabaš,* homemade tallow soap that she had long ago made herself for the ritual washing after death. She had not wanted us to use store-bought soap as it might have been made of fat of dubious provenance. Nanna also left some gold to pay for her burial, with the remainder to be distributed to the poor and to help children pay for their education. She had also left instructions for Muhamed to arrange a *hatma* and dedicate it to Babba and herself on Laylat al-Qadr, the twenty-seventh night of Ramadan. If at all possible, she wanted it done in the Great Mosque in Prijepolje, where her brother Hafiz used to pray. She died on Tuesday, March 27. I had heard her say long before that the *suvaldžije,* a special kind of angels, would not come to the grave of anyone dying on that day to ask what he or she had accomplished in this life. The deceased—Allah knows best—thus would not be disturbed at the start of their eternal life in the Hereafter. I remember her telling me that Thursday evening and Friday, the day of *džuma,* had been ordained as the day for God's good creatures to die, just as every day on which death finds us is God's day.

Lale and my colleague Dragica's husband, Pera, took care of everything to do with the burial and getting people to the cemetery and back home. Muhamed dealt with the imams, giving them as a gift for the mosque the remainder of the black fabric with which she was covered. Muslims in Belgrade were buried in coffins. The Bežanija cemetery was small and old. The Muslim section was at the far end, next to a garden in a little valley full of plum trees. Nanna was buried beside the path separating the cemetery from the garden. The Soldiers' League had turned the garden into a memorial park with a little obelisk and a few stars in the grass, in memory of those who had been brought there from the Staro Sajmište Camp by the Belgrade city police and killed during World War II. Not far from Nanna's grave I found the grave of a Red Army soldier, a young man named Aydin, who had been killed at the age of nineteen during the liberation of Belgrade in 1944. The Soldiers' League of New Belgrade looked after his grave.

Whenever I went with my helper, Smail, to tidy up Nanna's grave, I used to think that my mother was not in some crowded cemetery but rather in a high, sunny place with meadows wherever one looked. Her cousins had once lived in Belgrade, and now here she was again, far from Babba's grave in Sarajevo and Hatidžehanma's and Hasan *efendija*'s in Istanbul. My aunt Arifa died in Belgrade but was buried in Prijepolje, and Hafiz was buried at his ancestral home in Hisardžik. Thus these were our ties to our country, where we had lived for centuries. I once asked Muhamed, who came to visit Nanna's grave once a year, whether we should move her to Prijepolje. "No," he replied. "There's no need." Later I had a modest *nišan* made for her with an inscription picked out in gold: "Fatima Hadžišehović, a religious teacher from Prijepolje, 1895–1968, Al Fatiha."

Kenan was very sensitive as a baby and liked it when people paid attention to him. He loved being outdoors and noticed everything around him, especially animals. While Nanna was alive, it was she who prepared Kenan's meals. They would have breakfast together, telling each other stories that Kenan remembered for a long time after her death. They always waited to have lunch with me. As soon as I returned from work, I would take Kenan and his bowl of food and we would go out to Ada Huya, the island on the Danube linked by a long causeway to the land and meadows. There we would stop beside some chickens or a cow in the fields, so Kenan could look at them as he ate. Sometimes we would walk along the Danube's sandy banks and watch the boats passing, and sometimes we would sit alongside a fisherman, of whom there were always some there. By eight o'clock Kenan would be in his cot with a bottle of warm milk gruel made of toasted rice. He was not bothered by the babble of voices all around, for we lived in a single room and sometimes had guests. He always slept peacefully until early the next morning.

Even while still very small, Kenan loved picture books. He would lie or sit beside me and look at the pictures and ask me to read the stories. Sometimes while reading I would skip a few sentences to make it shorter, but he would immediately bring me back. He did not miss anything. He learned entire texts by heart, asking me to point out the words for him with my finger while he recited.

We fed him with a small spoon as a baby, just as he had learned in the hospital. When we changed over to feeding him from a bottle he became accustomed to having a pacifier. One pacifier that he particularly liked almost fell apart, but he did not want it replaced. Kenan liked to hear the story about the disobedient wolf cubs that annoyed their mother. She would leave them in their den and go out to look for food. The cubs would leave the den and run to the nearby bushes or a little farther to the stream, which attracted them with the sound of its cool, clear water gurgling and splashing over the stones down the slope. The mother would return and find them gone and immediately go looking for them. "Ah, there you are, you little rogues!" she exclaimed when she saw them. They would run happily to their mother and jump excitedly around her. Then all of them would return home for breakfast. The she-wolf would come to our window, so I always left a little food out for her to take to her children. Kenan would smile when he heard this. One day, however, I had to give her the pacifier, since she needed one for her cubs and had no money with which to buy one. He was delighted that she had found a pacifier after all. I had already bought him a replacement, but he did not want it. Thus, he finally gave up sucking.

On Saturdays and Sundays, Kenan and I used to visit the Belgrade Zoo in Kalemegdan or the Pioneers' City in Košutnjak Park. We knew every path, as well as the temperament of all the animals in the zoo. Rabbits like fresh grass, birds like grain, and the roe deer enjoys little branches with the leaves still on; they all got something. Sometimes Kenan would drive the pony traps. We would linger by the monkeys and then go visit Buca the hippopotamus. Sometimes we found him asleep in the water, and sometimes he would snort angrily, sending a jet of water spurting up. We did not like the reptiles and would go rapidly through the crocodile and snake house to the pool that was home to sea animals that liked fish. This was where the penguins lived, lined up in rows as if they were in the army. We would throw grain to the ducks, geese, and pelicans in the little river where they swam, dived, or preened their feathers while standing on the green verge that extended beyond. The zebras, gazelles, and Indian cattle grazed nearby. It all seemed quite normal, as though we were in a meadow. Farther on, one climbed up toward the bear pen. The polar bear enjoyed the winter, with its ice and snow, and in summer would lie around lazily or sway to and fro to cool off. We used to throw fruit to the brown bear, which we regarded as our own. If the fruit did not roll down of its own accord, he would roll them down into the water with his paw to wash them before eating them. He ate nothing without washing it first!

Sometimes we would go to the zoo in the afternoon when there were fewer visitors and watch the keepers feed the animals. The lions would lick their chops when they had eaten their fill and then wander off lazily to stretch themselves out and rest, blinking. In the early evening, the parrots would become talkative with the keepers, their voices perfectly mimicking the humans' voices.

Kenan recognized the wolves from the story, but those in the zoo did not look so "terrible." If we were fortunate, we would see the wildcats climb up and hide in the rocks. At one time the zoo had a lynx, a species that was almost extinct in Europe. I especially liked the goats. They were very sociable, running up for the little branches we offered them. They had kids, of which there were always plenty of different colors: ruddy, black, and party colored. The kids sought every opportunity to suckle from the nanny goats' full udders and when they had eaten their fill they would wriggle their little tails. That always made Kenan smile. He would stay there beside them for a long time while I sat on a stone to catch my breath and light up a cigarette. Kenan did not like the camels, which always seemed cross with us, but I visited them. "They are the providers of the Arabs," I would tell him. By the time we reached the camels' cage, it would be time to leave.

When Kenan was a little older, I would take a day off and we would walk around town. Both of us went to the hairdresser in our salon in the Belgrade Palace in Terazije. We would eat lunch in a restaurant and then go to Tašmajdan, where Kenan would play at motorcar racing. Bulka was particularly close to Kenan. She used to make preserves for him—the kind that we were not allowed to give to others. She sewed his clothes and bought him a school satchel to carry when they went out for a morning walk. She photographed him dressed up like a schoolboy with the satchel beside him, standing almost as tall as he did. However, if Kenan disobeyed her, she had her own little Kenan who would call and ask her to come over to his place. Kenan would have preferred the other little Kenan not to exist, and he would always try to find out where he was and whether he was going to appear. I did not much like it that she made him jealous in that manner.

In September, 1967, Kenan began going to Marko Orešković Elementary School near our apartment. He found it difficult to get used to doing his homework and to coming home earlier from the playing fields outside the house. When Nanna died the following year we had difficulty getting used to the empty flat and Kenan to spending the entire day in the school's common room. We solved it by having my neighbor Milica take care of him until I got home from work. In the morning, the two of us would leave the apartment together and go to his school, which opened very early. I would then continue on and catch the Vinča bus, which left at 6:20 A.M. right there on Lenin Boulevard. When we sat down to dinner, we would talk about how to learn from books, about what some concept meant. He learned easily. He had Derviš's intelligence, but he also reminded me of my father. I told Kenan the most important word in learning was *why*. If a pupil cannot answer that question logically, it means he does not understand, I explained. He thus would always wait for my question and then rush in with "Why?" and begin to laugh.

In September, 1975, Kenan enrolled in the Ninth Belgrade Gymnasium, where he placed first in the entrance examination. He received no rewards for his success, though. I patted him on the back and gave him a quick hug, and he smiled and put on a little bit of an air. Nevertheless, he understood it as a matter of course and so did not boast. He did not spend all his time with children whose parents were better off; he preferred to associate with everyone. Even while Nanna was still alive we combined all of our funds and planned together what to buy. He began earning money doing odd jobs while still young, washing the windows of new buildings and working in shops during the summer. In this way he was able to save money for annual vacations and buy books on subscription. When he earned his first "wages," he very seriously put his earnings with mine and began reckoning what had to be purchased. His seriousness seemed comical to me, and I remember thinking, that's how communism came about. But I was glad to know that someone else would take account of our household expenses and thus relieve me.

At gymnasium, Kenan was a *vukovac.* These were the pupils who received top marks in every subject. He did not know how to draw or to sing, and I think that the teachers made him a gift of those marks. He liked geography best. At home he read books and spent a long time making extracts from the *Great Atlas of the World* and the encyclopedia of the natural world that we had purchased on installments. He typed the material out on an old typewriter. I was usually working at the kitchen table when he announced his "results" from the other room. It seems the distances between cities, continents, and some important geographical points differed from atlas to atlas. He knew about the problems of mapmaking that gave rise to this phenomenon and would continue with borders that were "not natural" between individual countries. He then would determine which state had occupied more territory and state that for this reason "there must be war."

In addition to geography, he was interested in Latin. The Latin teacher and the teacher of what was then Serbo-Croat told me that if there were a higher mark than five, they would have given it to Kenan. Grammar came easily to him. He would write out Latin expressions for me and I displayed them at work above my desk. The first one he wrote down for me was "*Bona causa triumphat,*" which means "Good things triumph." Next he wrote, "*Surdo fabulam narare,*" meaning, loosely, "It's useless to speak to someone who isn't listening to you." Kenan's Latin phrases remained on display in the Vinča laboratory after both of us left Belgrade, a symbol of hope that, with God's help, justice would prevail in the war in Yugoslavia.

More than fifteen hundred students applied for the Faculty of Medicine in Belgrade in 1979, and about five hundred were accepted. The future students had to sit for an entrance examination in Latin, biology, physics, and chemistry. Kenan had spent the summer studying after choosing medicine as his subject, much to my surprise. When the time for the exams came, Kenan went. Upon his return, he said more about whom he had met in the faculty than about the exams themselves. The day the results were to be given out, Tito was returning from Havana from a conference of nonaligned countries. A huge welcome had been prepared and traffic was banned in the city. I had asked an acquaintance from the faculty to look at the list of students who had been accepted, and when I called her, she said his name was not on it. Surprised, I decided to check for myself. I took a roundabout route, using some of the suburban buses, and barely caught the last tram for the faculty at Đeram Market on the Boulevard of Revolution. A huge crowd of people had already poured into the city and thronged around the Parliament building.

I finally reached the faculty, but no one was there, only a huge list posted in the entrance hall. It bore the names of all those who had passed and all those who had not. I began to look for his name at the bottom of the list, since I trusted my acquaintance. No, it was not there. I was about to move on to the list of those who had not passed, when I looked up and saw Kenan's name at the very top, following the five candidates for scholarships from the Tito fund, who had gained some additional marks. Stunned by the realization of what it all meant, I sat down on the steps. My Kenan was among the top candidates to be accepted as a medical student in Belgrade!

I at last set off down the hill to catch the Number Seventeen bus, feeling light as a feather. There was no bus, but I was able to flag down a taxi and finally reached home after taking a roundabout route since the traffic ban was still on in the city. Back at home, I found Kenan all smiles. "Where have you been?" he asked. "I've been looking for you all over Vinča." I gave him a quick hug and replied, "I can't believe you are going to be a medical student, Kenan."

Immediately after Kenan's enrollment in the university, I set off on an official trip to the Saclay nuclear center in France. Kenan came along to see Paris and take a break after the arduous entrance exams. It was hardly any more expensive to take him with me, just a little extra for the journey. We took the train after I exchanged my first-class ticket for two second-class seats and a couchette. There was also very little difference between the off-season rate for a single bed and that for two in the Paris hotels where we stayed.

I had experienced health problems the whole of the previous year and felt certain I had an ulcer. I went to the hospital, but they did not diagnose the problem correctly, probably because the illness was not yet far enough advanced. So, I did not even have the proper medicines.

Subha Sadović, my friend from Prijepolje, had lived in Paris since 1962. Soon after our arrival I went to visit her. While I was there, I had an attack. Subha took me to her doctor, who referred me to the hospital. Since it was the weekend, he also prescribed some medication for me. It did not make me feel any better, so I stayed at Subha's. On Monday morning I was suddenly taken ill. Kenan took me to the hospital, where I had no trouble getting in with my passport and the doctor's prescription. Some people also came from work to help me. After they took an X ray I was placed in a ward. By evening I was running a high temperature, so they transferred me the next morning to another hospital, Saint Lazare, near the Place de la République from where the Grand Boulevard leads to the center of Paris. They put me in a little suite, like the other patients. There was a television in the room, as well as a small bathroom.

Kenan, who stayed with Subha, visited me every day with her. Both of them were very worried about me. I wanted to make things as normal as possible, so I urged Kenan to see the sights of Paris and put to use the few words of French he had already managed to pick up. He returned home the following week. As we parted, I asked him to go straight home and not to go wandering about. I was very ill and wondered if I would ever see him again. I watched him until he disappeared down the corridor. He could have ended up alone. They sent me to a third hospital, where I underwent a small operation to open up a vein in my chest through which to give me a larger infusion of medication, instead of an intravenous drip in my already bruised arm. As soon as they returned me to the ward they began intensive treatment. Every evening, two nurses wearing masks over their faces would come, open up the vein again, and insert a new bag of medicated infusion. And so it went, night after night, with nothing to eat. The first few days were tough. Perhaps the medication was what caused me to have hallucinations that I was at the edge of some abyss where I had gone with Nura and Rabija, floating on a green islet by the water. Then the scarlet blood would spurt onto the wall opposite my bed and I would awaken from the nightmare with a fever. The night nurses were older and rather resembled the nuns, who also lived on the hospital grounds. After a few days I felt well enough to chat with them a little. They were amazed that I knew entire sentences from the French classics by heart, and even more so that I had learned them at gymnasium as part of the normal curriculum. No one learned more than we did about others and less about ourselves.

I began to lose weight. I lost more than ten kilos in a month, going down to fifty-two kilos. I could not stand any excitement, not even calls from the doctors or my Vinča colleagues. Since my bed was close to the nurses' room, as soon as they began to stammer on the telephone I knew that it was for me. The most they could manage of my surname was "Madame Hadži"—everyone is known in France by their surname prefaced by the appropriate title. Then one day I heard Dragica's drawl: "Muna, how are you?" I could barely muster a response. That evening I had another high temperature, so they kept me isolated to avoid any further excitement. Every two or three hours they would take my blood pressure and measure the sugar in my blood, and I was X-rayed every day. The doctors, convinced I would pull through, encouraged me. After less than a month, they stopped my treatment, examined me thoroughly, and said I was on the way to recovery. Indeed, I *did* feel better. The head doctor also told me what the diagnosis was: they had found Crohn's disease in the sigmoid part of my large intestine. The disease manifested itself as inflammation of the mucous membrane that spread deep into the tissue, which could lead to perforation of the intestine and life-threatening internal bleeding. It was my good fortune that they had succeeded in preventing this with the treatment they had given me.

I had become so used to eating nothing that I began to be seized with anxiety when they told me that I could begin to eat normally again. It seemed to me that I would not know how to chew or how to move my jaws. When they stopped the infusions, they brought me a nasty-tasting green vegetable soup. I was able to sip only a little of it. It was much the same at dinnertime. The next morning, they brought me white coffee with chicory, some overdone bread, butter, and jam—just like what I had eaten in Kolonija during the war. I had a little real food for lunch: meat, steamed and browned vegetables dressed with butter and lemon and sprinkled with chopped parsley, and for dessert some tart-tasting strained fruit. It was all unsalted, since I was still on cortisone, but the herb-flavored food was tasty and savory even so.

When I first fell ill, I could not even think, let alone pick up a pen. It was as though I had forgotten how to write. I gradually regained my strength, and when I finally began to eat, it returned even more rapidly. I could watch television programs, too. I began with nature programs and switched midstream to historical programs about ancient civilizations. Finally, experts on ballet even managed to arouse my interest in that discipline, which I had never liked before. That year, 1979, was the first year of the fifteenth Islamic century, according to the Hijra calendar. Several programs were dedicated to this event, and for the first time I saw and heard on television scholars from Al-Azhar and other Islamic universities.

There were no restrictions on visiting hours to the hospital. Subha used to come and visit me after work, and some others from our part of the world came, too. One day they brought me a tapestry to embroider. I also began to read our newspapers, which were regularly available in Paris. Surfeited with French, I began to read slowly at first, being so tired, but after a while I read everything from front to back. I had already begun my convalescence. I started by taking a bath. The nurses helped me get into a wheelchair and then to the bathroom. I washed in cold water, which was a real pleasure for me. They also gave me physical therapy, and one day I was able to stand on my own two feet. Step by step, helped by the therapist, I would walk the few meters to the conservatory, which was full of greenery. I took pleasure in everything, and there, sitting in a comfortable armchair, I watched a group of students doing their practicals, clustering round the doctors in the corridor as they explained to them the work of the hospital. If Kenan had wanted to study abroad, I could have managed his studies in Paris. The value of our dinar was high at that time, and I could almost have managed his fees from my salary.

I slowly returned to life. One day I mustered the courage to go alone to the central, well-lit bathroom. Out of caution I sat on a chair and splashed myself with water, much as we used to do when taking *abdest.* I enjoyed it so much that I felt even stronger. I recall, too, the day when I first went out of the hall where the physical therapy exercises were conducted, and down into the little park between the buildings. We came back by lift, since my legs were shaky, but I was soon able to use the stairs, stopping to rest on each step.

The day finally came for me to leave the hospital. Since I was still on medication and a strictly salt-free diet, I went back to Subha's place.

After convalescing for a week I went back to work on a shortened schedule, as noted on my hospital discharge form. I was warmly welcomed at work, where everyone did all they could to make my job easier for me. It was difficult for me to cope after all I had been through, but I simply had to work. There were no long-stay or sick leave facilities in their hospitals. I laid out the map I had been given and worked out the best route on the metro: one that allowed me to get around the corridors on moving walkways, since I suffered from painful inflammation of the calves after I began to use my legs. In fact, I did not surface until I got to the Institute's bus stop.

I returned to Belgrade in December. After my final medical checkup I was prescribed medication and given detailed diet instructions. I was also given a letter for my doctor outlining the diagnosis and giving a detailed description of the analysis and the X ray findings. Fortunately, there was a convention between Yugoslavia and France regarding medical treatment. Since I had become ill on the job, my expenses were covered by our insurance, but I paid for the checkup in the clinic and for my outpatient prescriptions. My neighbor in Belgrade, a doctor, took me to the Military Medical Academy to see Prof. Milovan Elaković, who monitored my illness for years afterward. His treatment was similar to what I had received in the hospital in Paris. During the checkups he told me to be prepared for "long-term therapy" that would be adjusted to enable my system to take a break from the medication and to gain strength with the aid of additional vitamins and minerals. I had been expecting this, since the French doctors had carefully explained the nature of my illness to me.

After three months I began to eat salted food, but I now found it unpleasant: it was too strong and tasted nasty. In fact, I learned that it is possible to get used to many different ways of life and still be happy if we have no other choice. I continued working throughout all of this, which helped distract me from my illness. The following year, 1980, I went to Paris for a checkup. While I was there, I found the file containing all of my doctor's findings. I went there twice more after that. When, some years later, I sent a postcard to the doctor who had treated me in Saint Lazare, I received a letter in reply that really cheered me up, especially the comment, "Bravo for your health and your courage." It was only then that I understood just how ill I had been.

Kenan was in his third year at the university. After taking his exams in February, 1982, he went off to Sarajevo and Prijepolje for winter vacation. Upon his return to the university he displayed none of his usual enthusiasm. He told me he had quarreled with his girlfriend about mixed alliances that had no future. It seemed to me that that was his problem, so I tried to draw him into a detailed conversation about employment opportunities in Sarajevo, a place he had always liked. A relative of mine, Nakija, came to visit and gave him a gold chain for his birthday. When Kenan left to see Nakija off, I went to the kitchen to make him fritters, his favorite dish. Soon, however, they both came back. The moment they came in, I knew something was very wrong. Nakija told me that I should tell him about his father. She said she had already said something because the subject was troubling him. A shiver went through me as I joined them in the room. "All right, Kenan," I said. "I will tell you about your father, but first let us eat and calm down a bit." Nakija tried to save the situation with good humor plucked from thin air. "Come on now," she said, a broad smile creasing her face. "I was frightened for no reason, and now, you see, Allah willing, all will be well. I'm glad it happened." It was all we could do to get our food down in the tense atmosphere.

When we finished eating it was time for Nakija to leave, and Kenan left again to see her to the station. Upon his return, I asked him if we could put off our conversation about his father until the next day. I stayed home from work in the morning. After a brief search, I found the little purse in which I kept Derviš's pictures and letters, and showed them to Kenan. I tried to present his father to him as a good man and said that we had drifted apart because we took different roads: my motive was to get an education.

At first it seemed like Kenan would get over it, but the situation only got worse. He was unable to sleep, and finally we decided to get a doctor's help. We went together, and after all the formalities of furnishing personal and family information, we chose a woman doctor. As chance would have it, she was from Sarajevo. After talking to Kenan, she called me in and explained that Kenan's crisis had to do with his father, that he was distraught because he knew nothing about him. She suggested that we both come again, Kenan to talk to her, and I to talk to another psychologist in the same medical center.

Thus we started a kind of therapy based on conversation. I took sick leave in order to be with him and he stopped going to lectures at the university. I was trying to help him. We would take walks away from the city streets, on Mount Avala and in the woods nearby; we talked and talked, but there was no sign of improvement. I made visits to the psychologist, talking to someone for the first time about everything that had happened, but Kenan did not want to go to the doctor anymore. I called Sakib, another relative, to ask if he would see him as a physician. The woman doctor had felt from the beginning that it would be good for Kenan to see his father. "It is not urgent," she said, "but it would be very beneficial for Kenan if his father would agree to talk to me." After Sakib had a short talk with Kenan, as we were saying goodbye in the corridor, I asked him to get me Derviš's address and telephone number. "Just the address and his number at work," I repeated. "I want to know once and for all what he thinks about being a father." It was the first time I had said Derviš's name and that crucial sentence in the presence of another person. Sakib was surprised by my resolve. He just looked at me and said, "Fine!"

Why had I not told Kenan earlier? I had known about this big problem all along. I also had come up against the question of what might happen when he eventually did find out. He might go looking for him and, if he encountered rejection, start out on some other road: skipping school or keeping bad company, for example. I had always thought of myself as a good mother, but then the woman doctor told me I was a good person for not having burdened anyone else, but not a good mother. Suddenly, the idea of the goodness in me began to break down. Whatever happened, the truth had to be told. I came to that conclusion at the end, although I had sensed it from the beginning. What truth? There is nothing worse than rejected love—only the illness of a child is worse. I was never brave enough to actually say that simple answer.

From the beginning of March until April 9, the two of us wandered around in that nightmare. One Friday evening the telephone rang. Kenan was lying down, so I answered it. "Hello, it's Derviš." Had I misheard? I could not believe it. "Who?" I asked. He repeated: "It's Derviš." I was silent. "How are you?" I forced myself to speak: "Fine." Then, after a brief pause, he said: "I would like to meet you tomorrow morning at eleven. Could you meet me at the Mercator store?" My voice sounded like someone else's when I mumbled, "Yes" in a halting manner. "So, what have you been doing?" he continued, trying to overcome my lack of cordiality. "Nothing in particular." There was a short pause. "Fine," he responded. "So long until tomorrow." The phone clicked when he hung up.

I went into the other room. "Kenan, your father called." Kenan sat up. "What does he want?" he asked, as though it was of no importance to him. "He would like to see you and asked if he could first talk to me to make the meeting easier." "Fine," he said, and then added as though to himself, "Perhaps he is a good man." The next day I went to the Mercator and Kenan stayed home. I had no trouble recognizing Derviš despite all those years we had been apart. We greeted each other and shook hands, trying to behave like good friends meeting after a long interval. We headed for the Hotel Putnik around the corner. Inside, we sat at a table opposite one another in the almost empty restaurant. Overcoming some reluctance, I outlined Kenan's situation to him. I told him that I would also like to know his position on being a father and to hear just one word: "Yes" or "No."

Derviš did not give me a direct answer to anything. He slumped back in his chair and said that he was not satisfied with his life. I could not believe it! Were we going back to the beginning again? What sense did it make to keep on saying the same things after so many years? However, squeezed by Kenan's problem and the lack of sleep, nothing else was important to me at that moment. Fatigue and Kenan were the only things of which I was aware. I was worried about having left Kenan alone for so long and wanted to leave. Each time I got up to go, Derviš would stop me. Several times I went off to telephone Kenan.

It was getting dark when we finally got up to go. Derviš suggested that he meet Kenan in this same place at five the next afternoon. It was drizzling outside. My apartment was not far away, but he offered to drive me. Although I did not want that, I fell back on old custom and, out of politeness, did not refuse. Derviš stopped the car near the front door of my building, turned toward me, drew me to him, and began to embrace me. I pulled away, afraid of attracting the attention of neighbors or passersby. My resistance brought him to his senses. He laid my head on his shoulder and said softly, "Just like this for a little bit." We stayed like that for a few peaceful moments and then he broke the silence with these quiet words: "Nothing has changed. I knew from the beginning when I saw you that nothing had changed. I knew it as soon as we started talking." The tangle of my circumstances began to throb inside me. How can it not have changed? I thought. So many years of being alone—and then there was Kenan. I saw the unbridgeable divide and realized there was no point in saying anything. I pulled away, already skilled at covering internal confusion with external coolness, and said, "Until tomorrow, so long."

Of course, it would have been impolite—and, what is more, cruel—to turn my back and go into the building, so I stood there to see him off.

Kenan was waiting for me. I told him my impressions, and when he asked whether paternity was possible, I repeated Derviš's words. We met again the next day at the same place. Derviš and Kenan greeted one another. We spent about two hours in a spontaneous conversation and then went home. I was fearful about Kenan's reaction that night, about spending it alone with him. Once we were in the apartment, Kenan laughed and said that he had seen Derviš before. I was surprised, "When?" He said that he had followed me to the Mercator the day before when I went to meet Derviš. "You sneak, you," I said. "And there I was, worried about how I was going to introduce you." Somehow, his reaction dispelled my fear and our awkwardness. We sat down to drink coffee. Kenan lighted a cigarette and the two of us fell to talking, making fun even of ourselves as we exchanged observations.

We began to keep company. Derviš would sometimes come for a short while, sometimes for longer. The doctors thought it would be beneficial for Kenan to see his father as much as possible. When Derviš called him, they would go out together. I had again gone back to work, but I continued to see the psychologist. During our discussions she explained to me figuratively that my feelings for him "still were not spent," that they were still "burning" because we had broken off so abruptly and they had neither "found an outlet" nor the "substitute" of another relationship. Kenan's doctor once told me I had "transformed my sexuality into work," and that they had not had such a case for a long time. On another occasion, the psychologist remarked that my politeness, which did not allow me to stand up against anyone, derived from the excessive authority that Derviš represented for me, since I came from a background in which the male members of the family were to be respected.

Nevertheless, the two of us kept going around and around the same topic. It was clear to me that Derviš wanted to pick up where we had left off. But did I want that? At the beginning, the most important thing for me was his attitude toward Kenan. However, his announcement that there was plenty of time introduced a new element into our relationship. We quickly became a threesome. If Derviš was not there, Kenan would usually ask, "Has our friend called?" He seemed constantly concerned about this. He began to feel a little better and soon started going out on his own. Kenan began to compare my social status with Derviš's competence and his family's affluent lifestyle. I could see that our former life and outlook was being shattered. Maybe some people are able to make better lives for themselves in other ways, but we could do so only by working. Suddenly, my views were old-fashioned. It seemed to me that the atmosphere in which he had grown up did not suit Kenan. The differences in outlook that had led Derviš and me to break up now began to be felt in our home. "Look at what's really important, what attracts you; perhaps you'll be better able to find out for yourself what you want," I advised him. "I wanted to have a family, not be left alone"

As a practical step, I bought a booklet entitled, *The Law on Family and Marital Relations and Legislative Norms.* I discovered that I no longer had the right to apply for confirmation of paternity. It could only have been done prior to Kenan's eighteenth birthday. After that, Kenan had until his twenty-third birthday to apply for paternity proceedings—and he was already twenty-two! It was the first time I saw these regulations. We went on in this manner until the beginning of 1983. In the meantime, Kenan returned to university after a year's break.

In March, 1983, I invited Derviš to talk about things. We went out to Kalemegdan one afternoon and I said that he was wrong to treat our relationship with Kenan as though we ourselves did not exist. "You must answer the main question," I told him again. "I must have an answer within the month." I said all of this like a robot, in a cold, tired voice. Derviš had again become a stranger to me.

I was surprised when he did not change the subject. He agreed, asking only that I give him about three weeks. Derviš had a tram to catch, so I set off for my bus. A moment later he caught up with me. We continued together in the direction of Zeleni Venac: wretchedly, painfully, sadly, along streets full of people, yet to us they might as well have been deserted.

I talked continually to Kenan about his relationship with Derviš. Quite a while earlier, Kenan had told me he had decided to go to the courts to apply for confirmation of paternity—unless I felt I could not bear to go to court. "That would be the only reason for me not to do it, Mama," Kenan said. "I'll go along with it if that's what you want, but I would like to know why you are doing it." I was surprised by his reply. "Someone must tell Derviš that he cannot do everything he wants at other people's expense," he explained.

I knew that Kenan was both fighting for Derviš's affection and rebelling at the same time. On all his documents, even after he finally acquired a father, he kept my surname and would write my name in the box labeled "parents." This shows that he not only was no stickler for formality, but that he was also ashamed of having been rejected, of being different from "real" children.

After about three weeks, Derviš called me. He had come up with a plan that would enable us to do what we wanted. He said we must go formally to the court and file a case against him. At first I did not understand and resisted the idea. Finally, I asked him a simple question: "Do you have any doubts?" I received no answer, but the threads were beginning to come together—from too many blows and yet another misfortune that had befallen me. Earlier, when Kenan was having his crisis, a Turkish woman of my acquaintance had visited me and awkwardly confided that she knew about the "indignities" that had been disseminated about me in our circles in the Sandžak, Belgrade, and Turkey—no doubt in order to protect Derviš and his family's reputation. The worst of it all for me was the discovery that Derviš had spoken to people from our mutual milieu in this way, referring to nonwhite foreigners as "blacks" and suggesting that the reason I had been punished by the Party was because I knew foreigners.

Wandering about Kalemegdan trying to convince each other, we came to the café and went into the garden. We sat down, I do not know why, and he ordered something to eat. We did not eat anything, however. I continued to try to persuade him and to press for what was right, and when I again went too far, Derviš looked up at me and raised his voice. "Munevera, do you really want to destroy my marriage? What *do* you want, in fact? It's not my fault that such a fuss was kicked up about you. You don't know how dangerous a person can be and you don't know what life is." He shook his head, expressionless, yet somehow changed in a way that I did not recognize. That was that, then. He had finally admitted to my face that his marriage was important to him, and at the same time revealed what he really thought about me. I thought that Derviš had associated himself with hearsay. "Listen, Derviš, I've kept quiet so far, but if I begin to talk about what I know, a lot of people will be hurt." I threw everything in his face, from Sarajevo onward. I knew that I was going beyond the boundaries of decency. I expected him to really flare up, but he simply said, "You won't do that." I jumped up from the table and ran outside, leaving him there. He caught up with me at the entrance and began to hug me in full view of the customers in the garden. "Don't go," he said breathlessly. I extricated myself and made off for the tram, but he again caught up with me. "I came today to be with you, forget all these stories," he said. I stopped under the eaves of a shop, leaning against the closed door, and felt sobs welling up inside me. "I'm going to pray to God to get us out of this mess and hope that the worst doesn't happen," I answered. Despite all the acrimony I pulled myself together, knowing that Kenan was waiting for me at home. I really had nowhere to go, torn between the two of them, just as Derviš probably was with his family. "Those were the walls around us," I thought. Everything subsided within me and I let myself go with the flow of events. I finally agreed to go to court. He explained to me what it would be like. He had a cousin-in-law, Meho, a prosecutor or a judge, I forget which, who knew the procedure. I just needed to meet with him. So, we met in Mercator and found seats in a little café. I looked at this Bosniak who "could take care of everything." Meho told me that it was "nothing," that it should have been settled much earlier. "If we were in Bosnia," he added, "it would be dealt with in two hours," but here "we have to engage an attorney, write the charge, and go to court." We agreed. They urged me to come to the grill at Slavija. Derviš called Kenan, who was at home, and he came to join us, not knowing what it was about. We had lunch. I even enjoyed the barbecued lamb. I felt calmer. After lunch, we separated outside the café near Derviš's apartment and even shook hands, which I did with Derviš as though he were a stranger.

Derviš and I finally realized that we had to speed things up. We went to see the lawyer, who told me to bring all the facts, and that I could describe the case myself. I wrote it all down, very much in brief: how we got to know each other, our relationship, what our intentions were. Derviš came to see what I had written and the three of us sat down together in the room. When he had finished reading, his face darkened. "This won't do," he said shaking his head. I saw that it was because I had written that we had embarked on our relationship with the intention of marrying. Until that moment I had not realized that there was any doubt about that intention. But we had had a relationship. "No," he said, standing by his decision. Kenan turned toward him and said, "Fine, Derviš. Are you my father?" There was a short pause. "Yes, I am," he barely managed to say, his voice soft. "Then why do you want to go to court? It's hypocritical," Kenan replied. Derviš became angry, got up to leave, and said angrily, "Look for another father, both of you." He reached for his coat at the door, but I could see that he was reluctant to leave. Perhaps he was now aware that we could really go to court, and not just put up a pretense. I felt uncomfortable at the way Kenan had undermined his father's authority, at his being able to talk to him in that way. "Go into the kitchen,

Kenan," I said. I took a fresh sheet of paper. "Dictate to me," I said, turning to Derviš. He took out what I had written and reduced the whole thing to a few sentences, referring to a short period of—if I recall it correctly—less than a year during which we had been "lovers."

I had already seen that it was drawn up to show our relationship as having been a free and insignificant one, since there was nothing to be lost by doing so and it would be easier to achieve what we wanted in the court. However, when he used the word *lovers,* I knew that it was not his. He would not have gone so far, he had always declared the very opposite. Besides, it would have been a sin. To know that Kenan's mother had been his mistress, that would do. However, I decided that it would not do: "No, we weren't lovers, that's not how Kenan came to be. Do you really think I lived all these years alone just because we were lovers?" I looked straight at him as I talked, but I knew that our relationship had in fact come to the verge of being just that. Yet if it was, it was not that—I also knew that within myself. Derviš, write that we simply 'went out together.' It's the same as what they want, only just a little different. The word is not so crude but the relationship is irresponsible, which is what it was, since this is what we've come to." Derviš agreed and breathed more easily. Kenan filed the suit and I witnessed it.

Our hearing was scheduled for the beginning of June. I was a little uneasy about appearing in court for the first time in my life. There was a lady judge and two jurors in a small courtroom. The attorney was Derviš's. The procedure was briefly explained to us and the judge ordered Derviš and me to have a blood test to determine paternity. Kenan had already received the results of his test. We went to the Blood Transfusion Union above Slavija on Svetosavksa Street, where samples of our blood were quickly taken. They said they would send the results to the court. I had read about how this was done and seen that it could be determined with a high degree of probability whether someone was *not* the father, but not whether he was. For positive proof, very specific analysis was necessary.

We returned for the second hearing on June 28. The judge had already received the results, which she read. They did not rule out Derviš's paternity. When she was finished, the attorney rose and announced, "They do not wish to proceed further and are withdrawing the charges." But the judge denied his request, ruling that "the court must proceed and reach a verdict." The judge then called on me to testify first. I briefly told about how we had "gone out together" for three years. The judge asked if Derviš had known about my pregnancy and, if so, when. I replied that he had not known at first. Finally, the judge asked me whether our relationship had been with the intention of entering into marriage. In accordance with what we had agreed, I replied, "No, we were just going out." From the judge's question, however, I realized that she accorded importance to our intentions in this case.

She asked Derviš fewer questions, including whether he had known about the birth of the child, to which he responded that he had. He clearly was uncomfortable, and I breathed a sigh of relief when the hearing ended. We rose to leave, and the judge turned to Derviš. "Are you married?" Derviš seized the opportunity to say a little about his situation: "Yes, I am, for many years, and I have two children." The judge nodded and said, "Introduce the children, they should see each other."

I came first for the verdict. The judge received me and said that she had reflected for a long time about me. She said that she too was married. The verdict had not yet been typed out, so I went outside to wait. Then Derviš arrived. We sat in the antechamber, waiting. "Are you satisfied?" he asked, adding hurtfully, "You have won a Pyrrhic victory." Then he repeated, "But only a Pyrrhic victory." I tried to explain to him that I had only done it for Kenan's sake, so that he would no longer have to leave the box for "father" empty, which always upset him the most whenever he had to fill out forms. He clearly did not like that explanation; he was very dour and could not handle the situation. I gave up, turned away, and looked into a void.

Derviš got up and went to make a telephone call. Then he read the newspapers. I did not say anything else. They called us to come for the verdict and to sign. We took the papers separately and once again found ourselves in the antechamber, silently walking down the steps. We left the Hall of Justice, me setting off for the railway station after a brief "good-bye," and he to catch a taxi. He made at first as though he were going to get in, then turned toward me: "Get in, I'm going to Brankova Street, we can go together." I just waved and continued down the street so I could breathe more freely. I did not sleep all night, staring vacantly into space, with a pounding in my head that felt as though I was being hit with a hammer.

The following day I went to pay the attorney. We had shared all of the costs. The attorney welcomed me by saying, "Now let's go on." He raised his eyebrows a little. "With what?" I asked. "To claim damages for Kenan for previous years, of course," he replied. I was sad to have to say, "No, Kenan doesn't want that, but we can ask him." The attorney looked at me and said, "And the surname." I shook my head. "No, not that either, he said he wants to keep his current surname." The attorney looked bewildered. "I don't know what's going on," he said. "Derviš can't make up his mind. He was here one afternoon before the court with his family, something is troubling him."

I looked at him vacantly from the armchair. "You are to blame," he said angrily. "You let things run on, you were there, you should have pushed harder." I shook my head. The attorney finally said: "That's not how it's done, to be thrifty when there's no need, there's no point." Trying to talk to the attorney about feelings and to go to court was also pointless. He saw everything realistically; the only thing that mattered to him was facts. Still, I was glad he was on my side and Kenan's—even though he was their attorney, too.

I thanked him and, unsure about what else to expect, asked, "Is this final?" He nodded. "Yes," he said. "His father's name will be registered on the birth certificate." A few days later I went to the municipality of Savski Venac to check for myself. I requested a copy of Kenan's birth certificate. The box for the father's name was indeed no longer empty. I put the birth certificate, the verdict, Derviš's letters, and a small plastic bag with some presents together and said with finality, "This is for you, Kenan."

Epilogue

The Breakup of Yugoslavia

Belgrade's postwar period ended one Saturday in the summer of 1965. While going to work through town, I noticed some people running along the streets, and on Knez Mihajlova Street a crowd had gathered outside the shops, but I paid no attention. Later, on my way home that afternoon, I stopped to buy bread and oil, but in vain; the shop was still open, but its shelves were bare and would not be restocked until Monday. "Why?" I wondered aloud. "The reform has been introduced; prices are changing," the shop assistant replied. I went home uneasy, like everyone else. By Monday, everything had changed. The major differences in price affected all but those articles whose price remained government controlled: certain kinds of bread, milk, and so on. We became accustomed to the high cost of living. Thankfully, the state granted additional benefits for people receiving low wages. For a while, however, it seemed as though things would be different: there were many job redundancies, unprofitable enterprises were closed. Nevertheless, after a while it seemed as if the old lifestyle had returned. The day-to-day talk of reforms came to an end, and things settled down—even in newspapers and on the radio. Yet, all this notwithstanding, there remained a sense of insecurity.

We had everything in those days. Our shops were full of exotic fruits and chocolate, and many boutiques selling luxury goods and large department stores were opened. People used to go to Trieste to buy Italian fashion clothing. Later, visas were abolished for the majority of countries and crossing the border was just like going to another city. The Yugoslav passport was highly regarded, and our emigrants found jobs in European firms trading with the East and other countries. Tourist agencies organized travel on credit payment terms and enterprises sent their women employees to Rome, Paris, or Moscow for Women's Day on March 8. The country did business with Libya, Iraq, many African countries, and later the Soviet Union. We knew that our affluence was based on loans, but people went on believing that the situation was the state's concern, not ours.

Yugoslav society was slowly stratifying itself again on a different basis from the prewar capitalism. Income was created by workers assigned a quota, "individual agricultural producers"—as the peasants were called—

and by artisans and independent professionals. On the other hand, there were many consumers: Party, union, and state officials. The song "Comrade Tito, this can't go on, one works and seven to write it down," described the situation well. Firing people did not exist in practice; it was hard to take responsibility for leaving someone jobless. No matter how badly and incompetently they did their jobs, unproductive employees received almost the same benefits as the good workers. In order to provide for everyone, the government had to reduce the pay of qualified workers and those who worked against a quota, and raise the taxes levied on the peasantry.

Two classes of professionals soon emerged. Politician-professionals—people called them "politicians"—ran institutions and were elected or appointed to the regional, republic, or federal administration and the Party apparatus. Workers identified as being the "most competent" were awarded their positions based on merit and lived off their "pay."

The other class of professionals consisted of experts. They could barely live on their pay and had little prospect of being allocated an apartment. They advanced slowly in rank and employed members of their families had difficulty finding better positions.

Politician-professionals were often rectors and deans of faculties. They managed large enterprises as well as urban administration services. The firms favored by the state were known in all the republics without exception. Banks and the army were in the forefront for prerogatives. A junior official in a bank or the army often had a total income exceeding that of a university professor. Politicians were allocated staff apartments. Their children, even those with poor qualifications, were often employed in well-paid jobs or foreign branch offices. Technocrats went on official trips and procured equipment for firms and licenses from foreign companies. Once they had acquired the necessary skills, most founded their own companies. In their later years they secretly bought out socially owned enterprises for little money, making deals with those in the country's management structure. Faced with social and moral disintegration, there emerged a stratum of disaffected people. They generally were young, highly qualified people, who found it increasingly difficult to find employment. They were without prospects or social status and in the humiliating position of having to be supported by their parents. It was easy to win them over to nationalism.

The state penalized science in particular, fearing its independence. Researchers barely managed to scrape out a living in relation to their contribution. Given these circumstances, specialists, professors, and anyone else who could sought additional income working at more than one post: in newly opened faculties in the interior, as experts in large organizations, or in the military. Young researchers tried to leave the country by whatever means they could, learning foreign languages, and, while still at university, establishing links with foreign institutions. They left immediately after graduation instead of joining our institutes. The result was that Yugoslav science became more and more outdated.

The 1970s in Yugoslavia saw a succession of political events. In the autumn of 1968, student demonstrations broke out in Belgrade. The whole of the city was on its feet, as if some general performance was beginning. It was unimaginable that demonstrations could resolve anything in a society that was disintegrating ever more rapidly and becoming ineffective. All they could do was shake things up a little and bring a breath of fresh air. If nothing else, for the first time the great slogans were to be seen on the Kapetan Mišina edifice: "Down with the red bourgeois!" demands for freedom such as, "We want freedom of speech and work"; and the appeal to the workers to ally themselves with the students, "Workers with us!"

People would come out for a walk in the afternoon to see the spectacle and the military, brought in trucks and left to wait at the corners of the streets by Students' Square and Revolution Boulevard around the law and engineering faculties. Lectures were held, with public platforms, at the philosophy and law faculties. The students hoped for Tito's support, but it did not happen. The Party organization in Vinča was with the students. As always when reforms are called for, the Party stood by those calling for them, but not so explicitly as to bring the Vinča workforce out to the demonstrations. Nor did it go further than written expressions of support. Yet the demonstrations did take place, and no one publicly dispersed, arrested, or beat the students as had happened in 1954. The slogans remained in place for a long time.

Serbian liberals had their own republic program: the modernization of the economy. The mass movement in Croatia in 1970–71 called for greater political and economic autonomy. A new Yugoslav constitution was adopted in 1974. The republics became even more independent, and Yugoslavia acquired a rotating collective presidency. Nationalism, still insufficiently clearly distinct from the liberal movements, awoke and led to quarrels among the communists.

Yet another topic contributed to the inflammatory situation of the time: the nationality of Muslims-Bosniaks, which had been recognized in 1971. In 1968–69, the Institute received a letter saying that Bosnia was inviting tenders for a loan for the construction of roads and schools. The Bosnians in our laboratories had collected funds and subscribed to the loan. In addition to Belgrade's Energoproject, Energoinvest in Sarajevo was penetrating ever more successfully into the global market. Bosnian engineers, doctors, and professors worked in Arab countries. Bosnia and the Sandžak obtained their own Muslim ambassadors in large numbers. The practice from the Ottoman period and the First Yugoslavia continued whereby the Islamic Religious Association sent students to religious schools in Islamic countries, particularly to Al-Azhar University in Cairo. It was at this time—1971, I think—that the Islamic Theological Faculty was opened in Sarajevo and the Christian Theological College in Belgrade, closed after the war, again began to operate.

I knew that the majority of Serbs did not recognize the Muslim or Bosniak nationality. I was surprised, however, by the views of some of my Croat colleagues. They were equally if not more opposed to it. It was difficult for Muslims in such surroundings, the same thought constantly intruded on me. Muslims would have a considerable struggle until they could win their own place, if they won it at all. In my conversations with Serb colleagues, they would usually say, rather awkwardly and out of consideration, "Well, Muslims are really Serbs of Muslim faith, aren't they?" If I tried to explain, they would take refuge in "history," making it impossible to engage in a serious discussion. Now I saw that the Croats had the same intention: they wanted Muslims to be Croats. I thought about it and came to the conclusion that there were major reasons for the leadership at the very top level in Yugoslavia and in Bosnia to evaluate the nature of this danger and to do what should have been done at the second session of the National Antifascist Liberation Council of Yugoslavia in 1943: introduce all three people groups in Bosnia at the same level and rectify the injustice against the Bosniaks, already more than a century old.

On October 11, 1985, Kenan passed forensic medicine and graduated. He spent the next year as a faculty internist at the University Hospital in Belgrade. In May, 1986, we moved into a new apartment. Upon completing his internship in October, 1996, Kenan went into the army for a year and underwent further medical training at the Military Medical School in Banjica in Belgrade. Dragana, his faculty friend, accompanied him to the army post. She called me on the telephone to say that Kenan had gone unwillingly into the barracks grounds in Banjica, turning to wave to her as she stood at the gate. "Go on Kenčo, don't worry," said Dragana, herself a little agitated. It was hard for me, too, but military service was compulsory. It was a "debt to the country and a sign that a young man had become a mature person," as our people used to say. He attended lectures at the Military Medical Academy for the first six months of his term. After passing the exams, he was sent to practice in the Garrison Clinic of the Sarajevo Military Hospital.

Kenan obtained a job as a doctor in Travnik, Bosnia, in 1988. He married Azra that September, and on October 29, 1989, my grandson Amir was born. The following year, Kenan took a job in Sarajevo and began to specialize in internal medicine. Azra served as a lawyer in the Land Registry Department of New Sarajevo Municipality and they rented an apartment in Sarajevo's Dobrinja district, close to the airport. I went to pay them a visit in November, 1991. The war had largely flared up in Croatia. In Sarajevo the First Congress of the Party for Democratic Action (SDA) was held. The SDA was the Muslim political organization founded in 1990 by Alija Izetbegović. There was great interest in the delegates' speeches and the congress' conclusions, although the working sessions were held behind closed doors. War was in the air. Everyone was uneasy about what would happen, although they could not yet foretell the magnitude of the disaster in Bosnia.

When I returned to Belgrade, Kenan accompanied me to the early morning bus that left from the railway station. The railroad connection between Sarajevo and Belgrade had already been cut because it went through the war zone in Croatia. Our farewell was like many others. Kenan stood beside the bus and then on the parking lot until it left the station. Later, he telephoned to say that he had the feeling we would not see each other for a long time, if at all. Indeed, the years go by and we remain separated, like many others from the former Yugoslavia.

The bus went via the Han Pijesak and Zvornik Mountain regions. I knew that these areas were a hotbed of Serbian nationalists and most likely the first to be attacked—especially Han Pijesak of ill repute, with its military potential on which the JNA had squandered part of our national wealth. I looked out the window at the sleeping houses and had a presentiment that this might well be my last journey through our homeland and that ghosts could appear at any moment.

Immediately after we left Bosnia near Zvornik, Serbian military and police patrols appeared on the Brotherhood and Unity Highway that runs from Zagreb to Belgrade. They were strutting about as though the whole world was theirs. Meanwhile, the Muslims on our bus were frightened and sorrowful when we saw what was being done and that border checkpoints had already been set up.

At the beginning of April, 1992—on the third day of Bairam, I think—the Chetniks attacked Sarajevo. I listened to Sarajevo radio all night during the attack. It appeared to me that the city's defenders had, to some extent, been caught napping by the attack. Nonetheless, Sarajevo held out. Because of the danger in Dobrinja, which being near the airport was the first district to be attacked, Kenan sent Azra, Amir, and Azra's mother to Belgrade. He managed to get them on a military aircraft carrying the families of officers from Sarajevo to the military airport of Batajnica, in Belgrade. Osman, Azra's father, and Kenan succeeded in getting through the cornfields to the center of

Sarajevo. Thanks to Osman's knowledge of the terrain, they managed to get past the Chetniks unobserved. They left everything: Azra's father's apartment, Kenan's rented apartment full of household goods, as well as the house belonging to our cousin, Ahmo Šehović.

The telephone links between Sarajevo and Belgrade continued functioning until August. Because it was dangerous for her to be in Belgrade, Azra had gone to Vienna as a Bosnian refugee. In November, Kenan called me via a radio ham; we could barely hear one another. Macan, one of Kenan's university colleagues who had succeeded in making contact with Kenan, called me once more from Banja Luka. That was it. The Seventh-Day Adventist Relief Organization (ADRA) became active during that period, so I sent Kenan and my relatives in Sarajevo parcels, some money, and warm clothing via that organization. Derviš called me at about the same time to ask about Kenan and Azra. I gave him Azra's address in Vienna. He said that he had left Sarajevo with his family and was now living somewhere "between Istanbul and Germany." This meant that he had activated his previous business contacts in Europe and had involved his son in the business. He told me briefly about the sufferings of his relatives in Banja Luka who were expecting to go abroad, some of them to the United States.

How complicated and contradictory our lives had become! The people who had drawn Kenan to Sarajevo were leaving the city, and Kenan—Belgrade-born, not even a Bosnian—stayed there to defend Sarajevo and to share the city's misfortunes, helping people and hoping for the best. The war had placed Kenan and his university companions, like the rest of the people in Yugoslavia, on opposing sides. The Serbs sent Macan, who had been working as a doctor in Banja Luka in 1991, to the front in Croatia; Abdul-Adi returned to Novi Pazar to help the people of Sandžak; and Dragana, a native of Belgrade, found work in the University Hospital there.

Reflecting on life in Belgrade just before the war began, I saw that something very bad was approaching. Outlets of firms from other parts of Yugoslavia were disappearing. On the basis of the Law on Associated Labor they were taken over by the workers employed in them. It meant little, however, as goods of all kinds were no longer arriving. Nationalism was on the rise everywhere, over the radio and television, in the newspapers, even on the street. Belgrade was becoming filled with outsiders—dirty, disheveled, drunk, and carrying weapons. Music that included the most sinister Chetnik songs was blaring from every direction—from restaurants, stores, beauty salons, and people's apartments. Knez Mihajlova Street became the meeting place for "folklore" gatherings at which young people wearing Chetnik caps and Serbian and Montenegrin peasant costumes sang and delivered speeches about the glory of the Serbs and the "injustices" befalling them. Peddlers sold Serbian banners, cassettes, and books with hate-mongering and rabble-rousing titles calling for revenge for the injustices perpetrated in Tito's Yugoslavia. Everything contributed to the excited state. News items appearing under bold headlines were filled with descriptions of battles and the "liberation" of particular "Serbian" cities: Vukovar, Sarajevo, Dubrovnik. It was only a matter of days before the stronghold of the mujahideen and Ustaše would pass into the hands of the "liberators."

Refugees arrived from all directions. More and more graves were marked "NN," which presumably meant that the name of the deceased was not known. There were amputees, heads swathed in bandages, and the hospitals held more than a few young men who had been paralyzed by their wounds.

Reliance on government authority disappeared. It was evident that officialdom was working hand-in-hand with the underground and that lawlessness and the heedless use of power were not far away. Restaurants, bars, and stores selling luxuries sprang up, and entertainment and receptions were organized in the most expensive hotels for the new class being created no one knew how. Television was promoting new "business" people, among them bankers who seemingly had sprung up out of the ground. No one knew from where they had come. They were offering large projects, especially for the building of Belgrade. Dafiment Bank, Dafina, and Vasiljević became rich bankers paying interest rates of 15–20 percent per month on hard currencies. Long lines formed in front of their branch offices. People would get in line the night before, some of them bringing benches to sit on while they waited to deposit their money. Regular travel connections were established with Cyprus and Greece, where money was being invested. Workers were working less and less. Many were placed in a waiting status, but they continued to receive their paychecks. The black market in money and foreign currencies was flourishing around the Zeleni Venac market and other parts of the city.

At the same time, ordinary people felt profoundly insecure and many young people began fleeing abroad. Most people, however, went about their business in silence, occasionally grumbling about the high prices. The elderly and the poor would search through their wallets and purses for a few dinars with which to buy one or two articles in the supermarket, vying with one another for the cheaper rye bread, of which there was never enough—just as milk was always short. Nevertheless, although there was some grumbling, people put up with it all. There were no strikes or protests because most thought it was worth sacrificing for the "Serbian cause," all the while expecting victory. People believed that victory would result in all the Serbian lands, which had simply sprung up from nowhere, being united into a Great Serbia.

In our building and those around us, the celebrations of holidays, saints' days, birthdays, and weddings began on Friday and continued on Saturday and Sunday. Spirits soared as the *kolo,* a South Slav circle dance, was danced outside. The large apartment building I lived in pulsed with the music. As the night wore on, voices became raspy and fatigued from the food, drink, and festivity. If you stood too close to a window, you might be killed. At times I slept in the hallway, where there were no windows. At night I expected someone to break into the apartment; every time the building's front door opened could have meant disaster for the non-Serbs living there.

One night, a gang of youths banged on my door, rang the bell for several minutes without stopping, and slammed against the door in an attempt to break into my apartment. On my second call for police assistance I mentioned where I worked and officers finally came and arrested them. When I opened the door at the request of the police, I saw in the corridor drugged young men with glassy eyes and a fixed stare. Once I complained out loud about the situation at work. I was told that the youths were riffraff and that they had picked my apartment at random. I could see that people were unwilling to call problems by their right name. Not long afterward, I began to be disturbed by late-night telephone callers demanding that I move immediately, otherwise "your apartment will be blown up in half an hour." Because they used the Croatian instead of the Serbian word, I concluded that they identified Muslims with Croats. Banners reading, "Croats and Muslims out of Zemun," appeared on the light poles in Zemun. It was about that time that the Franciscan convent moved from a nearby park, where it had stood near the Zemun Hospital for more than 170 years.

I was still tutoring schoolchildren in the building to bring up their bad grades in mathematics, physics, and chemistry, just as though nothing was happening. I had good relations with my neighbors, but their guests who did not know who I was spoke openly against the Muslims. When the hoodlums banged on the door that night no one had dared to appear, although my neighbors living on the same floor must have heard and seen the attackers in the lighted hallway. I was also putting them in an awkward situation. They feared their children might be injured because of me, as some of the mothers told me in confidence. "Do you have anywhere to go where you would be safe, at least for a time?" they asked. When I shook my head, they advised me to put a different last name on my door. However, the list of tenants that had been posted on the wall for years had already disappeared from the entrance hall.

Friends—both Serbs and others, even some of my associates at work—were concerned about what might happen and some tried to help me by inviting me into their own homes. "Muna, I myself could not have believed how it is until I saw them beating the Shiptars with my own eyes on the Boulevard. I do not know what to tell you," one colleague said dejectedly. There were also cherished colleagues like Dr. Stefanović, who had the strength and humanity to ask me while riding on a bus, "Do you have any news from Kenan?" Others would add: "Why doesn't he come here? What is there for him there?" While conversing on the commuter bus with a long-standing associate whose work kept him well informed, I told him that Kenan was living close to the airport on Dobrinja, and perhaps would be better protected because the airfield was guarded by the Yugoslav People's Army. "No," he replied, "it is not the army we used to know. Tell him to get out of there." I felt a stab of fear and a shiver and began to worry about Kenan.

Ljilja invited me downtown to live with her. "It is true we are next to the Parliament if they drop bombs," she said, referring to the Americans. "But still, it is safer for you here," she said, flip-flopping as she considered what might be the best option. My situation became still more painful when I saw that everything in the Institute was changing, too. The most active people were the younger ones from the outskirts, the auxiliary personnel who over the course of a weekend would receive loot—or perhaps some of them even went themselves to loot dwellings in Slavonia and other plundered parts of Croatia. They would take appliances and sell them covertly in the administrative building in the Institute.

They turned up the 3 P.M. news on the radio on our Vinča buses to keep us informed about the frontline situation. Cities and regions were falling like houses of cards. An atmosphere was being created in which everyone was against the Serbs, but they rejected all ultimatums and were winning the day on the battlefield. Junior associates sitting in comfortable buses who before would snooze now discussed which tenants in their apartment buildings might be from other republics of the former Yugoslavia, and whether they had already been fired from their jobs. "Before, they would not even have known if the person in question was a Montenegrin; even they were suspicious, someone from Croatia three generations back, someone supposedly a Muslim. How did they overlook that? There it is, somehow they paid no attention before."

Couriers, cleaning women, people who made coffee for the office, workmen in the skilled trades, and the policemen who "guarded" Vinča usually took the front seats in the bus just behind the driver. They would talk about events, reporting figures on expulsions in Croatia and Bosnia in terms they understood, in easy confidence, leaning in the driver's direction. Our drivers deliberately imposed the atmosphere by selecting the radio stations and turning the volume up for newscasts, which not everyone wanted to hear, but to which no one could object. It was best to keep silent. Those who had knowledge from "confidential sources" usually had encouraging news about Kosovo, from which quite a few of them came. They talked about ways of pacifying the Shiptars and about the money policemen and others could earn when the government sent them to take over the civil service and the hospitals, finances, and mines from the Albanians. In a short time, with the additional wages and per diems for working in "exceptional" circumstances, they could buy a car.

I usually sat near the middle of the bus, where I could listen to the most distinguished specialists, members of the academy, and intellectuals argue about "the historic rights of the Serbs" and express surprise that others did not share their opinion on this issue. Listening to them talk, one always heard that the Serbs were the greatest fighters, that they had created Yugoslavia, and that others had taken advantage of what they had gained, taking everything away from the country and finally betraying it because they were unreliable and ready to sell out. Somehow, the opinion ran through all this that non-Serbs were dishonorable when it came to holding the country together. The talk of my physicians and members of the academy who had been my professors and acquaintances particularly affected me. Many of them had spent years in foreign capitals, enjoying all the benefits afforded them in Tito's Yugoslavia.

In all the conversations, even the well-intentioned ones, you could feel the anger against the Muslims. They had nothing good to say about them, the most that could be expected was sorrow that they would suffer. They were amazed that Muslims were unable to see which side to take in the fight between the Serbs and Croats. The Muslims were altogether discounted. I heard housewives, educated people, and even those I had helped at work say the same thing. They simply could not see the facts. "God himself made their hearts hard and their eyes blind." Was that happening now? I wondered as I said farewell to people I knew and departed from them on a kind of one-way journey. And what was His warning to us when we experience these sufferings and humiliations? I directed the same question toward myself in the name of all our country's Muslims. Nevertheless, we had to learn to live together. We had only this one country and it was our home and hearth. How then is one to act? That question surfaced again and again.

At night I could hear from my apartment the distant rumbling of tanks on the Belgrade–Zagreb highway and what sounded like heavy trucks moving westward. Hearing the more frequent overflights of aircraft and helicopters led me to suspect that the nights were full of heavy fighting. I thought about Kenan and wondered whether he was alive. I would go out onto the cold balcony to feel the chill and freeze and see whether I could stay outside, which had become a way of life for our fellow citizens in the camps and in Sarajevo without heat, food, or water. No, I could not stay long in the freezing weather of my own free will, not even as a mother, although my Kenan was experiencing that in Sarajevo. So what is one to say?

Our afternoon bus to New Belgrade sometimes took us past kilometer-long convoys of vehicles full of men mobilized in the army and heading westward on the Zagreb–Belgrade highway. The vehicles were from everywhere and bore the markings of the companies from which they had been taken. Mostly young people sat in the back of the trucks under tarpaulins, some of them holding liquor bottles, their fingers raised in the victory sign. The young women who ran out of the apartment buildings in New Belgrade and stood with their children along the highway and threw flowers at the convoys made a particularly striking sight in this sendoff of "liberators." It seemed to me that they were more excited than the fighters themselves. I watched all that from behind the curtain in the bus window, wondering what country I lived in. We were fighting each other in a country that had belonged to us all until the day before yesterday, and even when things were going very hard on us, as was the case now, we should have been more sensible in parting company. How quickly people forget everything! Those same apartments from which the women came running were built mostly for military personnel with the greatest conveniences, created by our own hands, just as the weapons they were carrying had been paid for by our work.

What I had always been afraid might happen—even since back in 1941–45, which made life in our otherwise beautiful country rather bitter—had come back again. I looked at it rationally, just as a man reconciles himself to death when he discovers he has no other option. The fact had to be faced that Yugoslavia was dead if one wished to survive. I thought to myself that they were not sorry that they were destroying the country and wondered if they were even aware of it. Some kind of universal segregation prevailed in Belgrade: by nationality, by origin, by conviction, and by everything else. People no longer listened to the same newscasts. The people I knew, my associates, hurried to hear the broadcasts from Belgrade radio and television stations, believing them. It seemed as though people had grown tired of the accumulation of problems in Yugoslavia since Tito's death and the end of communist rule. They found themselves in a vacuum and now were discharging their frustration, relatively painlessly for themselves, because it still was mostly a question of someone else's skin. I tried to listen to the foreign stations: the British Broadcast Corporation (BBC), Radio France International (RFI), the Voice of America, Sarajevo, and Zagreb, which could still be heard, and I watched Studio B, which was more critical and somewhat more objective. The weekly news magazine *Vreme* (*Time*) and the daily newspaper *Borba* also carried news from other sources, featuring columns and interviews with individuals in the opposition and from the other republics. Yet even they did not dare to take an opposing view or talk about the essential problems, so it was impossible to break through the news blockade. All of this was still more difficult in the interior of Serbia and Montenegro. Nowhere did one see or hear anything that did not originate on Radio-TV Belgrade or the daily newspaper *Politika,* which at that time was truly sinister, a hotbed of hatred and evil. I had read *Borba* since 1949 and *Politika* since 1953, but *Politika* truly disgusted me. *Večernje novosti* (*Evening News*), which had the most incompetent news people—their only skill, or so it seemed, was lying—was still more sinister. I wondered how it was possible that even the people I knew, whose intelligence and power of judgment I never doubted, could believe that which clearly was not the truth. How could Dubrovnik and Vukovar be Serbian cities? From whom were they liberating Sarajevo? I seemed to be witnessing some kind of conversion. Pressured as they were by the knowledge of atrocities that their own people were committing, was it impossible for them to admit guilt and easier to believe in a lie? They found justification in assuring themselves of the thought, "They are doing the same to us." Thus the sentence, "They are all alike," which would ease the burden of communication between the victim and the one committing evil, gained currency among neighbors of differing origin and among workmates.

The laboratories lost the life and openness they once had. Our cordiality was insincere; everyone held to his own truth. Whenever I walked into some department, my younger associates and a number of the older ones, including those who had been Party members until yesterday, would turn off the radio because they had been listening to stations that were savagely and openly nationalistic. It was a sad thought, knowing that educated people were consuming that kind of news. I wondered how these young people had been shaped when their upbringing was so strained, as though a snake were hatched in one's own bosom, and how had we nurtured them and helped those snakes to become so strong? I could see that their upbringing both at home and in school had contributed to this. I would say the home was the nest and the school was the bosom.

It was similar in Kosovo in 1981–83, where, in fact, it began with those demonstrations. We were doing field experiments. People were being killed in the vicinity, but we went on working. When the autonomy of Kosovo and Metohija was abolished, I think it was April, 1989, I happened to be in Vranjska Banja (Vranjska Spa) again doing experiments, when the police used weapons to smother the demonstrations in Bujanovac, killing some of their own citizens in the process. That same day, they were preparing for national festivities and dancing the *kolo* on Terazije, a central thoroughfare in Belgrade. It was the same atmosphere that I had experienced as a young girl in Prijepolje in 1941 as I watched from the school window and saw the *kolo* danced through the market in celebration of the coronation of King Petar II Karađorđević. Those who led the *kolo* were killed by the same ones in whose name it was being danced.

In the end, my disgust passed over into action. I had begun to see myself as a wicked intellectual who was "doing science" as though nothing were happening, yet all the while people were being killed, suffering in camps, being driven from their homes, the women cruelly raped, and the Muslim nationality being destroyed. I knew that Kenan had lost everything in his apartment, that the people in Pale had looted everything. He had lost cherished family mementos, as had Azra, my daughter-in law, and many others. Someone had appropriated those things.

I wondered if in Hitler's Germany educated people had been indifferent like this, had simply gone on doing their jobs? I recognized the situation I had heard about, the one in which educated people who refused to acknowledge the truth were more to blame than those who overtly committed evil acts. They had allowed evil to develop without protest or resistance because their silence spared them. I could never live with myself if I turned into that kind of intellectual.

I finally became firm in the realization that I could no longer pursue scientific research under these conditions and would have to leave. But where? To Turkey? What would I do there with no money or work, when I could not even speak the language? I had long wanted to improve my English and get to know the United States, a country with the latest technology, to visit libraries and perhaps do something worthwhile for some future country arising on the soil of the former Yugoslavia—Bosnia, for example.

I had the feeling that the work I had done up to that time at Vinča was completed. I had begun to lose projects because people presumably were hesitant to collaborate with a Muslim woman. Thus, the money we needed to carry on could not be obtained from the usual sources of financing: powerful companies and special-interest communities in science that were nationalistically oriented. All the Muslims who had worked in important positions in hospitals, banks, Belgrade television, and government institutions—not to mention the army—had, along with other non-Serbs, lost their positions or been demoted far down the ranks. Even a neutral stance that had wedded them to the changes and the war could no longer help them. Or perhaps they came from mixed marriages and were already committed by their upbringing. Whatever the case, successful newspapermen, correspondents, broadcasters, professors, and physicians all lost their jobs and positions in summary fashion, only to see their places taken by "patriots."

That was how I finally chose to come to the United States and uncertainty.

Appendix

Science Caught in the Political Crosswinds

In my day, the institute at Vinča was called the Boris Kidrič Institute of Nuclear Sciences after Boris Kidrič, a Slovene who was a member of Yugoslavia's inner circle of leadership. At the time the Institute was founded, he was the minister for the economy and science. His bust was placed in a small park beside the library and in front of the Physics Laboratory and administration building. When, around 1991, the name was changed to the Vinča Institute of Nuclear Sciences, the bust was quietly removed from its foundation, while the pedestal, evidently awaiting the placement of some Serbian great from the field of science, remained.

The Institute was built in 1948, some fifteen kilometers south of Belgrade, very close to the prehistoric settlement of Vinča on the Danube River, which is the subject of much research in Europe and even worldwide.

The laboratories were housed in one- and two-story buildings scattered through the parks and undulant grassy grounds in which grew various types of beautiful trees and shrubs. The broad walkways and paths between buildings were bordered with flower bushes that continually changed their color and scent according to the blossoming season of their particular plants. On a leveled-off area of the grassy slope there were two nuclear reactors, plus the modern building housing the "hot" laboratory with its high smokestacks.

When it was founded, Vinča was not only the largest nuclear institute, it was the largest scientific institute in Yugoslavia. It had laboratories dedicated to basic and applied research, a hot laboratory, so called because of the high level of radioactivity generated, two reactors, one of them made in Russia, laboratories for reactor materials, electronics laboratories, a radiation protection laboratory, a medical center with a laboratory for nuclear medicine, and numerous workshops and auxiliary services.

Basic research was being done in physics, chemistry, and biology, oriented toward nuclear fields, so that there were several specialized laboratories in these fields, five in the physical sciences alone.

Vinča, also had a well-established computer center, and a powerful management called the "Administration Building" headed by Vinča's director. The director, although he had an official car and his own chauffeur, usually took the regular Vinča buses that went to every quarter of the city. In fact, people were not bothered by formality in Vinča.

Because of the reactor, Vinča always had a medical team and telephone receptionists on duty. It also had living quarters for foreign students, doctoral candidates, scientists on long-term research projects, and our own researchers who worked at night so that they could take a nap and a breather from their experiments.

Vinča obtained its initial cadre educated in the field of nuclear sciences in the following manner: first, it provided jobs for students who had graduated from the university in various specializations, and then sent them to nuclear centers in Europe, America, and the Soviet Union. They received their doctorates abroad or did their experimental work there and then returned home to defend their dissertations in various departments of the universities. Once they returned to Vinča they were placed under the supervision of the senior scientists and university professors who created the Institute. It seems to have been the quickest and most efficacious way to develop individual fields.

At the time I was taken on by the Institute, there were a number of well-known specialists and professors. Academician Pavle Savić was head of the Physical Chemistry Laboratory and Vinča's founder. A French scientist, Prof. Robert Walen, and Pavle Savić established the Physics Laboratory. Professor Aleksandar Milojević, later the mentor for my doctoral thesis, founded the Detection Department, and Prof. Đorđe Bek-Uzarov, of Russian origin, the Radionuclide Metrology Department. Academician Dušan Kanazir in the Molecular Biology Laboratory served as president of the Serbian Academy of Sciences in the 1990s. Dr. Zdenko Dizdar, who built the laboratory for high radioactivity and the production of radioisotopes (the so-called Hot Laboratory) was Bosnia's postwar industry minister. Professor Milorad Mlađenović, a Sarajevan and founder of nuclear spectroscopy, worked in our laboratory and was an associate of European nuclear laboratories. Professor Fedor Borelli, who originated from a well-known Italian aristocratic family from the Adriatic coast, was the head of our laboratory and a professor at the Faculty of Electrical Engineering. Academician Slobodan Ribnikar of the Physical Chemistry Laboratory was a member of the Ribnikar family, founders of the newspaper *Politika,* and Dr. Petar Martinović, a highly regarded biologist, was an old associate of American institutes. Professor Afgan Naim, the only Muslim in a major post, was a specialist in the energy industry and an associate of world institutes in that field.

One of Vinča's important virtues was the diversity of its people and the quality of its personnel. The researchers, especially at the beginning, came from all parts of the country. Young specialists did their advanced specialized training in Vinča from various institutions and hospitals in the country. Quite a few its scientists and researchers considered themselves Yugoslavs rather than belonging to any particular nationality. There were few Albanians and Muslims. In the first place, there was our medical doctor, Fadila Čemerlić, a true Bosnian woman, communicative and easygoing. Her husband Ahmed was an engineer in the Electronics Laboratory and later dean of the Faculty of Electrical Engineering in Sarajevo. A biologist, Dr. Fadila Popić, was a Mostar woman in a mixed marriage. Later, Dr. Nurudin Bijedić, a theoretical physicist, joined us from the University of Zagreb.

I often heard it said that Muslims could not get jobs at Vinča and that is why there were few of them. However, I think that was not the case. Vinča required a certain extra effort. There was the issue of whether persons could find housing and live in Belgrade with their family, or did they prefer to be in Sarajevo or somewhere else in one of the Muslim communities being developed and offering better living conditions.

Beginning in 1960, a large number of researchers came to the Institute to gain experience and prepare theses. They came largely from Asian and African countries, as well as a few from the West and from the Eastern Bloc, although that was more a part of scientific cooperation. A few Muslims from Islamic countries were doctoral candidates in the Physics Laboratory, including my friend Dr. Kamal Buraei, a geophysicist from Cairo University; Dr. Abdul Vahid, who later founded Pakistan's High-Energy Physics Department; Dr. Ahmed Nazifi from Afghanistan; and a few others. There were also some Albanians, founders of the group for physical sciences at Priština University in Kosovo, who were doing their doctorates in our laboratory.

There were two kinds of researchers at Vinča. Some worked mainly on service measurements, construction of instruments, technical design, and less on actual research. Some of them were highly paid managers and directors of programs Vinča conducted for business enterprises. People were selected for these higher technical positions according to their experience and the success of their work. Researchers who achieved the higher scientific positions after finishing their doctoral studies belonged to the second group. They were scientists and became involved in research as they progressed through the various grades from junior scientist to scientific adviser, which was on the same level as a university professor. The chief investigators for an international scientific project had to be people with a bibliography of world significance.

In time, the master's degree and publications became a precondition for doing a doctoral dissertation. The doctoral candidate had to have at least two publications in foreign or domestic scientific journals. Since there were few scientific journals in Yugoslavia, we published abroad. The best journals, of course, were those whose articles were most often cited.

Vinča had various forms of technical and scientific communications at home and abroad. Researchers communicated their findings at domestic conferences, symposia, and congresses. Scientists had the right to go abroad to study once every two years and attend conferences even more frequently—provided, of course, that they had papers to present. Their travel was financed by funds from the republic's scientific budget. Design councils for projects in the technological field could send specialists abroad on any particular type of assignment they saw fit.

Our domestic gatherings were interesting. The Yugoslav Society for Protection from Radiation had existed from the beginning and was very active. Symposiums were held every two years in various parts of the country. I remember the festive atmosphere at the opening of a symposium in Banja Luka sponsored by the Rudi Čajavec Institute in October, 1967.

The plenary sessions were held in the hall of the Yugoslav People's Army. Researchers from all the nuclear centers, university departments, military institutes, and many other smaller institutions, military personnel, the president of the municipality of Banja Luka, and factory managers were assembled in the overcrowded hall. It was more festive and the papers were more serious than at some congresses. I wondered why this was so important; I thought perhaps some of the regional centers, in this case Banja Luka, were competing to show how up-to-date they were, and that is why they were more ambitious. Later, I realized on the basis of the projects we did why there was so much pomp and ceremony at a symposium.

There also were dinners and lunches in well-known tourist spots. We went to Jajce, where the foundations for the Second Yugoslavia were laid at the second session of the AVNOJ on November 29, 1943. Most people were staying in the Hotel Bosna, and every day we passed by the Ferhadija Mosque, which today is no more, because vandals born out of the "spontaneous" Serbian nationalistic events destroyed it in 1992.

Another symposium that has remained in my memory occurred in Priština, the capital of Kosovo, in the fall of 1977. The topic was environmental pollution in industrial centers such as the cities in the Kosovo basin. Truly eminent specialists and university professors came from all over Yugoslavia. This was the first time I had ever visited Kosovo. When we entered Kosovska Mitrovica aboard a bus, visibility was limited to eight or ten feet from the ground. A mist of bluish-white gases hovered over us as countless tons of poisonous gases and metallic dust were being spewed into the air.

The plenary sessions were held in the hall of the Executive Council of

Kosovo and Metohija, while the working groups met at Priština University. The number of participants was small in some of the narrowly specialized groups, which allowed us to discuss things in great detail. I was surprised when colleagues of ours whom I had known earlier delivered their papers in Albanian, although they had graduated from universities elsewhere in Yugoslavia. Translation was time-consuming. I saw that this was a regular thing except in the plenary sessions. When I asked a colleague why they were speaking Albanian when they knew we could not understand it, he explained it was because we were in an official provincial institution.

When we returned to the hotel, we would pass through crowded streets during the evening promenade. The Albanians would stroll along one side of the street while the others stayed on the opposite side with no intermingling. Scientists commented on these events in our hotel rooms. I wished the Albanians well: to enjoy progress, to have their own university, but I did not understand whether this kind of division was necessary. Being from a mixed environment, I could better understand people's relationships and I knew that that kind of separateness would eventually erupt.

In the hall of the Executive Council, while waiting for sessions to begin, I took the opportunity to get to know the cleaning women. They knew very little of my language and I even less of theirs, but gradually I understood some of what they were saying and they what I was trying to communicate. One woman, no longer very young, told me that she was the sole breadwinner in her family, that she had seven children and a husband who occasionally found work in the market. Her children were going to school and she received the family supplement. They got by, she said, by scrimping. Rarely did she buy anything at retail, not even bread, meat, or clothing. The household dealt directly with the farmers in the villages, where she bought things in bulk, by the sack or the drum. She prepared wool and spun it herself, and her oldest daughter knitted sweaters, socks, and other things for the children. The family bought meat only occasionally, and she prepared vegetables her husband brought home from the market whenever he was hired to sweep up. They had only a few dinars to spend on incidentals. After conversing with them for two or three days, I realized that it was possible to survive that way.

When I left, I was grateful to those women who had explained to me how the unemployed and those with small incomes get by. Their handiwork and their rural connections rescue them. They have children, who in turn go to school. The future must be for them.

The decentralization of the federation upset Vinča's programs. It became a Republic of Serbia institution. In 1963 Vinča numbered more than fifteen hundred personnel, including about three hundred doctors and masters of science. After the Federal Atomic Energy Commission was disbanded, whole sections of laboratories were shut down—especially those having to do with the production of isotopes, which were linked to the reactors. The Republic of Serbia had quite a few unwise investment projects and dissatisfied workers who were threatening strikes. No one had the time to pay very close attention to Vinča during that period, so it was left almost to itself.

Particularly fierce battles were waged over decentralization in the Institute's Communist Party. Two tendencies stood out. One that I will provisionally call "centralistic" wanted to preserve Vinča as a whole with central financing, whereas the other was led by young people in the engineering sciences who wanted independence for their laboratories. The former were doomed to fail because a similar process was taking place in our society at large and had generated this process at Vinča. Any laboratories that could operate at all independently were detached as separate entities. Instead of one general director, the previous laboratory heads became directors. All of the administrative structures were transferred from the central to the laboratory level, while those at the Institute level remained virtually intact. This was manifested almost to the point of absurdity after 1976, when the Law on Associated Labor (basic rules for self-management) began to be applied even to science.

It was hard to find work. There were not many institutions in need of our knowledge. Industry had not reached the level where it was seeking high technology, nor did it have any great amount of money. The enterprises were operating with foreign licenses. Funds for science and funds for development still remained at the federal and republic levels as a source of financing for Vinča. However, what came from them was less than half of the needed revenue. One reliable and long-term source of financing was the Yugoslav People's Army. At one time, early on, the JNA had its own sections in Vinča's laboratories where its specialists did their work. Later, when it opened its own institutes, the army pulled out its specialists and transferred them there. The JNA switched to concluding contracts on projects with Vinča in which the army would specify the type of research. This was especially true in the period after 1975. It is of interest that the JNA usually did not engage for the project the most able researchers, especially those who had spent a long time abroad, or the best laboratories. In addition to that research, there was also mostly targeted research relying in part on military or, more accurately, strategic programs for the future. These were laid on a broader foundation, and sometimes several institutions cooperated on them. Vinča's crisis and self-management also had a good side. The shortcomings of the Institute's various laboratories and services were gradually exposed and income was based on contribution, all the way down to the individual, so that it became evident who was worth how much and how much each could contribute. It soon became clear that skilled and specialized personnel were being paid the least while making the largest contribution.

Beginning in 1960, Vinča prepared for the registration of the RA reactor with the International Atomic Energy Agency (IAEA) in Vienna, as well as for the production of radioisotopes. Several of the Institute's laboratories were engaged in nuclear reactor operation control projects.

When I began working at the Institute, the reactor's neutron flux (determining the reactor power) was measured by so-called activation analysis methods. The activation method consists of setting up in the reactor a target for the neutrons: gold, sulphur, iridium, or cobalt folia that become radioactive. On the basis of the folia's measured activity, its radiated time, and some numerical parameters, one can establish the neutron flux. My colleagues Prof. Vladeta Urošević, the late Dr. Vlasta Bulović, and Prof. Đorđe Bek-Uzarov were measuring the radioactivity of the cobalt and gold folia radiated in the RA reactor, which were then sent to England for checking at the Harwell National Laboratory. A few weeks later, the chief of our laboratory, Prof. Fedor Borelli, received a message from Harwell saying that our measurements were correct and proposing that our results be published.

My first solo assignment was the measurement of the radioactivity of iodine-131, which in those days was used for medicinal purposes and which was beginning to be produced in the Hot Laboratory. Because of the importance of iodine, the IAEA in 1960 organized a project involving the comparison of iodine-131 in which more than thirty international laboratories participated, including our own. The IAEA-authorized laboratory made a solution of iodine-131. All participants were sent two sealed ampoules with several milliliters of solution, plus the orientation values of their activity. The project lasted about two months. Most of the staff remained in the laboratories until late afternoon or late into the night. The results were computed on the basis of the Greenwich Mean Time (GMT) of a given date. The laboratories were obliged to fill out a questionnaire, giving the name of the method used as well as a description of each step taken, accompanied by numerical data. The different methods of measurement have their own theoretical boundaries, so their quality varies. The method or methods used by a laboratory depended on its financial situation.

We finished our measurements at the end of January, 1961, completed the questionnaire and sent the results to the IAEA. After two days, the agency informed Dr. Zdenko Dizdar, the Institute director, that the results were good. A few months later, the IAEA sent a communiqué listing the laboratories and their ratings. Ours was rated among the best laboratories in Europe.

I worked on Yugoslav nuclear projects from 1966–71. We presented reports on our work before a project committee at joint meetings in Belgrade, Zagreb, and Ljubljana. The hotels where the sessions took place usually were full of participants from all over the country. Sometimes the discussions involved heated topics, such as daring research projects or results that evoked conflicting opinions. One such case was our experiment in the "fuel element" project, in which I happened to participate.

A separate task of the project was to determine the dynamic for the creation of gases in the fuel in the experimental channel of the reactor. On the day of the experiment, our team gathered in the reactor room; we had an operating permit and a certified list of participants. I stood on the platform with the engineer who directed the team's work. We began the experiment at 1 P.M. with the reactor set at zero power. The measuring devices for pressure and other parameters in the experimental fuel element indicated that the experiment had begun normally. The reactor's power increased gradually. At each power change, my engineer colleague increased the pressure of the carrier gas in the fuel element and checked its temperature. I carefully followed each step he took with one of my own. Extractions from the fuel element were made in the small chamber, where the pressure was lowered for safety purposes. One stage of the experiment at a given reactor power level lasted over two and one-half hours. I asked my colleague how many step-ups were taken in the change of the pressure inside the fuel. The value he stated seemed to me to be excessive and told him so. He answered that it was not. I thought, I guess this is how engineers work: they do not split hairs the way we researchers do. I also had a second thought: men do not like women mixing in their business. I kept quiet and continued my work.

Somewhere around three in the morning, the pressure in the fuel element disappeared. The pointer went down to zero, but the temperature continued to rise. We began to check the connection wires and the packing on the gauges, thinking that maybe there was damage in the chamber itself. The engineer contacted the reactor operators. Engineer Ivan Močilnik, one of my young coworkers, stayed with me. Having worked together a long time, we were accustomed to moving quickly, as well as in making decisions about an experiment. After half an hour of poking the apparatus, everything appeared to return to normal, but we still did not find the damage. The engineer increased the pressure, keeping it at the same level, while I took the sample from the chamber. When I brought the samples to the measuring unit, I noted that there was no needle on the radioactivity gauge. At first I thought it had fallen off, then I noticed that it was all the way over to the right, completely beyond the scale. It had simply stuck to the measuring unit and was not moving. I understood that this was an indication of high radioactivity of the gas in the balloon. Almost at the same moment, the operators announced that the reactor's exhaust gases had increased in activity. We stopped the experiment at that point, but our work was not finished. We had to identify chemically the released gases. It was already time to begin the morning's tasks. While we were finishing our analysis, the reactor safety committee met. The results of our analysis confirmed that the fuel element's jacket (shield) had burst.

I went home after undergoing some medical tests and lay down in bed. Suddenly, it seemed as if the whole bed, with me in it, was spinning around. The lesson I learned from that experiment was that delicate and complicated experiments are best done by smoothly running teams whose members discuss every step in advance. Here, among other things, the human factor—which is the source of unpredictable mistakes—plays a definite role. It is clear that if the quality of the fuel element and its packing were not good, there could be an accident. However, if we had changed the pressure in smaller increments, I think we would have noticed the unexpected change in radioactivity and stopped the event in time.

I was given the mission of creating a primary standard for tritium measurement in late 1971. Tritium is the radioactive form of the element hydrogen and the fuel of future reactors. The sample was tritiated water whose radioactivity I had to define exactly, that is, absolutely. The methods of "absolute measurement" are based on physical-chemical processes in which the reactions between the components go "to the end," or have a yield of 100 percent. At that time, only a few laboratories made use of such a standard, employing the so-called Internal Gas Counting Method. Among them were one in America and another in Belgium, which we emulated. Our task was to create something similar in our workshops at Vinča, while at the same time making maximum use of domestic materials. We threw ourselves into our work, examining world literature on the subject, and discussing variants with machine engineers and machinists. In the end, there appeared in the laboratory a glass and metal vacuum system. One of the pieces of the apparatus was a detection system consisting of five metal detectors identical in construction but varying in diameter and length. In the winter of 1972, we began the testing the standard of tritiated water (HTO) purchased from the Geel Laboratory in Belgium. It was said that the North Atlantic Treaty

Organization had built this laboratory, which was visited by Professor Bek-Uzarov and master of physics Ljiljana Dobrilović. It was they who brought me documentation concerning their apparatus.

Measuring gases takes a long time. Even though we worked conscientiously, we did not confirm the value of the standard indicated in the Geel Laboratory certificate. Some of our detector combinations gave lower values and others higher ones. After checking our apparatus and methodology, we had to stop. It was clear that there was a hidden (systematic) error somewhere in our system. These are the worst because they can neither be removed nor compensated for by repeating the measurements. Our detectors were steel cylinders, closed at the ends by Teflon insulation through which passed a fine, central wire, a so-called anode with very high electrical tension. The Americans used the same device.

We had little time left to finish our project. Kamal, our former doctoral candidate from Egypt, came to our aid. At that time he was working on detection mechanisms. Ivan and I had gone back to examine the literature on the construction of detectors and on electrical discharges in them. We were close to a solution when we went to the library one evening to take another look at Dr. Wilfred Miller's work. "Ivan," I said, "the line on Miller's graph is like ours, except for the fact that he has it drawn through two points. But we have three, one of which always deviates. So, this is the problem: we have three points, whereas two will never show a systematic error. I wonder if we might find something in the old literature." Ivan looked up from the sheet he held in his hand. "Muna," he replied, "let's look in Reed. He's the one who developed this method. Something is lacking in our design."

Fortunately, we found a work that had been published in the *Review of Scientific Instruments* ten years earlier. There we found a line with three points and all three on line! And the design of the detector was given as well. The anode had been visibly thickened at the ends near the Teflon. The designer had thus created an "empty space" at the ends, which avoided the influence of the deformation of the fields running from the insulator. Even though the surface of the Teflon insulator in our devices had been smooth, it was not sufficiently homogenous to handle the effects of the current.

We returned to the lab, removed the detectors from the apparatus, and thickened the anodes at the ends with an ordinary piece of needle from a syringe. We later refined this approach. As soon as we finished, we again began to take measurements. Kamal sat in front of his calculator, which he had found in a junk pile and fixed. (Evidently, our new electronic devices were too loud for him.) He would check my figures and wait for the values before inserting them into the formula. Ivan measured the impulses at the various plateaus, while I, standing over him, followed the values one by one. After two hours, we got our preliminary results. Kamal added them up and voila! All the points were almost on a straight line.

We immediately called our chief, Professor Bek-Uzarov, on the telephone to tell him the news. We also invited our coworkers in the other building to come for coffee, which we prepared on our old hotplate sitting on the corner of the table where we had assembled our detectors. It was against regulations to keep food where we were working with radiation, but who could worry about every detail? Besides, coffee is not food. Since it was already late at night, some people got ready to go home, while some stayed on and continued working. In those days we had folding cots on which I used to like to take a nap. Ivan preferred to doze off in an armchair. Kamal, who lived in an apartment at Vinča, would always sit until the early morning hours.

When our work was published, we received more than a hundred postcards from researchers around the world asked for copies and additional information.

In 1972, our Metrology Department organized the First International School for the Measurement of Radioactivity, to which scientists came with their lectures from more than thirty of the best-known laboratories in the world. I presented two papers with my colleagues. Today this institution is still working, bringing together laboratories from around the world. The meeting was held in the former holiday resort operated by the Federal Atomic Energy Commission in Herceg Novi. Kenan was with me. As a rule, he would play chess with the symposium participants or members of their families. The participants were accompanied by their wives, who could enjoy the warm water of the southern Adriatic or visit nearby Dubrovnik.

At the conclusion of the gathering, the scientists visited our facilities in Belgrade. They expressed amazement that we had obtained such good results while working in poorer conditions compared to theirs. In those days we held world-class rank in many fields of science.

I went to the IAEA laboratory in Vienna for the first time in 1971. My task was to examine the agency's apparatus for measuring low radioactivity in nature, which we intended to copy. The agency's headquarters was located in the very center of Vienna, but later moved to the outskirts, in the handsome UN Organization Center. Specialists from various countries worked at the IAEA as temporary or permanent employees. The agency's projects were carried out everywhere in the world. It was the cofinancier of numerous projects and helped individual countries equip their laboratories. After the 1963 earthquake in Skopje, the Macedonian Institute for the Application of Isotopes had received from the IAEA in Vienna a modern laboratory for measuring low concentrations of tritium in natural waters.

Well-paid physicists, chemists, and engineers staffed the IAEA's laboratories, but they did not have the right to publish the results of measurements, which were sent to the main project managers, whose seats were usually on the upper floors. The managers interpreted the results with their teams, which included specialists from countries in which the projects were carried out. The papers were then published in agency publications or in international journals.

The agency had a competitive procedure for selecting specialists as either temporary or permanent employees. The criteria were good references, a sound knowledge of languages, and evidence of organizational ability. Those who had dealt with both administrative matters and science had a better chance. Specialists also were appointed to the IAEA by countries who sent their own representatives. In both cases, a specialist first had to pass a selection process in his own country. Specialists who had the support of foreign research centers had a better chance of success. The selection of such specialists usually involved an "introductory procedure." They first had to be promoted in their native countries for having worked well on agency projects. There then followed a period of collaboration between such specialists and others from foreign laboratories in Europe, and finally appointment to the agency. Over time, powerful outposts staffed by specialists in my field were created in Germany, France, Holland and Poland.

In 1971, the high standard of the officials was visible. The IAEA had its own shops selling luxury food and drinks, cigarettes at low prices, national food in the restaurants, and bread from various countries. At noon, wives and children would come for lunch so they could spend some time with their husbands. The children would run around the luxurious hallways. Those who did not know about this custom were surprised to see children in the agency.

The last time I visited the agency was in 1990, before the war in Yugoslavia. I could tell from the old types of apparatus in use that the agency's funds had been curtailed. The quality of IAEA publications in the fields I knew about had fallen since individual research was outdated. The agency's specialists were no longer primarily researchers, but looked more like senior officials coordinating research projects. New scientific disciplines were appearing in European and American laboratories. The laboratories of developed countries with their own traditions and money easily moved on to new scientific disciplines and entered into collaboration with the agency, becoming its testing ground. It was evident that less-developed countries, despite the agency's help and encouragement, were unable to keep up the pace of work or open their own laboratories. The domination of those who possessed high technology could be seen by anyone who had observed a laboratory in any underdeveloped country, if it had one at all. It was not possible to find a single worthwhile instrument that had not been bought in one of the developed countries. It seemed to me that, as time went by, the laboratories in less-developed countries lagged ever farther behind—much more so than when I began working in the 1960s.

The extent of this unhappy state of affairs was still more visible and striking to me in rich but underdeveloped countries such as Kuwait, which is crying out for water. Kuwait has only a little fresh underground water that comes from the rare precipitation in its mountain regions, but the country has plenty of oil and money. It makes no difference, however, since it lacks experienced specialists and developed laboratories. At one time, the government had developed plans to obtain freshwater by desalinizing seawater and pumping it into natural reservoirs formed by the massive porous rock on which Kuwait lies, and then use it like any other underground water. A project of this kind in which I took part was initiated in 1989 by the Kuwait Institute of Science. Its laboratories were full of instruments; almost anything one could want for one's work was available. However, I found that Kuwait was wholly dependent for this on the developed countries whose specialists it engaged.

Glossary of Bosnian Terms

A Note on Spelling and Pronunciations of Bosnian (Serbo-Croat) Words and Names

C, c	is pronounced *ts,* as in *mats*
Č, č	is pronounced *tch,* as in *match* or *chalk*
Ć, ć	is pronounced similar to *tch,* but a thinner sound, more like the thickened *t* in *future* or *rich*
Đ, đ	is pronounced roughly like *j,* as in *jam,* or *g,* as in *George*
J, j	is pronounced *y,* as in *Yugoslavia* or *yet*
Lj, lj	is pronounced *li,* as in *million*
Nj, nj	is pronounced *ni,* as in *dominion*
Š, š	is pronounced *sh,* as in *shawl.*
Ž, ž	is pronounced *zh,* as in *Zhivago* or French *jour*
Dž, dž	is pronounced *j,* as in *John*

Bosnian Terms

abdest	Muslim ritual ablution before prayers. This includes washing the face, arms, and legs, rinsing the mouth and nose, and rubbing the neck, ears, and top of the head before prayer.
aga	Originally a military officer, later any gentleman or landowner. Often a title of respect in the Sandžak and Bosnia, regardless of the occupation of the person so addressed, e.g., Salih-aga, Ibrahim *aga* Mujaga, or Mujaginica (Mujaginca), the wife of Mujaga.
akšam (Ar. *magreb*)	The "sunset" or evening prayer.
Allah	The proper name of God in Arabic.
Amidža	Uncle, father's brother.
Babba or *babo*	Traditional name for *father* in the Muslim community in Yugoslavia.
Bairam	A very important Muslim religious holiday. Ramadan Bairam follows the month of fasting called Ramadan.
beg (Tur. *bey*)	A high-ranking official in provincial service. Often a title of respect in the Sandžak and Bosnia, regardless of the occupation of the person so addressed. The general term for *lord,* like Smail *beg* (Tur. Smail *bey*), Alibeg.
čaršija	Marketplace; bazaar.
Chetnik, Četnik	Serbian nationalist fighter.
efendija	Bosnian form for Turkish *effendi,* a title of respect, like *sir.* Initially used for government officials and members of learned professions
fes (fez)	A traditional Muslim conical hat.
Gymnasium	Secondary school consisting of eight years of education after primary school. The education system in the former Yugoslavia, like its successor

	countries today, is the same as that in many other continental European countries.
Hadž (Ar. Hajj)	The pilgrimage to the Kaaba, the holy place in Mecca, which takes place in the last month of the Islamic calendar. This requirement is known as the fifth pillar of Islam.
Hadžija (Tur. *hadži*)	Title given to one who has made the *hadž*.
Hafiz	Honorific title, given to one who knows the Qur'an by heart.
Hanuma (*hanma*)	Turkish word for *lady*. Often a title of respect in the Sandžak, e.g., Hatidžehanma.
hodža	Islamic studies teacher; *hodža hanuma* is a women's studies teacher.
Iftar	The evening meal when Muslims break their fast during Ramadan.
Imam	A Muslim religious leader; leader of a group during prayer.
Ićindija (Ar. Asr)	The third Muslim prayer during the day (midafternoon).
Islam	Literally to submit. According to Islamic belief, the religion of all the prophets of Allah confirmed finally by the mission of the Prophet Muhamed.
Jacija (Ar. Isha')	The fifth and last prayer of the day (nighttime).
kilim (ćilim)	Handmade woolen rug (*sag*) or carpet, woven in colorful folk or flower designs.
kitab	A book; leather bound in olden times.
Mujezin (Ar. Muazzen)	Man who proclaims the hour of prayer.
muftija (Tur. *mufti*)	Highest-ranking Muslim priest, expounder of the law, competent to issue *fetvas*—legal opinions/decisions.
Muslim	One who professes the faith of Islam or is born to a Muslim family.
Namaz (Ar. Salat)	Obligatory Islamic prayer during the day; the second pillar in Islam.
Nanna, Anna	Mother, commonly used in the Sandžak
Nišan	Muslim headstone.
Partisan	A Yugoslav soldier during World War II who fought against the occupiers under the general command of Marshal Tito.
Paša (Tur. Pasha)	Title of high-ranking official and soldier; Sandžak ruler.
Podne (Ar. Zuhr)	The second Muslim prayer (at noon).
Qur'an	The holy book of Muslims which, according to Islamic belief, Allah revealed to the Prophet Muhamed in Arabic.
Ramadan	Muslim month of fasting; the ninth month of the Islamic calendar.
Sabah (Ar. Fajr)	The Islamic morning (dawn) prayer.
Sandžak	Literally *banner* in Turkish. A military administrative area or province in the Ottoman Empire, established in the sixteenth century. Until 1912, its administrative center was the ancient Taslidža ("White Stone Town"), today's Pljevlje. Today, the former Sandžak is divided between Serbia and Montenegro.
Šejh (Ar. Sheik)	One of its meaning is Muslim religious and spiritual leader.
šerijat (Ar. *shari'a*)	Islamic religious law; a *šerijat* school to train judges for the Muslim court.
Ustaša (Ustaše, plu.)	A Croatian nationalist soldier.
Vakuf (Ar. *wakf*)	Muslim foundation; religious or humanitarian endowment.
zar	A wrapping Muslim women wear over their dress and heads when going outside the home.

Index

Italics indicate pages with illustations.
MH is the abbreviation used for the author, Munevera Hadžišehović